THE HIDDEN

HABITS OF

GENIUS

THE HIDDEN HABITS OF GENIUS

BEYOND TALENT, IQ, AND GRIT—
UNLOCKING THE SECRETS OF GREATNESS

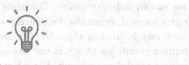

CRAIG WRIGHT

DEY ST.
An Imprint of WILLIAM MORROW

DEY ST.

HarperCollins books may be purchased for educational, business, or sales promotional use. For information, please email the Special Markets Department at SPsales@harpercollins.com.

A hardcover edition of this book was published in 2020 by Dey Street, an imprint of William Morrow.

FIRST DEY STREET PAPERBACK EDITION PUBLISHED 2021.

Designed by Paula Russell Szafranski

Library of Congress Cataloging-in-Publication Data has been applied for.

ISBN 978-0-06-289273-7

23 24 25 26 27 LBC 7 6 5 4 3

For our children,

Evan, Andrew, Stephanie, and Christopher,

and for Fred, Sue, and Sherry.

CONTENTS

INTRODUCTION   Hitting the Hidden Target   1

CHAPTER 1   Gift or Hard Work?: IQ or Many Qs?   11

CHAPTER 2   Genius and Gender: The Game Is Rigged   31

CHAPTER 3   Avoid the Prodigy Bubble   49

CHAPTER 4   Imagine the World as Does a Child   63

CHAPTER 5   Develop a Lust for Learning   77

CHAPTER 6   Find Your Missing Piece   99

CHAPTER 7   Leverage Your Difference   113

CHAPTER 8   Rebels, Misfits, and Troublemakers   135

CHAPTER 9   Be the Fox   153

CHAPTER 10   Think Opposite   173

CHAPTER 11   Get Lucky   191

CHAPTER 12   Move Fast and Break Things   209

CHAPTER 13   Now Relax   225

CHAPTER 14   Time to Concentrate!   237

EPILOGUE   Unexpected Outcomes   251

ACKNOWLEDGMENTS   255

NOTES   257

PHOTO CREDITS   313

INDEX   315

HITTING THE HIDDEN TARGET

Today, genius is all around us, from the helpful employees at the Apple Genius Bar to Baby Einstein products intended to make our kids smarter. The TV reality star Kim Kardashian is called "a business genius" and her husband, Kanye West, is said to be "a jerk who is also a genius." Alan Turing, Martin Luther King, Jr., Abraham Lincoln, Stephen Hawking, and Steve Jobs show up in contemporary films and are called geniuses. Then there are Academy Award–winning actors such as Daniel Day-Lewis and Eddie Redmayne, who portray the brilliant individuals in those films. Are they geniuses, too? The swimmer Michael Phelps is called a "locomotive genius." The tennis stars Roger Federer and Rafael Nadal hit "genius strokes." Yo-Yo Ma has been referred to as a "cello genius." The College of Business Administration of the University of Nebraska at Omaha offers an annual course titled The Genius of Warren Buffett. On May 23, 2019, Donald Trump stood before television cameras at the White House and declared himself "an extremely stable genius." Not to be outdone, North Korean leader Kim Jong Un has dubbed himself "the genius of all geniuses."

How do we explain this "longing for genius," as the writer George Eliot (Mary Ann Evans) expressed it in 1872?[1] Beneath our excessive popular use of this term rests a serious, timeless, and profoundly human desire to understand the unknown. To do so, we simplify, attributing the complex agency of many previous thinkers to a single, exemplary individual: "the genius." Often the genius assumes the qualities of a savior and thus gives humanity hope for a better world. At the same time, the genius provides solace—an explanation, even an excuse, for our own shortcomings. "Oh, well, no wonder, she's a genius!" But still we wonder: How is the magic trick done? What is hidden beneath the surface? Discarding the myths surrounding those exceptional individuals, what were or are their lives and habits really like? And what can we learn from them?

In 1951, doctors at Massachusetts General Hospital wired an EEG machine to the brain of Albert Einstein and watched the bobbing needle in an attempt to find the seat of his genius.[2] After Einstein died in 1955, an enterprising pathologist, the Yale-trained Dr. Thomas Harvey, extracted his brain and cut it into 240 neat slices that he and others could examine.[3] Although every nook, cranny, and sulcus of Einstein's cerebral matter has now been studied, neuroscientists still can't begin to explain how his imaginative thought process worked. Forensic pathologists in Salzburg have tried to match Wolfgang Amadeus Mozart's skull with the DNA of relatives in that city's St. Sebastian Cemetery.[4] Thus far, however, Mozart's genome remains elusive. Similarly, scientists in Milan are digging into the DNA of Leonardo da Vinci, but, again, no "genius gene" has been identified.[5] Why are we not surprised? Genius involves the complicated expression of too many hidden personal traits to be reduced to a single location and process in our brain or on our chromosomes. How an exceptional individual's traits work together to produce genius will remain a mystery. What these traits are and how they can be cultivated, however, is the subject of this book.

TO BEGIN WITH: WHAT IS GENIUS? THE ANSWER DEPENDS ON WHOM you ask and when. The ancient Greeks had several words for genius, among them *daemon* ("demon" or "spirit") and *mania* (a creative fury that consumed an inspired poet). We get our English word "genius" from the Latin noun *genius,* meaning "guardian spirit." In classical Greece and Rome, everyone had a guardian spirit, who, oddly, did not belong to him. From the Latin word *genius* arose the French *génie* and from it, in turn, the English "genie." Think of the genie waiting to emerge from the magic lantern in Walt Disney's *Aladdin* films. Think also of the candles on your birthday cake and the wish you make. Since Roman times, those candles and that wish have served as an annual votive offering to your genie, so that your guardian spirit might then do right by you in the coming year.

The list of recognized geniuses from the Middle Ages—Dante Alighieri, Geoffrey Chaucer, and Joan of Arc might come to mind—is short. Did the lights go out in the Dark Ages? No. Genius was simply co-opted and "rebranded" by the Catholic Church. In classical times one made a wish to one's genius; in the Middle Ages one prayed to a spiritual force with the name of a patron saint, not only for salvation but also to cure an illness or to find a lost comb. The great creations of the era—the soaring Gothic cathedrals, for example—were the handiwork of mostly name-less, faceless humans inspired by an external divine spirit, the Christian God.

With the Renaissance, transformative thinkers on earth re-gained a face and a name: Leonardo, Michelangelo, Raphael, and William Shakespeare were just a few such geniuses. Some Italian poets and painters were also dubbed *il divino,* as in *il divino Leonardo*—the divine Leonardo. Now they, too, like the saints, enjoyed divine powers as semideities. Their hands could shape the ideas that the mind of God might conceive. During the eighteenth-century Enlightenment, however, genius and God parted company. God withdrew, leaving the individual as the lone possessor of genius. Genius was now wholly immanent—it came with birth and rested within the individual.

Nineteenth-century Romantic sensibilities caused the face of genius to change yet again, becoming distorted, sometimes bizarrely so. Picture a lone, disheveled, eccentric misfit who suffers for his art. On cue appears Ludwig van Beethoven, the nineteenth-century poster boy for genius. He was, and certainly looked, a bit crazy, singing loudly to himself as he lurched through the streets of Vienna. Around the same time appeared the mad Dr. Frankenstein (in Mary Shelley's famous novel) and then the deformed genius Quasimodo (in Victor Hugo's *The Hunchback of Notre Dame*). Later, a brilliantly deranged Phantom would haunt the boards of the Paris Opéra—another disfigured genius.

Today, when we see a light bulb light up over a cartoon character's head, it serves as a visual symbol for that character's "bright idea." In truth, that act of genius—the creation of the modern incandescent light bulb—was the product of America's first research lab, Thomas Alva Edison's "invention factory" in Menlo Park, New Jersey.[6] Now Nobel Prizes in physics, chemistry, and medicine are usually awarded to two or three individuals in each discipline, suggesting that in modern times the scientific team has replaced the once solitary Einstein.

The fact that the word "genius" has changed meaning so often over the centuries tells us that genius is a concept relative to time and place. Genius is whatever we humans want to make it. A "genius" is whomever we choose to so designate. Purists will object to this transitory, populist approach. Is there no such thing as absolute truth and beauty? Are not the symphonies of Mozart and the equations of Einstein universal and eternal? Apparently the answer is no—it depends on whom you ask. The music of Mozart (1756–1791), although still revered in Western concert halls, has no special resonance among the citizens of Nigeria, for example, who have their own beloved sounds and musical heroes, such as the Afrobeat pioneer Fela Kuti (1938–1997). Einstein's explanation of gravity is merely one of four to hold sway since the ancient Greeks. Rays of genius in the arts and sciences are bent over time by different cultures and by each new generation that encounters them. Until recently, the history of the genius in the West was populated by "great men" (meaning white men), with women and people of color largely marginalized. But that is changing, and it is up to each of us to decide what constitutes exceptional human accomplishment.

Almost all dictionary definitions of genius include the words "intelligence" and "talent." We will explore what it means to be "intelligent" in chapter 1. As for "talent" as an essential component of genius, that misconception should be discarded immediately. As we will see, talent and genius are two very different things. The German philosopher Arthur Schopenhauer cleverly made this point in 1819: "A person of talent hits a target that no one else can hit; a person of genius hits a target that no one else can see."[7] A talented person deals skillfully with the immediately evident world. A genius, however, sees what is hidden from the rest of us. In 1998, Steve Jobs was quoted in *Business Week* as saying "A lot of times, people don't know what they want until you show it to them."[8]

As early as 1919, Nikola Tesla foresaw radio, robots, solar heating, and a cellular smartphone "not bigger than a watch."[9] Today two-thirds of the people on the planet are connected by the sort of internet phone that Tesla predicted. In 1995, while working at a quantitative hedge fund in New York, Jeff Bezos observed that traffic on the internet had increased 2,300 times over the previous year; he also realized that driving from store to store was an inefficient way to acquire merchandise. He envisioned Amazon and started with books. Twenty years later, his company had grown into the world's largest e-commerce marketplace, selling nearly every product imaginable. The only absolute in life, it turns out, is change, and the genius sees it coming.

To be a genius, by our modern definition, requires not merely hitting the hidden target but also hitting it first. Originality matters. But it was not always this way in the West. The classical Greeks, for example, thought the capacity to imitate Homeric poetry a mark of genius. Similarly, since ancient times, the

Chinese have assessed value according to the degree to which the new emulates the best of the old. And it is interesting to note that in modern Chinese culture, group accomplishment continues to trump individual achievement. Westerners began to see things differently around 1780. Beginning with the philosopher Immanuel Kant, who considered genius to be "the very opposite of the spirit of imitation,"[10] and continuing with British, French, and U.S. patent legislators, originality became a litmus test for exceptional accomplishment, one that protected an individual's intellectual property. Western faith in the "self-made man" and the "rugged individualist" dates from this time, and it maps well onto the traditional notion of genius in the West. But does original genius rest within the society or the individual? Perhaps we need a definition of genius for every culture at every time throughout history.

To set a framework for this book, let me give you my definition for today: A genius is a person of extraordinary mental powers whose original works or insights change society in some significant way for good or for ill across cultures and across time. In brief, the greatest genius produces the greatest impact on the greatest number of people over the longest period of time. Although all human lives are of equal value, some people impact the world with greater force. I emphasize the words "change society" in my definition, because genius is creativity and creativity involves change. Obviously, it takes two to play this game, an original thinker and a receptive society.[11] Accordingly, if Einstein had lived on a desert island and had chosen not to communicate with others, he wouldn't have been a genius. If he had chosen to communicate with others but they hadn't listened or had chosen not to change, again, he would not have been a genius. Unless Einstein effects change, he is no Einstein.

With the importance of creativity in mind, we see that many individuals popularly referred to as "geniuses" today are merely celebrities. To identify the true geniuses, we can begin by removing the majority of actors, actresses, and performers. Talented as they may be, those who work through something already formed by someone else—a screenplay or a musical composition, for example—are not geniuses. Creativity and creation are key, which is why Kanye West, Lady Gaga, and Beethoven, but not Yo-Yo Ma, may be considered geniuses. The same goes for most great athletes: as impressive as the record-breaking Phelps and Federer may be, they score no creativity points. Others invented the game. What about billionaire financial wizards, such as Warren Buffett? Needless to say, amassing money is different from effecting change. Money is a fuel of genius but is not genius per se. The genius rests in what is done with the opportunity money affords.

Eliminating all these false positives allows us to focus on the actions of the real geniuses as defined above. What constitutes "real genius," however, is not always clear cut; never will there be unanimity of opinion. By including Jeff Bezos, Jack Ma (the enterprising Chinese counterpart of Bezos), the entrepreneur Richard Branson, and the abolitionist Harriet Tubman as I do in this book, I may be casting my net too widely. Likely you will not agree with all my pronouncements on genius or on who is and who is not one. If you do not agree—bravo! As we will see, contrary thinking is one of the hidden habits of genius.

THIS BOOK CAME TO BE WRITTEN AFTER A LIFETIME OF OBSERVATION and study. I have spent my career surrounded by people who are exceptionally gifted at one thing or another—math, chess, classical music, creative writing, and other fields of endeavor. Yet I found myself not especially gifted at anything, only a B+. If you are a prodigy with a great gift for something, you can simply do it and may not be aware of why and how. And you don't ask questions. Indeed, the geniuses I met seemed too preoccupied with committing acts of genius to consider the cause of their creative output. Perhaps only nongeniuses like myself can attempt to explain genius.

"If you can't create, you perform, and if you can't perform, you teach"—that is the mantra of conservatories such as the Eastman School of Music, where I began my education as a classical pianist. Unable to compose or to earn a living as a performer, I moved on to grad school at Harvard, earning a Ph.D. and becoming a classroom teacher and researcher of classical music history—a musicologist, as it is called. Eventually, I found employment at Yale teaching the "three B's" of classical music: Bach, Beethoven, and Brahms. Yet the most fascinating character I met was an M: Mozart. He was funny, passionate, naughty, and hugely gifted, wrote music like no other, and seemed like a decent human being. One of my several trips to Florence caused me to research its native son Leonardo da Vinci. I quickly saw that Leonardo and Mozart had many of the same enablers of genius: extraordinary natural gifts, courage, a vivid imagination, a wide variety of interests, and a "go for broke" approach to life and art.

To how many other geniuses did these common agents extend? Enter Shakespeare, Queen Elizabeth I, Vincent van Gogh, and Pablo Picasso. Eventually, that cohort of great minds became the basis of a Yale undergraduate course that I created called Exploring the Nature of Genius. Year after year, increasing numbers of students enrolled. As you might expect, Yale students did not line up for the class to hear about a definition of genius or to track the history of the term over the ages. Some wanted to find out if they were already geniuses and what their futures might hold. Most wanted to know how they, too, might become a genius. They had heard that I had studied geniuses from Louisa May Alcott to Émile Zola and had identified a common set of personality traits. They, like you, wanted to know the hidden habits of these geniuses.

But what are they? Here is a preview that summarizes the principal focus of each chapter in this book:

- Work ethic (chapter 1)
- Resilience (chapter 2)

- Originality (chapter 3)
- Childlike imagination (chapter 4)
- Insatiable curiosity (chapter 5)
- Passion (chapter 6)
- Creative maladjustment (chapter 7)
- Rebelliousness (chapter 8)
- Cross-border thinking (chapter 9)
- Contrarian action (chapter 10)
- Preparation (chapter 11)
- Obsession (chapter 12)
- Relaxation (chapter 13)
- Concentration (chapter 14)

IN ADDITION, THROUGHOUT THESE CHAPTERS, I OFFER PRACTICAL insights about genius such as these:

- IQ, mentors, and Ivy League educations are greatly overrated.
- No matter how "gifted" your child is, you do him or her no favor by treating him or her like a prodigy.
- The best way to have a brilliant insight is to engage in creative relaxation: go for a walk, take a shower, or get a good night's sleep with pen and paper by the bed.
- To be more productive, adopt a daily ritual for work.
- To improve your chances of being a genius, move to a metropolis or a university town.
- To live longer, find your passion.
- Finally, take heart, because it is never too late to be creative: for every youthful Mozart there is an aged Verdi; for every precocious Picasso, a Grandma Moses.

IN THE END, READING THIS BOOK LIKELY WON'T MAKE YOU A GE-nius. It will, however, force you to think about how you lead your life, raise your children, choose the schools they attend, allocate your time and money, vote in democratic elections, and, most important, how to be creative. Unlocking the habits of genius has changed me and my view of the world. Perhaps a careful reading of this book will change you as well.

CHAPTER 1

GIFT OR HARD WORK?

IQ or Many Qs?

"There is no answer! There is no answer! There is no answer!" one hundred eager undergraduates chanted in the first session of my "genius course," as I urged them on. Students typically want an answer to put into their pocket as they leave class that they can deploy later on a test, but I felt that it was important to make this point immediately. To the simple question of what drives genius—nature or nurture—there really is no answer.

This issue always caused debate in my class. The quant types (math and science majors) thought genius was due to natural gifts; parents and teachers had told them that they had been born with a special talent for quantitative reasoning. The jocks (varsity athletes) thought exceptional accomplishment was all hard work: no pain, no gain; coaches had taught them that their achievement was the result of endless hours of practice. Among fledgling political scientists, conservatives thought genius a God-given gift; liberals thought it was caused by a nurturing environment. Nature or nurture? Each side had supporters among my students. Similarly, geniuses throughout history have taken sides.

Plato said that the capacity to do extraordinary things was a gift of soothsayers and gods.[1] But Shakespeare seemed to place great faith in free will and independent initiative when he wrote, "The fault, dear Brutus, is not in our stars, but in ourselves" (*Julius Caesar*). On the other hand, in his autobiography, the English naturalist Charles Darwin declared that "Most of our qualities are innate."[2] More recently, the French philosopher Simone de Beauvoir declared, "One is not born a genius, one becomes a genius."[3] Back and forth the argument goes: natural endowment versus hard work.

Geniuses have a habit of not recognizing their own hidden gifts and leaving it to others. Giorgio Vasari (1511–1574), the acclaimed biographer of the great Renaissance artists, marveled at Leonardo da Vinci's innate talents with these words: "Sometimes in a supernatural fashion a single body is lavishly supplied with such beauty, grace, and ability that wherever the individual turns, each of his actions is so divine that he leaves behind all other men and clearly makes himself known as a genius endowed by God (which he is)."[4] One of Leonardo's gifts was keen visual observation; he had the capacity to "freeze frame" an object in motion— the outreached wings of a bird in flight, the legs of a galloping horse off the ground, the eddies of a rippling river. "The dragonfly flies with four wings, and when those in front are raised those behind are lowered," Leonardo recorded in a notebook around 1490.[5] Who knew?

Leonardo's archrival Michelangelo had a photographic memory and perfect hand/eye coordination that allowed him to draw lines in precise proportional relationships.[6] Tesla was a fast study because he, too, had an eidetic memory and could quote, among other things, every line of Johann Wolfgang von Goethe's *Faust*. Wassily Kandinsky, Vincent van Gogh, Vladimir Nabokov, and Duke Ellington were all born synesthesiacs; when they heard music or observed words or numbers, they saw colors. Lady Gaga is, too. "When I write songs," she said in a 2009 interview in the *Guardian*, "I hear melodies and I hear lyrics but I also see colours; I see sound like a wall of colours."[7]

In 1806, Ludwig van Beethoven, in the midst of one of his

famous temper tantrums, barked at the high-ranking Karl Max, Prince Lichnowsky, "Prince, you are what you are through the accident of birth; what I am, I am through myself. There have been and will be thousands of princes; there is only one Beethoven."[8] To this we might respectfully reply, "True enough, Ludwig, but you, too, are an accident of birth. Your father and grandfather were professional musicians, and likely from them you inherited, among other things, your gift of perfect pitch and musical memory."

Perfect pitch is heritable and runs in families, though it is a talent given to only about one in ten thousand. Michael Jackson, Frank Sinatra, Mariah Carey, Ella Fitzgerald, Bing Crosby, Stevie Wonder, Dmitri Shostakovich, and Mozart were similarly endowed with absolute pitch. Mozart was also born with an extraordinary phonographic memory (memory for sounds) as well as a motographic one, meaning that he could instantly move his hands to the right place or key on the violin, organ, and piano, coordinating musical sounds in his mind with the spot that would create them. All of his musical gifts were evident by the age of six. That could only be nature.

Twenty-three-time Olympic gold medal swimmer Michael Phelps has the body of a shark and sometimes races one.[9] But Phelps was born with an ergonomic advantage: he is the perfect height for swimming (six feet, four inches), has atypically big feet (flippers), and possesses unusually long arms (paddles). Normally, as Leonardo's famous Vitruvian man shows, a person's reach is equal to his or her height; Phelps's wingspan (six feet, seven inches) is, however, three inches longer. But Phelps, as suggested above, is no genius. Gifted as he is, he has done nothing to change the discipline of swimming or influence an event at the Olympic Games.

Simone Biles, whom the *New York Times* calls "the greatest American gymnast of all time," presents a different case.[10] Her extraordinary athletic ability has revolutionized gymnastics. On August 9, 2019, she became the first person to execute a double flip dismount from the balance beam and also a triple-double flip in a floor exercise, bringing the number of gymnastics skills named after her to four. Each new move required judges to create a new "difficulty point score." In contrast to swimmer Phelps, transformative gymnast Biles is short (four feet, eight inches), compact, and densely muscular. As a result, she can stay tightly tucked in twists and flips, thereby maintaining speed. "I was built this way for a reason, so I'm going to use it," she said in 2016,[11] referring to her compact frame. Yet at the same time, as she emphasized in a MasterClass online educational video in 2019, "I really had to focus on the fundamentals, such as doing the drills, doing a lot of all the basics, doing the mental work, so that I could be where I am today."[12] Nature or nurture?

THE EXPRESSION "NATURE VERSUS NURTURE" WAS POPULARIZED BY Francis Galton, a cousin of Charles Darwin, in his book *Hereditary Genius: An Inquiry into Its Laws and Consequences* (1869). Galton studied nearly a thousand "eminent" individuals—all but a handful being males of British birth, including some of his own relatives. You don't have to be a genius to guess Galton's opinion on the matter: genius runs in direct family lines and is hereditary; your potential is bequeathed at birth.

On the first page of *Hereditary Genius,* Galton said that it would be possible "to obtain by careful selection a permanent breed of dogs or horses gifted with peculiar powers of running, or of doing anything else," as well as "a highly-gifted race of men by judicious marriages during several consecutive generations."[13] Forget, if you can, that Galton's notion of selective breeding was the starting point for eugenics, which led to the death camps of National Socialism. Galton was simply wrong: you can't create a superhorse, or a "gifted race of men," by selective breeding.[14] To make the point, return with me to the 1973 Kentucky Derby and meet a horse named Secretariat.

On a sunny spring afternoon, May 5, 1973, I stood on the outside back rail at the three-quarter-mile post at Churchill Downs. In my hand I held two two-dollar "win" tickets, one that I had bought on a horse named Warbucks and one that I had purchased for a friend on the favorite, Secretariat. As the horses entered the track for their warm-ups, Warbucks appeared first, coming in at 7-to-1 odds. The horse seemed small, but perhaps there was no correlation of size and speed in horse racing. A few horses later, at 3-to-2 odds, appeared Secretariat, a huge creature with a massive chest and shiny chestnut coat. And he had swagger. If God were a horse, he would look like this.

Off they went. Secretariat won the mile-and-a-quarter race in one minute and 59^2/$_5$ seconds, and he still holds the record for the Derby and the other Triple Crown races as well. My horse came in dead last. Not having the gift of foresight, I waited in line for forty minutes to collect the three dollars on my friend's two-dollar bet. I should have given him the three bucks and kept the ticket to sell today on eBay. But who could then have foreseen the existence of eBay and that Secretariat, today called a "genius racehorse," would become the horse of the century and perhaps of all time?

Talent may be heritable, but genius is not. Genius—or exceptional accomplishment, in the case of a horse—is not generational but more akin to a perfect storm. At the time of the autopsy of Secretariat, his twenty-one-pound heart weighed twice that of his father, Bold Ruler. Secretariat came from a good but by no means exceptional bloodline, and he left no exceptional progeny. Of the four hundred offspring he sired, only one ever won a Triple Crown race. Similarly, most geniuses don't come from obviously exceptional parents.[15] Yes, there are six pairs of Nobel Prize–winning fathers and sons and one mother and daughter (Marie Curie and Irène Joliot-Curie).[16] Perhaps the more compelling case is the cohort of Johann Sebastian Bach and his three sons Carl Philipp Emanuel, Wilhelm Friedemann, and Johann Christian. But these families are the exception that proves the rule. Think of Picasso's four children (none was a brilliant painter), look at the art of Marguerite Matisse on the web, or listen to a piano concerto by Franz Xaver Mozart (supermusical ear but no imagination), and ponder why geniuses tend not to produce geniuses. Think of all the geniuses—Leonardo, Michelangelo, Shakespeare, Isaac Newton, Benjamin Franklin, Tesla, Tubman, Einstein, van Gogh, Curie, Frida Kahlo, King, Andy Warhol, Jobs, Toni Morrison, and Elon Musk—who seem to come out of nowhere. Einstein implied that ancestry is not a good predictor of genius when he said, "The exploration of my ancestors . . . leads nowhere."[17] The point is this: genius is an explosive and seemingly random event arising from a combination of many personal phenotypes—among them intelligence, resilience, curiosity, visionary thinking, and more than a dash of obsessive behavior.[18] Psychologists call it "emergenesis";[19] we laymen prefer the term "perfect storm." It can happen, but it's a long shot.

Galton didn't know of the work of Gregor Mendel, the genius who gave us a scientific understanding of the units of heredity called genes. Nor could Galton have known of Havelock Ellis's work *A Study of British Genius* (1904), which attempted statistically to demonstrate that geniuses are most often firstborn males, conveniently forgetting the female Elizabeth I (third child in birth order), Jane Austen (seventh), and Virginia Woolf (sixth), for example.[20] Today, the thinking of Galton, Mendel, and Ellis forms the basis of what is called biological determinism or the "blueprint for life" theory: your genes provide a template on which is engraved all that you will become. But as you might suspect, the predeterminative "blueprint theory" of genius is not the answer.

Perhaps the answer is to be found in the modern science of epigenetics. Epigenes ("outside the genes") are small tags attached to each gene in our genome. Our growth, from birth to death, is subject to the workings of these "on or off switches," for they control when and if our genes will express themselves. In simplest terms, genes are the nature side of things, epigenes the nurture. How we are nurtured, the environment in which we live, and how we control that environment and ourselves affect the activation of our genes. Again, epigenes are triggers of genetic development stimulated by the environment. As the neuroscientist Gilbert Gottlieb stated, not only do genes and environment cooperate as we develop, but genes require input from the environment to function properly.[21] Epigenes hold out the possibility that each of us can control what we become if we are willing to work for it.

Have you ever heard of a lazy genius? No. Geniuses have a habit of working hard because they are obsessed. Moreover, in public proclamations they tend to value their parental units of heredity ("gifts") far less than their own labors, as the following quotes from a few Western geniuses suggest: "If you knew how much work went into it, you wouldn't call it genius" (Michelangelo); "I should get discouraged if I could not go on working as hard or even harder" (Vincent van Gogh); "Genius is the result of hard work" (Maxim Gorky); "I didn't believe in weekends. I didn't believe in vacations" (Bill Gates); "There is no talent or genius without hard work" (Dmitri Mendeleev); "What separates the talented individual from the successful one is a lot of hard work" (Stephen King); "I worked very hard when I was young so I don't have to work so hard now" (Mozart); "People may not get all they work for in this world, but they must certainly work for all they get" (Frederick Douglass); "No one ever changed the world with a forty-hour work week" (Elon Musk); and "God gives talent. Work transforms talent into genius" (Anna Pavlova). I once believed that, too.

Here's a joke you may remember: A young musician arrives in New York City and naively asks, "How do you get to Carnegie Hall?" The response: "Practice!" I tried that, and it didn't work. Hard work has its limits.

My training in music started at age four on an Acrosonic upright piano with lessons from the amiable Ted Brown and within six years progressed to a six-foot Baldwin grand and the best teachers in Washington, D.C. To become a concert pianist—to be the next Van Cliburn was my aim—I entered and was graduated from the prestigious Eastman School of Music. By the age of twenty-two, I had practiced approximately 18,000 hours, yet I knew that I would never earn a dime as a concert pianist. I had every advantage: huge hands and long, thin fingers, the best training, and a strong work ethic. I lacked only one thing: a great gift for music. I was talented, yes, but I had no exceptional sense of pitch, musical memory, or hand/ear coordination, nothing extraordinary. I did, however, have one negative genetic endowment: I was susceptible to stage fright—not an asset when the difference of a millimeter on a piano or violin can spell the difference between success and failure. Still today, this "failure to launch" as a pianist causes me to ask: Does hard work alone transform talent into genius? Does practice really make perfect?

It does according to Anders Ericsson, the godfather of the discipline of performance expertise. Beginning in a 1993 article in *Psychological Review* and continuing through his coauthored book *Peak: Secrets from the New Science of Expertise* (2016), Ericsson posited that human greatness is not a genetic gift but simply the result of disciplined hard work, 10,000 hours of focused practice. Ericsson's evidence for the theory initially came from studies in which he and other psychologists tracked improvement in violinists and pianists at the Music Academy of West Berlin.[22] Students of similar age but different performing levels (from secondary school music teachers to future international stars) were correlated with duration and quality of practice. The finding: "We conclude that individuals acquire virtually all of the distinguishing characteristics of expert performers through relevant activities (deliberate practice)."[23] The promise of the 10,000-hour rule was attractive, and many people jumped onto the "practice" bandwagon, including first-rate humanists such as Nobel Prize winner Daniel Kahneman (*Thinking, Fast and Slow*) and David Brooks ("Genius: The Modern View"), as well as the popular bestselling author Malcolm Gladwell ("The Trouble with Geniuses" in his book *Outliers: The Story of Success*). But there's a problem—actually two.

First, at the outset, the Berlin psychologists failed to test students for natural musical ability. They did not compare apples to apples but rather compared the talented to the truly gifted. Extraordinary natural ability makes practice fun and easy, encouraging the participant to want to do more.[24] Parents and peers tend to be impressed by those to whom things come effortlessly, and they offer praise, thereby strengthening the positive feedback loop. Ericsson and company have confused cause and effect. Practice is a result. The initial catalyst is the natural gift.

Second, and more important, elite performance by definition involves "performing"—working through (Latin *per*) something that someone else has already formed (Latin *forma*). Exceptional performance can be useful if you are a math whiz searching for the square root of an impossibly long number, a card counter at a Las Vegas casino, an athlete hoping to clock a world-record time in climbing Mount Everest, or a concert pianist trying to play Frédéric Chopin's "Minute Waltz" in fifty-seven seconds. But someone else invented the game, the athletic event, or the musical composition. The genius gets to the top of the mountain by inventing something new and transformative: the aerial tramway or the helicopter. Practice may make the old perfect, but it does not produce innovation.

By now the attentive reader will have inferred the obvious: natural talent versus hard work is not a binary opposition. Genius is the product of both nature and nurture. To prove the point, I propose a contest. I call it "The $250 Million Race to Qatar." Our contestants will be two painters, Monsieur Paul Cézanne (1839–1906) and Señor Pablo Picasso (1881–1973). The aim is to create the most valuable painting ever sold to a potentate of Qatar. Because he was born first, Cézanne leads off.

As a student in Aix-en-Provence, Paul Cézanne, the son of a banker, showed more of a proclivity toward literature than toward art. Only at age fifteen did he receive formal training in drawing, and not until twenty, after a short stint in law school, did he vow to become a painter. After two years of learning his trade in Paris, he submitted works to the official Salon of the

School of Fine Arts for exhibition, but they were rejected. He resubmitted new works almost every year for the next twenty years, with the same negative result. Finally, in 1882, at age forty-three, came official acceptance.[25]

Pablo Picasso was born in the fall of 1881, the son of a painter, José Ruiz y Blasco. Young Picasso could draw before he could speak. His painting *Salmerón (Portrait of an Aged Fisherman)*, executed in an hour's time at the age of thirteen, is a masterpiece of psychological insight and painterly technique. An art critic, having seen other paintings exhibited by the boy, reported in *La Voz de Galicia* that "he has a glorious and brilliant future ahead of him."[26] Still not yet fourteen, Picasso gained admission to Barcelona's School of Fine Arts. As a fellow student said of the prodigy, "He was way ahead of the other students, who were all five or six years older. Although he paid no apparent attention to what the professors were saying, he instantly grasped what he was taught."[27] In his twenties, Picasso created the most stunning array of original paintings that the world had or has ever seen— the Rose Period works, the Blue Period works, the Harlequins, early Cubist masterpieces, and early Collage. Valued in purely monetary terms, he created his best paintings around age twenty-five.[28] Eventually, his *The Women of Algiers* (1955) would be purchased by Sheik Hamad bin Jassim bin Jaber bin Mohammed bin Thani Al Thani of Qatar for $180 million. Picasso, the possessor of huge natural gifts, was in a class by himself.

Monsieur Cézanne, however, continued to labor in his studios in Paris and Aix. By the late 1880s, at the age of nearly fifty, progressive artists were beginning to admire his unique emphasis on geometric forms and flat colors. During the decade before his death in 1906, a half century after he had begun art school, Cézanne created his greatest works.[29] In 1907, a retrospective of Cézanne's painting was mounted in Paris, and the young Turks of the art world attended—Picasso, Henri Matisse, Georges Braque, and Amedeo Modigliani among them.[30] "Cézanne is the father of us all," declared Picasso.[31] In 2011, Cézanne's *The Card Players* sold to the ruling family of Qatar for $250 million, $70 million more than had the Picasso.

But what's $70 million among friends? Let's call it a draw. Obviously there are two very different routes to creative genius, one immediately evident (gifts), the other more covert (laborious self-improvement). Both are needed, but in what proportions? The practice proponents say that more than 80 percent of outcome is determined by hard work, whereas other psychologists have recently suggested reducing that figure, depending on the field of activity, to around 25 percent.[32] To gain insight into the relative importance of gift and work, I queried Nathan Chen, a fledging genius in my Yale course.

As Simone Biles is today the number one–ranked female American gymnast, so Chen is the number one–ranked male American figure skater and likewise an Olympic medal winner. Chen was the first skater to execute six quads (a jump requiring four rotations) at an Olympic event, carrying the sport into a higher athletic realm and forcing judges to come up with a new metric of difficulty. Like Biles, Chen is comparatively short (five feet, six inches) and has a high muscle-to-weight ratio. What follows is the gist of what he has to say about gift and hard work.

In my opinion, there are genetic factors at work in this domain: height, bodily proportions, general strength, and capacity to quickly improve muscle memory. But there are, in addition, a number of genetic factors you can't really see and are more difficult to quantify. Among these are the ability to be calm in the face of stress and the ability to internally strategize and course-correct during a competition. So for me, I would say that it is 80% nature. The gold medal athletes get to an accumulated 100%—80% nature (genes and luck) and 20% nurture. For those athletes who are naturally at 60% (nature), they must maximize the 20% (work) in order to even think about competing against the top (as 90%–100% athletes).

Therefore, it's difficult to say which is more important, nature or nurture. They both have their importance, but at the end of the day, no matter how hard you train in your sport, *without* the genetic capacity it will be nearly impossible to be the best.[33]

Note that Chen astutely included "luck" among natural gifts, recognizing that it helps to be born with sufficient resources and educational opportunity. Finally, he suggests, whatever the ratio between gifts and hard work may be, in order to get to the pinnacle of what you choose to do, you must max out both.

WE HAVE LONG BEEN OBSESSED WITH ONE NATURAL GIFT IN PAR-ticular: IQ. Quantitative measurement of intelligence began in 1905, when Alfred Binet published a test designed to identify slow learners in the public schools of Paris so that they could thereafter be provided with assistance.[34] By 1912, the German term *Intelligenzquotient* (whence the English IQ) had become commonplace. Around the same time, the U.S. military started to employ a standardized test to screen for mental fitness and identify candidates for officers' training school. What had begun as an exercise in remedial education quickly became a gateway to elite status. After Stanford psychologist Lewis Terman began to study a group of gifted children with a minimum IQ of 135 (100 is considered average) in the 1920s, an exceptionally high IQ score came to be associated with genius. Still today, MENSA, a self-proclaimed "genius club" founded in Oxford, England, in 1946, requires for membership a verified IQ of 132. Some educators in the "gifted child industry" have gone further, identifying gradations of giftedness: an IQ of 130 to 144 as moderately gifted; 145 to 159 as highly gifted; 160 to 174 as exceptionally gifted; and 175 and above as profoundly gifted. But surely Stephen Hawking was right when he said in 2004, "People who boast about their IQs are losers."[35] Marie Curie never took an IQ test, neither did

Shakespeare, so how do we know how smart they were? Indeed, what does it mean to be "smart"?

IQ tests involve logic and employ the rules of math and language. Nowhere on an IQ test, however, are points given for creative answers or for expanding the possibilities of responses. The frustrated Thomas Edison identified the limitations of applying pure logic to a problem in 1903, chastising an uncreative apprentice in these terms: "That's just where your trouble has been, you have tried only reasonable things. Reasonable things never work. Thank God you can't think up any more reasonable things, so you'll have to begin thinking up unreasonable things to try, and then you'll hit the solution in no time."[36]

Reasonable logic differs from creative ingenuity; thinking inside the box, as the metaphor goes, differs from thinking outside. Strictly logical cognitive processing, of the sort involved in an IQ test, and creativity, of the sort practiced by an artist like Picasso, are two different things. Picasso likely would have agreed with Harvard's Stephen Jay Gould on the matter: "The abstraction of intelligence as a single entity, its location within the brain, its quantification as one number for each individual, and the use of these numbers to rank people in a single series of worthiness" may be ill advised.[37]

In 1971, the U.S. Supreme Court unanimously declared the use of an IQ test as a precondition of employment to be illegal.[38] The Scholastic Aptitude Test (SAT)—the standardized test widely used for college admissions in the United States—is not illegal, but it, too, is an imperfect standard by which to evaluate potentially transformative minds.[39] As recent economic data show, SAT scores reflect as much the income and education of a student's parents as they do the achievement potential of the student.[40] More than a thousand colleges and universities, including the prestigious University of Chicago, have dropped the SAT (and the similar ACT) as a requirement for admission.[41] In December

2019, students in a largely black and Hispanic California school district filed suit against the University of California system to stop it using such standardized tests, and six months later the board of regents unanimously agreed.[42] Like an IQ test, the SAT correlates with better grades in high school and the first year of college, as well as with later success and higher earnings in a few specialized fields.[43] Thus far, however, no one has demonstrated a correlation between such tests and the capacity to write a symphony or explained how Darwinian curiosity and patience can be measured in a three-hour exam.

Most recently, many American elite private schools, including Phillips Exeter Academy, the Dalton School, Horace Mann School, and Choate Rosemary Hall, have also dropped both Advanced Placement (AP) courses and tests.[44] "Students can often sense the tension that their teachers are feeling between wanting to honor the questions in the room, or the interest in the room, and wanting to prepare students for a test that's not set by the school," said Horace Mann head of upper division Dr. Jessica Levenstein in 2018.[45] Such "teaching to the test" not only constricts curiosity but also contributes to stress and grade grubbing.

On April 17, 2018, I was honored by Phi Beta Kappa at Yale University with the DeVane Medal for excellence in undergraduate teaching and scholarship. As I wandered around the room the night of the award ceremony and heard the things graciously said about me, I couldn't help but think of the irony. I had been a B+ student in high school and had not made the honor roll. I could never have gotten into Yale as an undergraduate—although it had a fine music program—so I hadn't applied. Although I had taken an array of disconnected courses, winter and summer, I had not graduated from college with honors. When it came time for graduate school, I had been accepted by Harvard, Princeton, and Stanford but not Yale. Never in a million years would I have been elected to Phi Beta Kappa anywhere. My wife, Sherry, was the smart one in the family (Yale *summa cum laude* and Phi Beta Kappa), but she had long ago alerted me to the fact that sometimes students reached the Phi Beta Kappa grade threshold by playing it safe—taking the courses that easily suited their natural gifts. Perhaps the legitimate members of Phi Beta Kappa were great test takers but not risk takers, more conformists than contrarian thinkers.

An article by Wharton Business School professor Adam Grant, called "What Straight-A Students Get Wrong," confirmed my suspicions. Published in the *New York Times* in December 2018, the essay argued that grades are not a reliable marker of success, let alone genius. Says Grant, "The evidence is clear: Academic excellence is not a strong predictor of career excellence. Across industries, research shows that the correlation between grades and job performance is modest in the first year after college and trivial within a handful of years. For example, at Google, once employees are two or three years out of college, their grades have no bearing on their performance." Grant's explanation: "Academic grades rarely assess qualities like creativity, leadership and teamwork skills, or social, emotional and political intelligence. Yes, straight-A students master cramming information and regurgitating it on exams. But career success is rarely about finding the right solution to a problem—it's more about finding the right problem to solve."[46] Grant's conclusion calls to mind a joke long kicked around the halls of academia: "The A students get hired to teach in the universities, and the B's get relatively good jobs working for the C's."

IF IQ TESTS, SAT TESTS, AND GRADES ARE UNRELIABLE PREDICTORS of career success, they are even worse predictors of genius. They generate both false positives (those who seem headed for greatness but aren't) and false negatives (those who appear to be going nowhere but ultimately change the world). There are, of course, the occasional true-positive geniuses who excel in school, such as Marie Curie (top in her class at age sixteen), Sigmund Freud (*summa cum laude* at his high school), and Jeff Bezos (*summa cum laude* and Phi Beta Kappa at Princeton). A reputable test of gifted youths at Johns Hopkins University identified the potential of Mark Zuckerberg, Sergey Brin (a cofounder of Google), and Stefani Germanotta (Lady Gaga).[47] On the other hand, in a famous "genius test" conducted at Stanford by Lewis Terman and colleagues from the 1920s into the 1990s, a cohort of 1,500 youngsters with IQs over 135 ultimately failed to produce a single genius.[48] As a Terman associate later reported: "There wasn't a Nobel laureate. There wasn't a Pulitzer Prize. We didn't have a Picasso."[49]

More important, consider these false negatives—those geniuses who might *not* have done well on a standard IQ test and would *not* have been elected to Phi Beta Kappa. Charles Darwin's early academic record was so poor that his father predicted he would be a disgrace to his family.[50] Winston Churchill was likewise a poor student, admitting that "Where my reason, imagination or interest were not engaged, I would not or I could not learn."[51] Nobel Prize winners William Shockley and Luis Alvarez were rejected by the Stanford genius test because their IQ scores were too low.[52] The transformative novelist J. K. Rowling has confessed to having "a distinct lack of motivation at university," her undistinguished record the result of spending "far too long in the coffee bar writing stories and far too little time at lectures."[53] Similarly, Thomas Edison described himself as being "not at the head of my class, but the foot." Einstein graduated fourth in his class of five physicists in 1900.[54] Steve Jobs had a high school GPA of 2.65; Jack Ma, the founder of Alibaba (the Chinese equivalent of Amazon), took the *gaokao* (the Chinese national educational exam) and scored 19 out of 120 on a math section on his second try;[55] and Beethoven had trouble adding figures and never learned to multiply or divide. Walt Disney was a below-average student and often fell asleep in class.[56] Finally, Picasso could not remember the sequence of the letters in the alphabet and saw symbolic numbers as literal representations: a 2 as the wing of a bird or a 0 as a body.[57] Standardized tests might have failed to recognize all those geniuses.

So why do we keep using them? We continue to rely on standardized tests because they are just that: standardized. A common set of questions can be used to evaluate and compare the cognitive development of millions of students, an advantage in countries such as the United States and China with large populations. To gain efficiency, we sacrifice breadth of understanding. Tests such as the SAT and Chinese *gaokao* set up a single metric for a single traditional problem, instead of encouraging strategies that question a premise or rethink a concept in an ever-changing world. They validate hitting a predetermined target rather than creating a yet-unseen one. They privilege a limited range of cognitive skills (math and verbal) above emotional and social interaction. The point here is not to suggest that testing to measure human potential should be ceased but rather that the test must be sufficiently broad, flexible, and nuanced to do the job. Although current standardized tests are efficient, they are too narrow in both intent and content to be predictors of success in life, let alone genius.

The choreographers Martha Graham and George Balanchine excelled in kinetic imagination; Martin Luther King, Jr., and Mahatma Gandhi in extrapersonal observation; Virginia Woolf and Sigmund Freud in personal introspection; James Joyce and Toni Morrison in verbal and linguistic expression; Auguste Rodin and Michelangelo in visual and spatial reasoning; Bach and Beethoven in auditory acumen; and Einstein and Hawking in mathematical-logical reasoning. The seven fields of human activity named above are the seven modalities of human intellect posited by Harvard's Howard Gardner—"multiple intelligences," he famously called them.[58] They are discipline-specific mind-sets from which creativity springs. Yet determinative within each and every one of these creative disciplines are multiple personality traits: intelligence, curiosity, resilience, persistence, risk tolerance, self-confidence, and the ability to work hard among them. I refer to one's capacity to deploy many such traits in the service of genius as the Many Traits Quotient (MQ's).

J. K. Rowling has sold more books (500 million) than almost any other living writer and created a reading frenzy among young people. In her 2008 commencement address at Harvard University, she extolled the virtues of failure and emphasized the importance of the imagination and of passion in life.[59] In a 2019 post on her website, she listed five personal qualities necessary to success as a writer: a love of reading (curiosity), discipline, resilience, courage, and independence.[60] If these personal enablers seem important to a genius like Rowling, why not construct a broadly based test to measure them? Perhaps our obsession with precollege tests such as the SAT and the *gaokao* is misguided. Perhaps instead of a test of things scholastic taught in school (the SAT), we need a more expansive Genius Aptitude Test (the GAT) that would involve MQ's.[61] Thus the GAT would come with subsections, among them the WHAT (Work Hard Aptitude Test), PAT (Passion Aptitude Test), CAT (Curiosity Aptitude Test), SCAT (Self-Confidence Aptitude Test), and RAT (Resilience Aptitude Test).

How high would a student need to score on the Genius Aptitude Test to get into Hogwarts or Harvard? Not high. Many experts today believe that the only intelligence tally needed to excel in the sciences is a threshold IQ score of 115 to 125. After that, there is almost no correlation between additional IQ points and creative insights.[62] The scientists Richard Feynman, James Watson, and William Shockley had scores no higher than that, and they won Nobel Prizes in their respective fields. The Graduate Record Exam (GRE), a standardized test instituted in 1949 for graduate schools, has a perfect score of 800. Most programs require a minimum of 700, employing it as a fast way to weed out "unqualified" candidates. But my own thirty years of experience reading applications to the Yale Graduate School suggests that a GRE score of only 550 out of 800 is sufficient demonstration of potential. Indeed, a 2014 article in *Nature,* titled "A Test That Fails," quoted William Sedlacek, professor emeritus of education at the University of Maryland, College Park, as saying he found "only a weak correlation between the test and ultimate success."[63] He recommended de-emphasizing the GRE and augmenting admissions procedures that measure other attributes—such as drive, diligence, and the willingness to take risks. As to what test score Sedlacek might be willing to accept, he says a 400 would be fine.[64]

Finally, is it possible that all Ivy League schools are themselves overrated?[65] A survey of Nobel Prize winners suggests that getting into Harvard, Yale, or Princeton is no more necessary to greatness than is attending *any* top 15 percent school.[66] Why, then, would American and Chinese parents try to falsify SAT scores and bribe admissions officers to get their child into a coveted "Ivy type" school? Precisely that sort of academic fraud has been going on, as was revealed in 2019 through an FBI sting called Operation Varsity Blues.[67] Why would parents risk fines and imprisonment to inflate scores on a test of questionable value? Why would they deprive their children of the opportunity to learn from failure and develop resilience? At Yale, Rudy Meredith—whom our daughter and I used to watch coach the women's soccer team—pleaded guilty to soliciting $865,000 to falsify the qualifications of two student applicants.[68] To make matters worse, almost annually at least one college or university gets called out for falsely inflating the test scores of incoming students.[69] But as I have said to generations of Yale applicants touring the campus with their parents, "In truth, there are at least three hundred great colleges in the United States, and it doesn't much matter which one of these you attend. What matters is not the school, but what is inside of you (or your child)."

But old myths—IQ is the gold standard of genius, the SAT is the gateway to success, anything less than Harvard, Yale, or Princeton is inferior—die hard. Perhaps we should take a step back and ask whether our reliance on metrics such as IQ and standardized tests and our fixation on elite education are nurturing the kind of citizens we want to lead our society. Do we privilege a system that rewards the natural gift of cognitive analysis

(IQ) or one that values multiple character traits (MQ's), including IQ? The number of false negative geniuses mentioned above—Beethoven, Darwin, Edison, Picasso, Disney, Jobs, and all the rest—suggests that genius is much more than IQ and that "smart" can mean many things. The challenge is to find a testing metric that discovers the hidden genius. Apposite here is a saying attributed to Einstein: "Everybody is a genius. But if you judge a fish by its ability to climb a tree, it will live its whole life believing that it is stupid."[70]

CHAPTER 2

GENIUS AND GENDER

The Game Is Rigged

I n 2014, Catherine Nichols, an aspiring novelist, undertook an experiment. She sent a query letter describing her unpublished novel to fifty literary agents under her own name, and then she sent the same letter to fifty agents under the name of "George Leyer" (wink).[1] "George" had his manuscript accepted for review seventeen times, whereas Catherine had hers accepted only twice. Even the rejections that "George" received were warmer and more encouraging than those sent to Catherine. Similar workplace bias correlated with gender or race has been observed in the process of reviewing job applications.[2] The surprising thing about the gender bias in the publishing business is that statistically nearly half of literary agents and more than half of editors at publishing houses are women.[3] The fact that women might have hidden biases against other women might come as something of a surprise; the fact that men have discriminated against women since time immemorial is not a secret to anyone. So successful have men been in excluding women from "the genius club" that even women have come to downplay their own importance.

Recently, I surveyed more than four thousand adults, asking them to name a dozen geniuses in Western cultural history. My respondents were all students, 57 percent women and most over age fifty, enrolled in One Day University, a continuing education program operating in seventy-three U.S. cities. The aim of my survey was to determine how far down the list of geniuses we would go before landing upon a woman. Even among this strong female majority of respondents, the first woman emerged on average in eighth place. Those named most frequently were scientists Marie Curie and Rosalind Franklin, mathematician Ada Lovelace, and writers Virginia Woolf and Jane Austen, with Curie named most often by far. There were no female philosophers, architects, or engineers at all.

This same disproportion arose early on in my "genius course" at Yale. Although Yale undergraduates are now fifty-fifty by gender, and although the "genius course" is a general humanities class open to all, annually the enrollment skews about sixty-forty male-female. Students at Yale and elsewhere vote with their feet, and, despite favorable course evaluations, women at Yale don't seem to be quite as interested in the notion of genius as their male counterparts. I have also noticed that when I pose a question or ask for a contrary opinion in class, predominantly male students respond. Once I realized this, I began asking a teaching assistant to keep track of the gender of each respondent and the amount of "airtime" consumed by each. The ratio, year after year, has been about seventy-thirty male to female.

Puzzled by this discrepancy, I soon found that others in the professional world, Sheryl Sandberg among them, had observed that in open discussion "alpha males" eagerly dominate, while women at first tacitly watch, sizing up how the game will be played.[4] And a 2012 study by professors at Brigham Young University, Princeton University, and Portland State University reported that at academic conferences women spoke significantly less than their proportional representation—their airtime amounting to less than 75 percent of that of men.[5] My initial 30 percent female engagement rate, however, was worse.

Speaking in public is one thing, but what was causing women to disengage from the subject matter I was teaching? Are women less excited by competitive comparisons that rank some people as "more exceptional" than others? Are they less likely to value the traditional markers of genius—things such as the world's greatest painting or most revolutionary invention? Are women somehow less interested in the very concept of genius? If so, why might this be the case?

A clue was to be found in a 2010 research report issued by the American Association of University Women titled *Why So Few? Women in Science, Technology, Engineering, and Mathematics.*[6] It emphasized that women have an uphill battle in STEM fields owing to the obvious stereotypes, biases, and unfavorable work environments in colleges and universities. Likewise, a 2018 report by Microsoft, "Why Do Girls Lose Interest in STEM?," suggested that the lack of mentors and parental support play a role.[7] I made the connection: fewer women probably opt for my "genius course" and fewer women embrace STEM fields because both have traditionally been constructed by and around men. Women have fewer role models (geniuses) to whom they can relate, and fewer contemporary mentors with whom they can bond. Why take a course in which the reading, once again, will be mostly about the triumphant accomplishments of "great men"? For these and other reasons, women have bypassed the STEM disciplines and the study of genius.

The historian Dean Keith Simonton, who has researched genius for more than forty years, has numerically demonstrated the underrepresentation of women in fields traditionally associated with genius. According to Simonton's statistics, women make up only about 3 percent of the most noteworthy political figures in history. In the annals of science, fewer than 1 percent of notables are women, a mere drop in an otherwise all-male sea. Even in the more "female-friendly" domain of creative writing, female luminaries constitute only 10 percent of great writers. In the realm of music, for every Clara Schumann or Fanny Mendelssohn, there are ten well-known male classical composers.[8] By way of conclusion, Simonton observed that although women constitute half the population, throughout history they have been depicted as "unimportant, inconspicuous, even irrelevant to human affairs."[9] One can choose to believe Simonton's statistics or not. But the question he ultimately poses is this: Does this so-called under-achievement arise from genetic inadequacy or from cultural bias? Many would consider the very question itself insulting, including the genius Virginia Woolf.

WOOLF WAS BORN IN LONDON INTO A WELL-TO-DO, UPPER-MIDDLE-class family in 1882. Although provided with books and private tutors, the low-cost homeschooling she received was a far cry from that afforded her brothers in expensive boarding schools and then at Cambridge University. Once when doing research on the poet John Milton, she was denied access to an unnamed "Oxbridge" college library because of her gender. Angered by the inequity and curious as to how such gender bias had come to be, she went in search of female geniuses throughout history. What she concluded was that genius is an all-male social con-struct, as she described in her famous essay of 1929, *A Room of One's Own*. Woolf's observations about exceptional female accomplishment—and the barriers to it—still resound today.

A quiet room (in which to write), money (to pay the bills), and time to think (about things other than child-rearing)—for Woolf, those were metaphors for opportunity, the opportunity histori-cally denied women. "Making a fortune and bearing thirteen children—no human being could stand it," she wrote. ". . . In the first place, to earn money was impossible for them, and in the second, had it been possible, the law denied them the right to possess what money they earned."[10] Thus as engines of intellec-tual capital, "women did not exist. . . . It was impossible for any woman, past, present, or to come to have the genius of Shake-speare,"[11] she wrote. Throughout history, she said, there had al-ways been this assertion: "You cannot do this, you are incapable of doing that."[12] Among those who set the "thou cannot" barrier was the famous educator Jean-Jacques Rousseau, who wrote in 1758, "In general, women don't like art, don't understand it, and have no genius for it."[13]

With defeat preordained for females, many female geniuses throughout history responded by disguising themselves and their gender. Jane Austen published *Pride and Prejudice* as an anonymous woman, and Mary Shelley did the same when she initially set loose *Frankenstein*. Other female geniuses assumed male *noms de plume*, including George Sand (Aurore Dudevant), Daniel Stern (Marie d'Agoult), George Eliot (Mary Ann Evans), Currer Bell (Charlotte Brontë), and Ellis Bell (Emily Brontë). Perhaps they would never enjoy the glory of recognition, but at least now their work had a chance of being published and read. How can a genius change the world if her work remains unknown?

The recognition Woolf gained and the issues she called out in her famous essay undoubtedly inspired and galvanized many female writers who came after her. The literary greats Toni Morrison (who wrote a master's thesis on Woolf), Pearl S. Buck, Margaret Atwood, and Joyce Carol Oates all wrote or write under their own names, and today women authors seem to enjoy the same status and power of voice as men. But if this is true, why did Joanne Rowling, Phyllis Dorothy James, and Erika Mitchell think it necessary to become J. K. Rowling, P. D. James, and E. L. James? Why did Nelle Harper Lee leave off the Nelle? Rowling was told by her agent, Christopher Little, that she would sell more of her Harry Potter books if she disguised herself as a man.[14]

"To write a work of genius is almost always a feat of prodigious difficulty," continued Virginia Woolf in *A Room of One's Own*. What made it difficult was that the world seemed indifferent to the extra weight placed upon a creative woman and that even men of genius were hostile to the notion that it should be lifted. "Accentuating all these difficulties and making them harder to bear is the world's notorious indifference. . . . [But what] men of genius have found so hard to bear was in her case not indifference, but *hostility* [emphasis added]."[15] Hostility is the child of fear—of losing authority, status, and wealth. The tendency to fear female accomplishment is part of what Woolf called "an obscure masculine complex." It consists, she said, of a deep-seated desire, "not so much that *she* be inferior, but that *he* be superior."[16]

To ensure their superiority, according to Woolf, males devised a simple strategy: make women look half size, and thereupon men appear twice as large. This she calls the "looking-glass," or magnifying, effect: "Women have served all these centuries as looking-glasses possessing the magic and delicious power of reflecting the figure of man at twice its natural size. . . . That is why Napoleon and Mussolini both insist so emphatically upon the inferiority of women, for if they were not inferior, they [the males] would cease to enlarge. That serves to explain in part the necessity that women are to men."[17]

Napoleon had indeed said, "Women are nothing but machines for producing children." Among those we consider great men, he was not alone in his misogyny. The poet George Gordon, Lord Byron, said of women, "They ought to mind home, and be well fed and clothed, but not mixed in society. Well educated, too, in religion, but to read neither poetry nor politics—nothing but books of piety and cookery. Music, drawing, dancing, also a little gardening and ploughing now and then."[18] Music? Why not, then, a female composer? The man of letters Dr. Samuel Johnson discounted that notion: "Sir, a woman's composing is like a dog's walking on his hind legs. It is not done well, but you are surprised to find it done at all."[19] A dog also came to mind when Charles Darwin contemplated marriage, carefully weighing the pros and cons of a dog versus a wife as a potential lifetime companion.[20] Said Picasso about dogs, "There is nothing so similar to one poodle dog as another poodle dog, and that goes for women, too."[21]

We might expect, or at least hope, that learned philosophers of the past might have risen above misogyny. But disappointingly, this was often not the case. Although we have Arthur Schopenhauer to thank for his remarkable metaphor "A person of genius hits a target that no one else can see,"[22] he seems far from the mark when he wrote in *On Women* (1851), "It is only the man whose intellect is clouded by his sexual instinct that could give that stunted, narrow-shouldered, broad-hipped, and short-legged race the name of *the fair sex;* for the entire beauty of the sex is based on this instinct. One would be more justified in calling them the *unaesthetic sex* than the beautiful. Neither for music, nor for poetry, nor for fine art have they any real or true sense and susceptibility, and it is mere mockery on their part, in their desire to please, if they affect any such thing."[23]

Surely, objective scientists might judge the world impartially. Yet an early neuroscientist, Paul de Broca, after whom "Broca's area" of the brain is named, declared in 1862 that brains are larger "in men than in women, in eminent men than in men of mediocre talent, in superior races than in inferior [read "African"] races."[24] Broca was incorrect, for brain size, it turns out, is mostly a factor of body size, not of gender or race. Perhaps the renowned theoretical physicist Stephen Hawking should also have kept quiet in 2005 when he stated, "It is generally recognised that women are better than men at languages, personal relations and multitasking, but less good at map-reading and spatial awareness. It is therefore not unreasonable to suppose that women might be less good at mathematics and physics."[25] That same year, economist and former Harvard president Lawrence Summers created a furor when he argued that men outperform women in maths and sciences because of biological difference, and discrimination is no longer a career barrier for female academics.[26] Shortly thereafter, he was encouraged to resign—and did.

Even the scientist Albert Einstein did not think beyond the paradigms of his day when he said in 1920, evidently with a tinge of misgiving, "As in all other fields, in science the way should be made easy for women. Yet it must not be taken amiss if I regard the possible results with a certain amount of skepticism. I am referring to certain restrictive parts of a woman's constitution that were given her by Nature and which forbid us from applying the same standard of expectation to women as to men."[27] Perhaps we should instead look to a different quote attributed to Einstein to explain the sexist and misguided comments of his contemporaries: "The difference between stupidity and genius is that genius has its limits." Stupidity, however, appears timeless.

TO BE SURE, THE TIMELESS STUPIDITY OF IGNORING THE INTELLECtual potential of half of humanity is deeply embedded in our culture. In Genesis, as later interpreted by Jewish and Christian writers, Eve is said to be "formed out of man," the mother of all things yet sinner and seductress. In Hinduism, according to the second-century B.C. Laws of Manu, no woman is independent, but each lives under the control of her father or her husband. Ancient Confucianism similarly advocated a hierarchical societal order based on gender differences. The three major Western religions—Judaism, Christianity, and Islam—traditionally segregated women during worship, giving them a place removed from the high altar or the central point of prayer.

Who dictated the laws of the world's great religions? Of course, they were the same male authority figures who set the rules for educational institutions in the West, including universities, professional schools, art academies, and music conservatories. Historically, only men were given the opportunity of a literate education, and only they went to university. The first woman to receive an academic degree was Elena Piscopia at the University of Padua in 1678. Bach moved to Leipzig in 1723 to take advantage of a free university education for his numerous sons, an opportunity not offered to his equally numerous daughters. A century and a half later, women were admitted to hear university lectures in Germany, but only if they remained behind a curtain. In 1793, they gained entry to the Paris Conservatory of Music but had to enter through a separate door; they were allowed to study musical instruments but not musical composition, creativity being deemed beyond their limited capacity. The Royal Academy [of Art] was founded in London in 1768 with two female members, Mary Moser and Angelica

Kauffman, but not until 1936 was another woman elected. Women painters were not admitted to the state-sponsored School of Fine Arts in Paris until 1897; and even then, as in London, they were barred from nude anatomy classes, instruction crucial to drawing and the very foundation of painting.[28] Nor could they gain normal access to other places necessary to their art. Among painters of animals in the nineteenth century, Rosa Bonheur (1822–1899) is perhaps the most famous for her realistic and detailed depictions.[29] But she had a problem: to get close to her subjects at horse fairs and slaughterhouses, she needed to wear pants rather than the long skirts usual for women at the time. "I had no alternative," she wrote, "but to realize that the garments of my own sex were a total nuisance. That is why I decided to ask the Prefect of Police for the authorization to wear masculine clothing."[30]

Women couldn't wear the pants. They couldn't vote in the United Kingdom until 1918 and in the United States until 1920. Marie Curie couldn't study the sciences or anything else at a university in Poland during the 1880s. Women couldn't attend the famed University of Edinburgh until 1889. In 1960, Harvard had one female full professor, Yale and Princeton none.[31] Women did not gain entrance as undergraduates to Princeton and Yale until 1969, and although women could attend Harvard classes as enrolled students at Radcliffe College beginning in the 1960s, Harvard did not officially merge with its sister school until 1999. The same year that Yale and Princeton went coed, 1969, the (male) dean of freshmen at Harvard, Francis Skiddy von Stade, declared, "Quite simply, I do not see highly educated women making startling strides in contributing to our society in the foreseeable future. They are not, in my opinion, going to stop getting married and/or having children. They will fail in their present role as women if they do."[32] No one at the time seems to have taken issue with von Stade, at least not in print. Without an education, women were assumed to be incompetent in financial matters, unable to get loans, have a credit card, or start a business without a male guarantor. In 1972, Michael Saunders, who now runs a

real estate company in southwest Florida with $2 billion in an-
nual sales, had an application for a business loan approved, only
to have it rescinded when the bank found out that Michael was a
woman. That same year, the U.S. Congress passed the Equal Opportunity Credit Act to end such gender discrimination. But as
José Ángel Gurría, the secretary-general of the Organisation for
Economic Co-operation and Development, ruefully concluded at
the end of a 2018 anti-bias report, "We are fighting centuries and
centuries of tradition and culture."[33]

Deeply embedded cultural bias has killed the creative careers
of many gifted women. The father of the fledgling composer
Fanny Mendelssohn issued this mandate to her in 1820 when
she was fifteen: "What you wrote to me about your musical oc-
cupations, and in comparison to those of [your famous composer
brother] Felix, was rightly thought and expressed. But though
music will perhaps become his profession, for you it can and must
only be an ornament, never the core of your existence. . . . You
must become more steady and collected, and prepare yourself for
your real calling, the only calling for a young woman—the state
of a housewife." Pressed by habitual self-doubts, twenty-year-old
Clara Schumann said the following in 1839: "I once believed that
I possessed creative talent, but I have given up this idea; a woman
must not desire to compose. There has never yet been one able to
do it. Should I expect to be that one?"[34] The promising composer
Alma Mahler was told by her husband, Gustav, in 1902, "The
Role of composer falls to me. Yours is to be loving companion."
Eventually the marriage ruptured, and the frustrated Alma ex-
claimed, "Who helps me to find MYSELF! I've sunk to the level
of a housekeeper!"[35] Sofia Tolstaya, who bore her husband, Leo
Tolstoy, thirteen children, saw her desire to create "crushed and
smothered." Although she edited and copied Leo's lengthy *War
and Peace* seven times, she left nothing creative of her own.

I have served a genius for almost forty years. Hundreds
of times I have felt my intellectual energy stir within me

and all sorts of desires—a longing for education, a love of music and the arts. . . . And time and again I have crushed and smothered these longings. . . . Everyone asks: "But why should a worthless woman like you need an intellectual or artistic life?" To this question I can only reply: "I don't know, but eternally suppressing it to serve a genius is a great misfortune."[36]

Many female geniuses were hidden from view for centuries because men wrote them out of history. Egyptian pharaoh Hatshepsut ruled from 1479 to 1458 B.C. and was called by the Egyptologist James Henry Breasted "the first great woman in history of whom

FIGURE 2.1: The head of Hatshepsut as sphinx, with beard, excavated from debris in the Deir el-Bahri, at Thebes, Upper Egypt, during 1926–1928. The monument dates from 1479 to 1458 B.C. and weighs more than seven tons (Metropolitan Museum of Art, New York).

we are informed."[37] So much statuary was produced during her twenty-year reign that nearly every major museum in the world has Hatshepsut monuments in its collection. Yet immediately after her death, the memory of Hatshepsut was systematically removed from Egyptian history. Statues of her were destroyed and inscriptions about her defaced. Her crime: Hatshepsut had made herself pharaoh (king), rather than playing the more traditional role of queen regent, and that, historians suggest, caused the destructive reaction. Not until the 1920s did archaeologists find and restore the once discarded evidence.[38] Today Hatshepsut can be seen in all her masculine splendor in the Temple of Hatshepsut in the Metropolitan Museum of Art in New York City (Figure 2.1). But back in the day, even wearing a fake beard was not enough to save a woman's fame from destruction.

The medieval nun Hildegard of Bingen (1098–1179) was no saint, at least not immediately. Instead, she was a "Renaissance man," a medieval polymath long before Leonardo da Vinci. Preacher, poet, painter, politician, theologian, musician, student of biology, zoology, botany, and astronomy—Hildegard of Bingen was all of those.[39] She corresponded with four popes (calling one an ass) and fought with Church authorities, who tried to silence her by placing her under interdict. For centuries after her death, Hildegard languished in obscurity. But beginning in the 1980s, with the advent of women's studies programs and feminist criticism, Hildegard's reputation as a medieval visionary was restored. In 2012, Pope Benedict XIII canonized her as Doctor of the Church, the fourth woman of thirty-five saints to be so designated.

Another female genius no longer hidden is the painter Artemisia Gentileschi (1593–1656). For centuries some of Gentileschi's works were attributed to male artists, including her father, Orazio, and the Neapolitan painter Bernardo Cavallino (1616–1656).[40] Did patrons not believe that paintings of such drama and passionate intensity as hers could be the work of a woman? But there is a story behind this art: As a teenager, Gentileschi had been

FIGURE 2.2: Genius changes the boundaries of convention, as can be seen in Artemisia Gentileschi's uniquely intense and dramatically expressive *Judith Beheading Holofernes* (1611–1612). Here Judith wreaks vengeance on the Assyrian general Holofernes (as told in the apocryphal Book of Judith). This is the first of five works painted over three decades in which Gentileschi depicted the bloody decapitation of Holofernes (Museo Capodimonte, Naples).

raped by her teacher and mentor, Agostino Tassi (1578–1644). The case had gone to trial, and Gentileschi had undergone a humiliating physical examination and torture by thumbscrew—a vise for crushing fingers—to prove her innocence.[41] The assailant was convicted but served no sentence; the victim was branded a woman of lost virtue. For decades thereafter, Gentileschi's paintings centered on acts of sexual aggression or female retribution for sexual assault (Figure 2.2). Many now consider Artemisia Gentileschi an artistic genius of the highest order, but in her day she was viewed mostly as a curiosity—a rare female painter in a man's world and a cautionary tale about the dangers lurking therein. Even today a vestige of this legacy persists. Remembered as much for her backstory as for the quality of her painting, Gentileschi is now known as "the #MeToo painter."

We could go on through the histories of uncredited, discredited, ignored, and unlucky female geniuses. The mathematician Ada Lovelace (1815–1852) was the first person, male or female, to realize that a nineteenth-century calculator need not be used only for math and numbers but could also store and manipulate anything that could be expressed in symbols: words, logical thoughts, even music—a "thinking machine," she prophesized. The daughter of the genius Lord Byron, Ada called herself a "natural genius" in mathematics. Today she is recognized as one of the first computer programmers, but she died at age thirty-six of uterine cancer, promise unfulfilled.[42] Rosalind Franklin (1920–1958) was an English chemist and X-ray crystallographer whose X-ray photographs provided the critical piece of information in the identification of the double-helix structure of DNA; the images were taken from her by male colleagues, and they, not she, received the Nobel Prize (for more on Franklin, see chapter 11). Lise Meitner (1878–1968) was an Austrian-Swedish physicist after whom chemical element 109, meitnerium, is named. She and Otto Hahn jointly discovered the process of nuclear fission in 1938–1939, the science behind the atomic bomb. But when the Nobel Prize in Chemistry was awarded in 1944 it went to him alone.[43] The signature style of art of the artist Margaret Keane (b. 1927), the subject of the Tim Burton film *Big Eyes* (2014), was appropriated by her agent/husband, Walter. Decades later, she sued, and a California judge demanded a "paint-off," which demonstrated that Mrs. Keane, not Mr. Keane, was the real creator of her unique "big-eyed waifs." The court awarded her $4 million, but by then Walter had squandered the money.[44]

Money is the great facilitator of human accomplishment regardless of gender. It is, as Virginia Woolf said, a proxy for opportunity. We know that women have enjoyed less monetary opportunity than men, being paid less for the same quantity and quality of work. In 1955, women in the United States earned 65 cents for each dollar earned by men. By 2006, the gap had narrowed to 80 percent, but it has not closed further since then.[45] The U.S. Women's National Team may have sued the U.S. Soccer Federation for equal pay in 2019,[46] and the #timesup movement for equal pay in Hollywood may have gotten attention at the Golden Globes that year, but the fact remains that within each racial and ethnic group in the world, a woman earns less than a man. Perhaps more important for genius, only 17 percent of U.S. startups are founded by women and to them go only 2.2 percent of venture capital funds from which to grow an idea.[47]

Aretha Franklin sang about something else on which women have historically been shortchanged: R-E-S-P-E-C-T. In 2018, the *New York Times* began to atone for the fact that since 1851 the vast majority of its obituaries had been men (about 80 percent are still that way).[48] To ensure recognition commensurate with accomplishment—and consequently more female role models—the paper launched the project "Overlooked," publishing memorial pieces on geniuses it had skipped, such as the novelist Charlotte Brontë, Brooklyn Bridge builder Emily Roebling, and the poet Sylvia Plath. Similarly, trade book writers and filmmakers have produced projects such as *Hidden Figures: The American Dream and the Untold Story of the Black Women Mathematicians Who Helped Win the Space Race* (2016), a bestselling book that became a hit film. Such initiatives alert us to cultural bias. Overtly or covertly, they urge us to remove it.

SOMETHING ELSE IS HIDDEN FROM OUR EYES: WOMEN EXHIBIT MANY of the same biases against women as do men. The authors of the book *Sex and Gender in the 2016 Presidential Election* have shown that whereas a majority of men look unfavorably on power-seeking women, 30 percent of women are biased against them as well.[49] A 2019 study, "Prejudice Against Women Leaders: Insights from an Indirect Questioning Approach," done at the Heinrich-Heine-University in Germany, tested 1,529 participants. When queried overtly, 10 percent of women and 36 percent of men were deemed to hold prejudicial views toward women leaders. When assured complete confidentiality, however, those numbers jumped to 28 percent of women and 45 percent of men.[50] Researchers have also discovered that not only were the women in these studies prejudiced against other women, they were often unaware of that fact. Psychologists call this discrepancy between self-perception and reality "implicit bias," "unconscious bias," or "blind-spot bias."[51] As the 2010 AAUW report *Why So Few? Women in Science, Technology, Engineering, and Mathematics* stated, such blind-spot biases, held by both women and men, are more difficult to eradicate because we are not aware of them.[52]

Remember Catherine Nichols's experiment? Female literary agents overwhelmingly preferred to review a manuscript of a novel sent out under a male pseudonym. In 2012, a group of Yale psychologists tested for bias among 127 science professors, men and women, asking them to review an application for a position as manager of a science lab.[53] An identical CV was distributed, sometimes under the name of a male applicant and sometimes under the name of a female. The male applicant was deemed preferable for the position, being judged not only more hirable but also worthy of a higher salary and of mentoring. Surprisingly, the bias against the woman was held in equal measure by women and men. Sometimes women are even more biased against women than men are. In 2013, Harvard researchers Mahzarin Banaji and Anthony Greenwald published the results of a "Gender-Career Implicit Association Test" that explored attitudes about women in the workplace and at home. They found that 75 percent of men held the predictable stereotype regarding the place of a woman, but so did 80 percent of women.[54]

The point of this is not to try to exonerate men by shifting the blame to women. On the contrary, the above studies show how effective men have been at subliminally ingraining gender bias. Historically, men have controlled most things, including social discourse about gender and about genius. If women today are just as likely as men to believe that a game-changing leader must be a tall, strong white man carrying a briefcase, who's really to blame?

Which brings us to the question of the allocation of genius by gender. Is there really a difference? Did Charles Dickens really have more literary genius than Louisa May Alcott? Did Thomas Edison, who is famous for his "genius is 99 percent perspiration" quote, really possess more tenacity than Marie Curie, who labored for years stirring vats of pitchblende under dangerous conditions? Why is Edison, not Curie, the poster child for perseverance? Indeed, the impressive, bestselling book *Grit: The Power of Passion and Perseverance* (2016) has no mention of Curie, nor does it have a discussion of, or index entry for, "women and persistence" or "women and grit." Why has this habit of female excellence been hidden from us? History demonstrates that to become and be recognized as a genius, a woman has needed an extra dose of grit.

The Nobel Prize winner Toni Morrison knew this. Consider her working arrangements when she was at her peak compared with those of fellow Nobel Prize winner Ernest Hemingway when he was at his. In 1965, Morrison was a single mother living in a small, rented house in Queens, New York. She would rise at 4:00 A.M. to write, then drive her two sons to school in Manhattan, where she worked as an editor at Random House, and pick them up when her workday ended to drive them home. After she put the boys to bed, she would go back to work. In 1931, the wealthy in-laws of Ernest Hemingway gave him the title to the largest and highest house on the island of Key West. There he spent his mornings writing in the separate studio attached to the house and his afternoons fishing. In 2019, the *Guardian* published an article by Brigid Schulte and the title says it all: "A Woman's Greatest Enemy? A Lack of Time to Herself." To carve out time to create requires extra grit.[55]

What might all this mean for the employers and spouses of women today? They should provide equal space, pay, and, perhaps most important, time. What might this mean for parents concerned with the happiness and future success of their offspring? Well, they should no longer dress daughters in the once popular T-shirt proclaiming "I'm too pretty to do homework, so my brother does it for me," for one. They should also be careful not to perpetuate gender stereotypes in more subtle ways. A recent article in the *New York Times*, "Google, Tell Me. Is My Son a Genius?," pointed out that parents today are 2.5 times as likely to ask online "Is my son gifted?" than "Is my daughter gifted?" and similarly 2.0 times as likely to inquire "Is my daughter overweight?" as they are for a son.[56] Thus, the current prejudice ratio for genius is apparently 2.5 to 1 against women. The game has been rigged for a long time and remains rigged because hidden cultural biases are difficult to discard, even for progressive, modern-day parents.

A final statistic, coming, again, from Professor Dean Keith Simonton and his book *Greatness: Who Makes History and Why*: Simonton posited that for every identifiable female genius, it is possible to name ten males.[57] If this is true, it would suggest, in the roughest of terms, that for every twenty potential geniuses, the empowerment of nine has been suppressed owing to gender bias. If you were running a business—let's call it the Human Potential Company—and nine out of every twenty geniuses working for you were kept underemployed, how smart would that be? Must stupidity, as Einstein suggested, really last forever?

Breaking a stupid habit requires action and begins with cultivating awareness. Understand that "the missing nine" are lost because of gender bias. Understand that the cause is culture, not lack of genetic gifts. Understand that women have the same hidden habits of genius as men and perhaps an extra dose of resilience. Think about the implications of the way you talk to your daughters about things such as homework and achievement versus the way you talk to your sons. Finally, if you recommend only one chapter of this book to your friends, colleagues, and family members, make it this one.

CHAPTER 3

AVOID THE PRODIGY BUBBLE

I n 2004, *60 Minutes* ran a special segment on Jay Greenberg, a twelve-year-old composer of extraordinary ability. In the piece, the young Greenberg, who sits at a computer to notate the music he hears, told host Scott Pelley that he had written five symphonies that miraculously seemed to stream through his head: "I just hear it as if it were a smooth performance of a work that is already written, when it isn't." Samuel Zyman, a professor at the famed Juilliard School of Music, commented during a follow-up report about Greenberg on CBS, "We are talking about a prodigy of the level of the greatest prodigies in history when it comes to composition. I am talking about the likes of Mozart, Mendelssohn, and Saint-Saëns." Violin virtuoso Joshua Bell, another prodigy, soon commissioned a concerto from Greenberg, which was recorded by the London Symphony Orchestra. Greenberg, all agreed, was a modern-day Mozart.

Enter another musical prodigy. In 2017, *60 Minutes* ran a special report on the English musical prodigy Alma Deutscher, also comparing that twelve-year-old to Mozart.[1] Like Mozart, Deutscher could name all the notes of the scale almost from birth, was composing by the age of four, and had written an opera for the city of Vienna at twelve.[2] Indeed, the opera, *Cinderella*, sounds very much like Mozart (excerpts can be heard on YouTube). Why are Greenberg and Deutscher, in fact almost all prodigies, compared to Mozart? Because Mozart is the gold standard.

On January 27, 1756, Leopold Mozart and his wife, Anna Maria (née Pertl), baptized their son Joannes Chrysostomus Wolfgangus Theophilus Mozart.[3] Later in life, Mozart would come to abandon the Greek-derived Theophilus in favor of the French Amadé or the Latin Amadeus—beloved of God. Genetically, this seems to have been true—Mozart had received divine musical gifts. He was a fourth-generation musician, part of a lineage that extended to five generations when his own two sons (neither of whom left progeny) followed in his footsteps to become musicians.[4] And it was the Pertls, not the Mozarts, who seem to have carried the musical genes. While his mother, Anna Maria, did not participate in the high-level music making in the family home, her father and her father's father were both church musicians.[5] Leopold Mozart, on the other hand, was descended from bookbinders in Augsburg, Germany. But what Leopold lacked in musical gifts, he made up for in ambition, which, as he recognized, could be realized through his son, Wolfgang.

Young Mozart seemed possessed by music. According to the testimony of his sister, Maria Anna (nicknamed Nannerl), he began playing on the keyboard at the age of three, showing special pleasure when he could pick out the "sweet" sound of the interval of a third (a span of three white keys on a piano with the middle one omitted).[6] The boy was not only a keyboard whiz, he was also a gifted violinist, and he seems to have picked up the instrument intuitively owing to his motographic memory (the capacity to see a note in a score and remember precisely the correct spot on the fingerboard to generate that pitch). The same was true for the harpsichord and organ, which he began playing at age six, although he had to stand while playing in order to reach the pedals. Mozart also had a phonographic memory. At age fourteen, for example, shortly after hearing for the first time a two-minute musical composition (Gregorio Allegri's "Miserere"), he wrote it down note for note. Perfect pitch, an eidetic memory for sounds, and an absolute motographic memory—the prodigy Mozart had it all.

With talent like this at hand, his bulldozer parent Leopold led Wolfgang and his gifted older sister, Nannerl, on a concert tour to the leading courts of Europe. Leopold's contacts and courtly manners cleared the way for an audience with the royals, and whiz kid Wolfgang delivered the musical goods. Heads of state, professional musicians, and amateurs alike gasped at the boy's extraordinary gifts. "A prodigy of nature and art" a citizen of Salzburg called him.[7]

BROADLY SPEAKING, THE WORD "PRODIGY" CONNOTES "AN AMAZing or marvelous thing, something out of the ordinary course of nature," and it is not necessarily tied to youth.[8] A three-hundred-pound turtle on the Galápagos Islands is a prodigy of nature, as is a four-thousand-year-old California redwood tree. Nevertheless, a "prodigy" is commonly understood today to be a young person possessing talents far beyond his or her years, a young person with the capacities of a mature adult. Picasso could draw at age three; John Stuart Mill at six wrote a history of Rome; and Bill Gates, on a math test of eighth to twelfth graders in Washington State, got the highest score—as an eighth grader.[9] To us, such talent is inexplicable.

As a culture, we are fascinated by the wunderkind. Consider the television show *Child Genius,* produced in cooperation with MENSA, which premiered in 2015 on the Lifetime network, where we saw eight-to-twelve-year-olds compete for the title "Child Genius" of the year. In the show young contestants—their IQs said to range from 140 to 158—displayed extraordinary feats of memory and calculation. Ryan was a math prodigy who instantly multiplied and divided four-digit numbers; Katherine could memorize a sequence of all fifty-two playing cards. Others could immediately recall wind speeds and barometric pressures in storms on particular days. The winner took home a $100,000 college fund.

More recently NBC has tried to satisfy our appetite for prodigies with the series *Genius Junior*—in TV game shows, "genius" and "youth" are synonymous. Instead of individuals, here teams of three preteens compete to win up to $400,000. As on *Child Genius*, exceptional performance is measured by math skills, as well as memory for geographical places and spelling (this time backward). The abilities of the young contestants on both programs are hugely impressive, but their expertise is limited to certain fields, those involving quantification and memory, skills that can be immediately validated in the form of a correct answer. In fact, prodigies generally first manifest in such formal, rule-governed domains as chess, math, music, and mnemonic processing. But are the contestants on *Child Genius* and *Genius Junior*, as the word "genius" suggests, really geniuses? They are not. They are simply prodigies.

The difference is that geniuses create. They change the world through original thinking that alters the actions and values of society. Prodigies merely mimic. They are extraordinary performers at a preternaturally early age. Prodigies do not, however, stand at the avant-garde of their field and change its direction. Although these children are precocious (from *precox,* a fruit ripe before its time), they come with an expiration date. If they have not begun to develop a personal creative "voice" by the age of seventeen or eighteen, they may never do so.

Take the cellist Yo-Yo Ma, for example, who was a child prodigy. Although his exceptional playing gives us great pleasure today, Ma readily admits that he is not a genius.[10] He is not a composer and will leave us nothing but interpretations of the works of others. Think of all those geniuses who hit their prime later in life, van Gogh, Cézanne, Jackson Pollock, Antonín Dvořák, Giuseppe Verdi, Michael Faraday, and Toni Morrison among them. Shakespeare did not reach the peak of his creative powers until about age thirty-six,[11] by which time Mozart was dead. Darwin's genius lay in his extraordinary patience; he did not publish his revolutionary *On the Origin of Species* until he was fifty. Some domains, especially the observational sciences, are predicated on long-term perception and measurement. To a degree, then, prodigy is "domain dependent." Ten-year-olds on *Child Genius* and *Genius Junior* can be math or spelling whizzes; they and others can also be prodigies in music or chess; but they do not write introspective novels. Mozart, however, had the good fortune of being naturally endowed in a field (music) in which exceptional capacity manifests early, and, unlike most prodigies, he also had the rare ability to create.

BACK TO THE BARNSTORMING MOZARTS. THEY DEPARTED SALZburg on September 18, 1762, and returned triumphantly on November 29, 1766—a journey lasting some four years. Traveling in high style—"noblement," Leopold called it—they moved about in their own private carriage drawn at times by six horses and with two servants to attend them. Their itinerary followed the money trail of the music-loving princes of Europe, proceeding through the major court centers north of the Alps: Vienna, Munich, Frankfurt, Brussels, Amsterdam, Paris, and London.

Everywhere Wolfgang was the darling of the royals. In Vienna, six-year-old Mozart sat on the lap of Empress Maria Teresa, who gave him a splendid set of clothes, and he kissed and excitedly proposed marriage to one of the empress's daughters (the future queen Marie Antoinette of France). At Versailles, Mozart stood next to King Louis XV at a New Year's dinner and was fed table morsels by the queen consort. Just how eminently presentable the Mozarts appeared in France at this time can be seen in a watercolor by Louis Carrogis de Carmontelle showing Leopold with violin and little Wolfgang at the clavier, his legs barely descending beneath the seat of his chair (Figure 3.1). Standing and singing is his sister, Nannerl. What about Nannerl? Was she a genius, too?

FIGURE 3.1: Watercolor by Louis Carrogis de Carmontelle done in Paris in 1763 showing the seven-year-old Mozart at the keyboard with his father, Leopold, and sister, Nannerl. Note that the feet of the diminutive boy scarcely descend the chair (Musée Condé, Château de Chantilly).

Nannerl Mozart was certainly a prodigy. A leading Enlightenment intellectual, Friedrich Melchior, Baron von Grimm, observed in 1763 that on the harpsichord "no one possessed a more precise and brilliant execution."[12] A Swiss journal reported in 1766 that she "plays the most difficult pieces by the greatest masters with unequalled neatness and accuracy."[13] The first compositions of Wolfgang Mozart were actually written in *her* musical notebook. So why have we never heard of her?

Nannerl was a prodigious performer but not a creator. No music exists today with her name on it. No music attributed to others survives in her handwriting—and we do have abundant examples of her script from the many letters she wrote. In none of her letters does Nannerl mention that she is composing or has the desire to compose. No contemporary accounts mention compositions by her. Nothing. Perhaps Nannerl Mozart did desire to be a composer, yet conventions of the day prevented her from becoming one. Perhaps she had the gift of creativity but not the opportunity. Given all of the discrimination female geniuses have faced over the centuries, this interpretation seems plausible. Indeed, this is the story line of the award-winning film *Mozart's Sister* (2010). Dramatic as her story in the film is, however, the historical documents tell a different tale. Nannerl Mozart did, in fact, receive the same encouragement, lessons, and instructional materials as her younger brother. In the case of the Mozart siblings, the significantly different outcomes were caused not by gender discrimination within the family but rather by the boy's extraordinary capacity for original musical creation.

BY THE TIME THE MOZARTS REACHED LONDON IN 1764, Wolfgang had assumed the role of youthful creator and Leopold that of paternal promotor. Eight-year-old Wolfgang played harpsichord and organ before King George III and Queen Charlotte at Buckingham House (later Palace), and to ensure that the British royal family would not soon forget them, Wolfgang presented

Queen Charlotte a memento: six violin/keyboard sonatas he had composed.

When a prodigy creates something extraordinary, there is the possibility that a hovering parent might have had a hand in it. We now know, for example, that the paintings of the four-year-old prodigy Marla Olmstead, also featured on *60 Minutes* (in 2003), were in part ghosted by her father, Mark.[14] But Wolfgang Mozart didn't need parental assistance in London, at least judging from Nannerl's memoirs. In the summer of 1764, Leopold Mozart fell ill, leaving the two children to amuse themselves quietly.

> In London, where our father lay dangerously ill, we were forbidden to touch a piano. And so, in order to occupy himself, Mozart composed his first Symphony for all the instruments of the orchestra—but especially for trumpets and kettle-drums. I had to copy it out as I sat at his side. Whilst he composed and I copied he said to me: Remind me to give the horn something worthwhile to do![15]

IF FURTHER PROOF OF ORIGINALITY IS NEEDED, BY THE TIME THE Mozarts returned to Salzburg in 1766, the now ten-year-old Wolfgang had written nearly a hundred works of this sort on his own, including forty keyboard pieces, sixteen violin sonatas, and at least three symphonies. In his preteen years, he composed a transformative masterpiece, Missa Solemnis, K. 139 (*Waisenhausmesse*) (1768), commissioned by and premiered before Empress Maria Teresa in Vienna.

WHAT ABOUT OUR MODERN-DAY PRODIGIES JAY GREENBERG AND Alma Deutscher featured on CBS? Although musical taste is personal, anyone who listens to Alma Deutscher's music would agree that it is more retrospective than progressive. Listen to her 2017 recording of Piano Concerto in E flat, available on You-

Tube. It sounds just like Mozart! Behind it is a young person of great talent possessing a musical ear capable of mimicking and responding to the musical style of her dead idol. But Deutscher's work looks backward 225 years, as might a scientist today hoping to find a vaccine for smallpox. Pleasing and impressive as it is, young Deutscher's music is in no way transformative. Neither is the music of Jay Greenberg. Now approaching thirty, Greenberg has moved with his parents to New Zealand, where he continues to study musical composition. Public notice of him has disappeared as quickly as it appeared. It turns out that the point of interest in Greenberg was not his film score–sounding music but rather the age at which he created it. To recall once again Samuel Johnson's reaction to a dog walking on his hind legs, we are impressed not by the creative value of the act but rather by the fact that it can be done at all.

Marin Alsop, the conductor of the Baltimore Symphony and the Vienna Radio Symphony Orchestra, knows Jay Greenberg's music well; in 2006 she recorded his tone poem *Intelligent Life* for distribution on a Sony CD. Recently, I had occasion to ask her why I had not heard much about Greenberg of late. "Had his music been written by a forty-year-old rather than a youngster," Alsop said, "few of us would have paid attention. It had promise but no distinctive voice; artistic voice is difficult to acquire without a life crisis."[16]

Why do so few prodigies become creators? What causes, or at least precipitates, the emergence of great art? What impels the true genius to shoot for the target to which others are blind? Is a life crisis the precipitating event from which springs an artist voice or a scientific vision? Are independence and resilience forged in the crucible of an early-life trauma? Of course, as Yoko Ono said, "No one should encourage artists to pursue tragedy so that they might become a good artist."[17] But the number of geniuses who have lost a parent, most often a mother, at a critical age is striking: Michelangelo, Leonardo, Newton, Bach, Beethoven, Fyodor Dostoyevsky, Tolstoy, William Wordsworth,

Abraham Lincoln, Mary Shelley, Clara Schumann, James Clerk Maxwell, Curie, Charlotte and Emily Brontë, Virginia Woolf, Sylvia Plath, Paul McCartney, and Oprah Winfrey. Is "genius the child of sorrow," as President John Adams said? Does pain generate a different worldview? Lady Gaga suggested as much when she stated in a 2009 interview in the *Guardian*, "I do think that when you struggle, your art gets great."[18] One quip of the poetic genius Dylan Thomas may be relevant here: "There is only one thing worse than having an unhappy childhood, and that is having a too-happy childhood."[19]

IN THE SPRING OF 1778, MOZART WAS ANYTHING BUT HAPPY. Indeed, most postteen prodigies are not.[20] For Mozart, his six-month stay in Paris (April–October 1778) was the low point of his life.[21] He had been ordered by his father, Leopold, to relocate to Paris to find a job.[22] Young Mozart had demurred because he had to leave behind his first serious love (she soon forgot him). To make matters worse, father Leopold sent mother Anna Maria along to Paris as a chaperone.[23] In Paris, Mozart's mother contracted typhus and suffered a slow death. Leopold blamed his son for failing to provide her with proper care. Finally, Mozart was unable to procure a job worthy of his abilities. Once youth disappears from the face of the prodigy, so does public interest. As he wrote in a letter on July 31, 1778, "What annoys me most of all here is that these stupid French seem to think I am still seven years old, because that was the age when they first saw me."[24]

Twenty-two-year-old Mozart in Paris was a miserable failure. Now alone, he had little money, no job, no girlfriend, and no mother—only a reproachful father. But Mozart's colossal failure proved to be the defining moment of his life. He had learned to rely less on the word of others and more on his own supreme gifts. He recognized that life could go on without "Papa," or anyone else, to offer constant advice and approval. Most important, he had experienced and survived a sudden and profound loss, which immediately gave to his music a new emotional depth, audible in the violin sonata K. 304, the only instrumental piece he ever wrote in the desolate key of E minor. In January 1779, Mozart limped back to Salzburg, but within less than a year he was gone. He moved away from his controlling father and to Vienna, where he created the remaining 95 percent of the masterpieces for which he is known today. Mozart had escaped the "prodigy bubble."

MOZART'S PARENT/TEACHER/MENTOR, LEOPOLD MOZART, WAS A superb guide, at least at the beginning. He surely accelerated Wolfgang's professional development, teaching the boy the basics of his craft and opening doors to the rich and famous, but Leopold became excess baggage and was left behind. Mentors can teach a young person how to network, assist in landing a job, offer praise and encouragement, and help the person move up the ladder of life.[25] Success is the aim (and that's what parents want). Mentors teach the status quo and how to mimic it but not how to create something new. What parent/teacher/mentor ever said, "Move as far away from me as necessary to find the best opportunities and establish an independent, questioning mind. Go and make bold, contrarian decisions. Implement a vision of the world far different from mine."? But that's how creative genius comes about.

Did Albert Einstein have a mentor? No, he disparaged his teachers, and they him. When he graduated from university at the age of twenty-one, he had so infuriated his professors that none would write a letter of recommendation for him. For four years (1901–1905), he was unemployable. Did Pablo Picasso have a mentor? Yes, one who chopped off the feet of pigeons, stuck them to a wall, and made young Pablo paint them so as to learn his craft. Picasso's father, José Ruiz, was a mentor by negative example, and around age seventeen the embarrassed Pablo began to sign his paintings with his mother's family name (Picasso), not his father's. As the grown Picasso later joked, "Don José was an exemplar by virtue of his ineptitude."[26]

The great fame of a few prodigies—Mozart and Picasso, for example—clouds our judgment. Their lives suggest that the prodigy-to-genius journey is the norm and that the state of being a prodigy is a necessary precondition to that of being a genius. But most geniuses, like Einstein, were, at the very least, "later" bloomers. Most creative writers and artists—people in non-rule-based fields—fall into the category of later-day geniuses. So, too, do most political leaders—Lincoln, King, Gandhi, and Angela Merkel, for example—who possess the capacity for empathy. Of the seven most prominent creators of the twentieth century studied by Howard Gardner in his book *Creating Minds: An Anatomy of Creativity Seen Through the Lives of Freud, Einstein, Picasso, Stravinsky, Eliot, Graham, and Gandhi* (1993), only one, Picasso, was a prodigy. Martha Graham did not dance until age twenty, the same age T. S. Eliot took up poetry. Sigmund Freud changed interests several times and only at forty came to the subject he developed into psychoanalysis. Einstein was an excellent student in STEM subjects, but, as my Yale colleague and Einstein biographer Professor Douglas Stone is quick to point out, "he was no prodigy."[27]

Why, then, "Baby Einstein"? The urge to anoint prodigious children as marvels to whose ascendant vector we can tie our own hopes and ambitions is strong. To satisfy it, in 2001, the Walt Disney Company began to market Baby Einstein (children's instructional media products) to hundreds of thousands of anxious, aspirational parents around the world. Babies and toddlers watched videos designed to improve their verbal skills, introduce the concept of numbers, enhance their color recognition, and reinforce simple geometric patterns such as circles, triangles, and squares. Soon Baby Einstein was joined by Baby Mozart, Baby Shakespeare, Baby Galileo, and Baby van Gogh. About the same time the so-called Mozart Effect appeared: its proponents said that listening to Mozart temporarily improved students' scores on an IQ test and made youngsters smarter.[28] Governor Zell Miller of Georgia budgeted $105 thousand to provide every child born in his state a CD of Mozart's music. The long-term expectation? That from prodigies would grow geniuses. Ultimately, the products proved to be disappointing. Neither the Mozart Effect nor Baby Einstein could be shown to enhance a baby's intelligence or creativity. The Walt Disney Company issued an apology and offered to return $15.99 for each product sold. As a 2009 headline in the *New York Times* laughingly advised, "No Einstein in Your Crib? Get a Refund!"[29]

Prodigy bubbles, too, often lead to disappointing results. Some prodigies, having been pushed too hard, burn out and leave their domain of activity forever. Others, who have been typecast by parents at too early an age, go on to find a new passion. "There is nothing in a caterpillar that tells you it's going to be a butterfly," said the futurist architect Buckminster Fuller. Still others continue to use their special skills and become prominent experts in non-rule-based disciplines such as psychology, philosophy, and medicine.[30] But most, like Jay Greenberg, simply disappear.

The problem with the prodigy bubble is that it is filled with unmitigated positive reinforcement, adherence to strict rules, tolerance for nothing but perfection, attention to a single activity, and excessively attentive, even domineering mothers and fathers—today's helicopter parents. In her book *Off the Charts: The Hidden Lives and Lessons of American Child Prodigies* (2018), Ann Hulbert described dozens of prodigies, all but one of whom are today wholly forgotten. She concludes with a cautionary note: "All too often, the impulse to herald youthful talents risks inspiring swelled heads and raising sky-high hopes that are likely to be disappointed."[31] Too often the prodigy is cut off, isolated socially, and stunted intellectually, a willing prisoner inside a suffocating environment.

Thus if you or your child have induction into the Pantheon of Genius as your goal, take a deep breath and relax—there is still plenty of time before your arrival. Until then, instead of training like a demon in a single rule-dominated discipline, try what is suggested here and in later chapters. Work to develop independence of thought and action and the capacity to deal with failure—maybe the "a trophy for all" approach to life is not realistic. Set a program of global learning instead of narrow specialization, and, most important, have as your goal developing the ability to learn not with mentors but alone. Not to be forgotten by parents is the importance of socialization as a way of building empathy and the capacity for leadership. Prodigies come in a few forms; geniuses come in many. Now would be the time to break the habit of coupling prodigy with genius; most geniuses never were prodigies, and most prodigies never become geniuses.

CHAPTER 4

IMAGINE THE WORLD
AS DOES A CHILD

On the evening of June 1, 1816, rain and lightning crashed down on the Villa Diodati on the south shore of Lake Geneva.[1] A group of British expats and fledgling geniuses had gathered for dinner and, inspired by the storm, they took up a dare: each would write a ghost story. Invited by Lord Byron, the guests included Percy Bysshe Shelley, his paramour Mary Godwin (later Shelley), her half sister Jane, and Dr. John Polidori. All were well under thirty years of age. Byron, the prototypical Romantic genius, had a reputation for being passionate, rebellious, self-absorbed, and brilliant. "Mad, bad, and dangerous to know" was the way Lady Caroline Lamb characterized him—after all, Byron had had an affair with his half sister. Percy Shelley was in the process of publishing his way into the pantheon of poetic greats known today as the English Romantics. Polidori would later write the short story "The Vampyre" and thereby put Dracula onto the literary map. But of the illustrious attendees, the one who has had the most lasting impact on the Western psyche and pop culture is Mary Godwin Shelley. That night, she began to imagine the first twitches of *Frankenstein*. She was only eighteen.

With *Frankenstein; or, The Modern Prometheus,* Mary Shelley helped create a new literary genre, the Gothic horror novel, a combination of the phantasmagorical and the murderous, whose progeny would later include other influential works, such as *The Hunchback of Notre Dame, The Strange Case of Dr. Jekyll and Mr. Hyde*, and *Phantom of the Opera*. The impact of *Frankenstein* on culture today, however, has less to do with Shelley's novel and more with the many films derived from it, including the Edison Manufacturing Company's 1910 *Frankenstein* and the definitive 1931 *Frankenstein* starring Boris Karloff.[2] The monster who lumbered into pop culture, however, differs significantly from Shelley's original Frankenstein.

Today, scientists are paying renewed attention to Mary Shelley's original message: beware the law of unintended consequences.[3] In Part II of Shelley's novel, Dr. Victor Frankenstein utters the following words, having been warmed, then suddenly burned, by the embers of a fire: "How strange, I thought, that the same cause should produce such opposite effects!"[4] Frankenstein was a creative genius who had the intent of advancing human knowledge. So, too, were Marie Curie, Albert Einstein, and James Watson and Francis Crick. The moral dilemma of Frankenstein— the need to weigh the positives of scientific discovery against the potential negatives and impose ethical standards—foreshadowed similar dilemmas that would be faced by Frankenstein's real-world descendants regarding atomic energy, global warming, and genetic editing.

HOW DOES A TEENAGER WITH NO FORMAL EDUCATION AND NO PUB-lications to her name deliver a moral lesson for the ages couched within a terrific story? How does someone from a seemingly stable, upper-middle-class home come to know of the dark side, "the mysterious fears of our nature"? And why, despite all the efforts of her later novels, was Mary Shelley never able to duplicate the success of her nineteenth year? The answer has to do with childlike imagination and adult reality.

No genius is an island; no idea is born *ex nihilo*. As a child of an upper-middle-class environment, Mary Godwin read widely, knew all about Ben Franklin's kite-flying experiment, and attended public lectures on chemistry and electricity, including discussions of Luigi Galvani's discovery of animal electricity. She was also rebellious and at sixteen ran off with Percy Shelley to Europe. Descending the Rhine River, the two impressionable youths passed within twenty miles of Frankenstein Castle and may have heard folktales about frightening events occurring thereabouts. From this experience she surely derived her character's name. But none of these external influences can account for the shocking originality of *Frankenstein*.

Instead, we must turn to Mary Shelley herself. In the introduction to the 1831 edition of *Frankenstein*, the author responded to a request from her readers to explain "How I, then a young girl, came to think of, and to dilate upon, so very hideous an idea?" In response, she said, "As a child I scribbled; and my favourite pastime, during the hours given me for recreation, was to 'write stories.' . . . but I was not confined to my own identity, and I could people the hours with creations far more interesting to me at that age, than my own sensations." She delighted in forming "castles in the air" and "imaginary incidents."[5]

Young Mary was an experienced writer, but only in her own imagination. A few evenings after that famous dark and stormy night near Geneva, she was privy to a discussion between Byron and Shelley about galvanization and the electrical experiments of Erasmus Darwin (a grandfather of Charles). She then went to bed but not to sleep. Instead she was held captive by her imagination in what she called "a wakeful dream."

> When I placed my head on my pillow, I did not sleep, nor could I be said to think. My imagination, unbidden, possessed and guided me, gifting the successive images that arose in my mind with a vividness far beyond the usual bounds of reverie. I saw—with shut eyes, but acute mental vision,—I saw the pale student [Frankenstein] of

unhallowed arts kneeling beside the thing he had put together. I saw the hideous phantasm of a man [the Crea-
ture] stretched out, and then, on the working of some
powerful engine, show signs of life, and stir with an un-
easy, half vital motion. . . . He sleeps; but he is awakened;
he opens his eyes; behold the horrid thing stands at his
bedside, opening his curtains, and looking on him with
yellow, watery, but speculative eyes.

I opened mine in terror. The idea so possessed my mind
that a thrill of fear ran through me, and I wished to exchange the ghastly image of my fancy for the realities
around. I see them still. . . . I could not so easily get rid
of my hideous phantom; still it haunted me. I must try to
think of something else. I recurred to my ghost story, my
tiresome unlucky ghost story! O! if I could only contrive
one which would frighten my reader as I myself had been
frightened that night!

Swift as light and as cheering was the idea that broke in
upon me. "I have found it! What terrified me will terrify
others; and I need only describe the spectre which had
haunted my midnight pillow."

THE ALCHEMY OF A FEW CHILDHOOD MEMORIES, A RECENT DISCUS-
sion, childlike night terrors, and a shockingly vivid imagination
worked to produce the most powerful horror novel and moral-
istic fable in literary history. What started as a dare progressed
to a short story and then, over the course of ten months, into a
full-blown novel. *Frankenstein* was published on New Year's Day
1818, with a first printing of five hundred copies, and it was generally reviewed favorably. No less a figure than Sir Walter Scott
commented on the author's "original genius."[6] The first edition of
Frankenstein was published anonymously, with a preface written
by Percy Shelley. Many critics assumed that such "original genius" could spring only from the mind of a man and thus attrib-

uted the novel to Percy himself. Mary Shelley wasn't credited as author until the publication of the book's second edition in 1823.

Fast forward to 1990. An imaginative young woman, Joanne Rowling, boarded a train in Manchester, England, heading to London. As she described the experience:

> I was . . . sitting there thinking of nothing to do with writing and the idea came out of nowhere, and . . . I could see Harry very clearly: this scrawny little boy, and it was the most physical rush of excitement—I'd never felt that excited about anything to do with writing. I'd never had an idea that gave me such a physical response. So I'm rummaging through this bag to try and find a pen or a pencil or anything. I didn't even have an eye-liner on me, so I just had to sit and think, and for four hours—'cause the train was delayed—I had all these ideas bubbling up through my head.[7]

What followed was a five-year journey between the imagining of the Harry Potter story and the completion of the first book, and they were not easy years for Rowling. She moved to Porto, Portugal, and from there to Edinburgh, Scotland, where, as a single mother of an infant daughter, she lived on welfare. "Let's not exaggerate here, let's not pretend I had to write on napkins because we couldn't afford paper," she has said. But she did live on a benefit check of £70 (about $130) a week, writing partly in her one-room flat but mostly in a local café called Nicolson's. Eventually, "after a large number of rejections," she found a publisher for *Harry Potter and the Philosopher's Stone:* Bloomsbury Press in London. Barry Cunningham, her editor at Bloomsbury, recalled in a 2001 BBC interview that, although Rowling had written only a single book, she had imagined the essence of the entire project. "And then she told me about Harry Potter—all through the entire series. . . . I realized, of course, that she knew exactly about this world and where it was going, who it was going to include, how the character would develop, and of course it was fascinating because this doesn't normally happen."[8]

The twenty-four-year-old Rowling could imagine great swaths of a fantasy world populated by youthful heroes and heroines. What she imagined went on to become one of the greatest successes in publishing history, generating not only books but also films, a play, a Broadway musical, and two fantasy theme parks, both called "The Wizarding World of Harry Potter." The link between the geniuses Mary Shelley and J. K. Rowling: both were young and imaginative, and both were afraid of things that went bump in the night.

AT WHAT AGE DOES A CHILD REALIZE THAT THE MONSTERS IN HER dreams or in movies and books are not real? Does the adult imperative to "grow up" encourage the loss of creative imagination? Neither Mary Shelley nor Joanne Rowling later surpassed the imaginary power she had displayed at ages eighteen and twenty-four, respectively. The rapper Kanye West spoke to this point in his 2010 single "Power." Beginning with a reference to the "purity and honesty" of "childlike creativity," he went on to include this couplet: "Reality is catching up with me/Taking my inner child."

Pablo Picasso initially lost custody of his inner child and had to work to get it back. "Every child is an artist," he said. "The problem is to remain an artist as we grow up."[9] Picasso contended that as a child he was preternaturally skilled at drawing, much like an adult. In fact, before the age of fourteen he could create realistic masterpieces. "When I was a child I could paint like Rafael," he said, "but it took me a lifetime to paint like a child." Atypically, Picasso's childhood works were not of the naive and playful sort. Creative play had been denied him by his mentor/teacher/father, José Ruiz, who had compelled his gifted son to create great art by copying the canonic masters, rather than allowing his imagination to run freely. "I had never had a childhood that was anything but a miserable effort at trying to be an adult," Picasso said.[10] "What one can consider an early genius is actually the genius of childhood. It disappears at a certain age without leaving around traces. It is possible that such a child will one day become an artist but he will have to begin again from the beginning. I did not have this genius, for example. My first drawings could not have been hung in a display of children's work. These pictures lacked the childlikeness or naiveté. . . . At the youthful age I painted in a quite academic way, so literal and precise that I am shocked today."[11]

Picasso seems to have destroyed almost all his childhood work. As he told it, he was forced to skip his artistic childhood but gradually willed upon himself the childlike imagination that provided a catalyst for later creative innovation. Critics such as Gertrude Stein found in Picasso's earliest Cubist works (1907) attempts to see and draw as children do, reducing art to the elementary forces of line, space, and color.[12] Later, around 1920, when Picasso entered his neoclassical period, he painted figures with cartoonishly large limbs, hands, and feet. That style Picasso attributed to a recurring childhood dream: "When I was a child, I often had a dream that used to frighten me greatly. I dreamed that my legs and arms grew to an enormous size and then shrank back just as much as in the other direction. And all around me, in my dream, I saw other people going through the same transformations, getting huge or very tiny. I felt terribly anguished every time I dreamed about that."[13] As Picasso said with his typical oxymoronic wit, "It takes a very long time to become young."

MARY SHELLEY, JOANNE ROWLING, AND PABLO PICASSO WERE ALL visionaries who hit hidden targets. Embedded in the words "visionary" and "imagination" are "vision" and "image." Picasso saw in images; Rowling saw a narrative attended by images; Shelley had a vision she expressed through words. Albert Einstein also saw things.

According to his own testimony, Einstein had a "bad memory for words and texts." Rather than seeing the physical world, as do most physicists, in abstract symbols and formulas, he literally envisioned it, using his very good memory for pictures and imaginary moving objects. "I very rarely think in words at all," he said. "A thought comes, and I may try to express it in words afterwards."[14]

In his autobiography, Einstein tried to explain the complex process of his imagination at work. For Einstein a sequence of "memory pictures" (*Erinnerungsbilder*) formed a "working tool" or "idea" that could later be expressed as mathematical formulas or as words. "I think that the transition from free association or 'dreaming' to thinking is characterized by the more or less preeminent role played by the idea. It is by no means necessary that an idea be tied to a sensorily cognizable and reproducible sign (word); but when this is the case, then thinking becomes thereby capable of being communicated."[15] Einstein called this mode of pictorial thinking first a "free play with ideas" and then simply "play" (*Spiel*).

From Einstein's mental play with images emerged his famous thought experiments. One came at age sixteen when, as he recalled, "I made my first rather childish experiments in thinking which had a direct bearing on the Special Theory [of relativity]."[16] What would the world look like if it were possible to grab on to a ray of light and travel at its speed? Several years later, as a young man walking between his apartment and his job at the patent office in Bern, Switzerland, Einstein daily passed the famous clock tower of that city. What would be the result, he wondered, if a streetcar sped away from it at the speed of light? (The clock would appear to have stopped, but a watch on the streetcar would keep on ticking, a point again pertinent to his Theory of Special Relativity.) Then, at about age twenty-six, Einstein imagined a person and things falling from a building at the same time; if the falling person saw only those things, would she perceive herself as falling? (No, all would be perceived as being at rest.) Later, when Einstein had his own children, he tried to explain the world to them using a childlike way of seeing things. Thus he expressed his great insight that gravity was the curving of the fabric of space-time (General Relativity) to his younger son, Eduard, with these words: "When a blind beetle crawls over the surface of a curved branch, it doesn't notice that the track it has covered is indeed curved. I was lucky enough to notice what the beetle didn't notice."[17]

Einstein was able to imagine the world as a child while keeping apposite scientific information in mind. J. Robert Oppenheimer, the "father of the atomic bomb," would say of Einstein, "There was always in him a powerful purity at once childlike and profoundly stubborn."[18] Einstein frequently cited the connection between creativity and a childlike mind. In 1921, he wrote to a friend, Adriana Enriques, "The pursuit of truth and beauty is a sphere of activity in which we are permitted to remain children all our lives."[19] And finally, toward the end of his life, he expressed it this way: "We never cease to stand like curious children before the great mystery into which we were born."[20]

The Magic Kingdom, the Wizarding World of Harry Potter, Adventureland—these are all fantasy worlds to which parents take their children to intensify and perhaps rekindle the sense of wonder of both parent and child. As imagined by the author J. M. Barrie, Peter Pan was the boy who refused to grow up; he lived in London but often flew to the fantasy world of Neverland. Michael Jackson modeled his life on that of Peter Pan, and he, too, chose not to grow up. (The dark side of Jackson's world was explored in the 2019 documentary *Leaving Neverland,* which focused on the artist's sexual abuse of two boys.) As Jackson once said to the actress Jane Fonda, "You know all over the walls of my room are pictures of Peter Pan. I totally identify with Peter Pan, the lost boy of Never-Never Land."[21]

By coincidence, when, in 1983, Michael Jackson first set eyes on the property that would become the Neverland Ranch, he was in the company of Paul McCartney. The two were collaborating on a music video, and ultimately Jackson would buy the copyrights to the lyrics of 251 Beatles songs. In terms of money earned in pop or classical music—a barometer of musical influence—the Beatles rank number one; Michael Jackson is number three. Jackson wrote his greatest hits before the age of twenty-three; nothing he did thereafter matched the musical or commercial success of his 1982 *Thriller* album. McCartney, arguably the primary creative force behind the Beatles (though some believe that it was John Lennon), was his most creative between ages seventeen and twenty-seven, before and during his success with the group. Try as he might, none of McCartney's later songs matched the impact of his early ones.

"The secret of genius is to carry the spirit of the child into old age," said the novelist Aldous Huxley.[22] Walt Disney (1901–1966) did just that and thereby transformed the world of entertainment. "I do not make films primarily for children. I make them for the child in all of us, whether we be six or sixty."[23] The story line of a Disney film is invariably a fairy tale or imaginary adventure. In addition to creating such megahits as *Snow White and the Seven Dwarfs* (1937), *Pinocchio* (1940), *Fantasia* (1940), *Dumbo* (1941), *Cinderella* (1945), *Treasure Island* (1950), *Alice in Wonderland* (1951), *Robin Hood* (1952), *Peter Pan* (1953), *Lady and the Tramp* (1955), *Sleeping Beauty* (1959), and *Mary Poppins* (1964), Disney created child-oriented TV shows such as *Disney's Wonderful World* and *The Mickey Mouse Club*, built Disneyland, and started Disney World and Epcot Center. What child in the West in the last fifty years has not played with Mickey, Minnie, Donald, Pluto, or Goofy? And it all began with a child-friendly character named Mickey Mouse.

"He popped out of my mind onto a drawing pad 20 years ago on a train ride from Manhattan to Hollywood," Disney recalled in 1948.[24] Thereafter, on TV, in animated cartoons, or in films, Disney himself always provided the voice, indeed inhabited the role, of Mickey. As a child growing up in Missouri, Disney lived near the Atkinson, Topeka and Santa Fe Railway line and became fascinated with railroads. In 1949, he had a quarter-size railroad built in his Los Angeles backyard on which he and his friends could play, and when he constructed Disneyland, he employed a half-size railroad to link its four realms: Adventureland, Fantasyland, Tomorrowland, and Neverland. Disney liked to ask, "Why do we have to grow up?"

Mozart never did. As his sister, Nannerl, said in 1792, "Apart from his music he was almost always a child, and thus he remained."[25] One of the external markers of Mozart the eternal child was his lifelong use of potty talk. Just as children do not fully understand, or choose to ignore, the rules of grammar and syntax, so they have yet to learn, or choose to ignore, what are considered inappropriate topics of conversation. Below is just one example found in a letter to a cousin that Mozart wrote at age twenty-one. It typifies at least a hundred such utterances coming from the mouth of our genius.

> Well, I wish you good night, but first shit in your bed and make it burst. Sleep soundly, my love, into your mouth your arse you'll shove. . . . Oh, my arse is burning like fire! What on earth does it mean? Perhaps some muck wants to come out? Why yes, muck, I know, see and smell you . . . and . . . what is that?—Is it possible. . . . Ye gods!—can I believe those ears of mine? Yes indeed, it is so—what a long melancholy note![26]

Then there are Mozart's musical canons such as the Latin "Difficile lectu mihi mars et jonicu," which when heard as a homonym in a Viennese polyglot comes out as "Lech du mich in Arch et Cunjoni" ("Lick my ass and balls"). We'll skip the "ca-ca, ca-ca, pu-pu, pu-pu" canon and others.

Childish, all this potty talk! But recall that stand-up comedians—Robin Williams, George Carlin, Richard Pryor, Mort Sahl, Lenny Bruce, Dave Chappelle, Sarah Silverman, Chris Rock, Amy Schumer, and so many others—were and are equally obscene. Notice how such comics invariably begin a routine—unless censored on live TV—with a barrage of profanities. Their aim is to call attention not only to themselves by their "bad boy" behavior but also to the creative process, as if to say "By these disruptive words I wish to invite you into a new world in which there are no barriers to full expression. It is now open season on things that we could not talk about before."

Mozart's jokes and scatological outbursts occurred mostly at night, when he was relaxing, being silly, and making new connections in an unconsciously childlike, playful way. His excessive profanity was simply a sign that he had gone to "Creativeland." The comic genius Robin Williams, with his toy soldiers, make-believe worlds, and coprolalia, often journeyed there. Another comic, John Cleese (*Monty Python's Flying Circus* and *Fawlty Towers*), in 1991 said this about "inappropriate" creative outbursts: "You have to risk saying things that are silly, illogical and wrong, and know that while you are being creative, nothing is wrong, there is no such thing as a mistake, and any dribble may lead to the breakthrough."[27]

Good things can come from imaginary friends. At age six, the painter Frida Kahlo repeatedly escaped through a window "with a little girl, roughly my own age" with whom she laughed and danced.[28] Charles Dodgson (Lewis Carroll) imagined Alice cavorting in *Alice in Wonderland* with an imaginary rabbit. Mozart, too, had an imaginary world and imaginary friends. His own childhood realm he called the Kingdom of Back, filled with citizens of his own imagination.[29] In 1787, he and his real friends were on their way to Prague for the premier of his opera *Don Giovanni*. To pass time, Mozart made up pet names for his wife, his friends, their servant, and even their pet dog. He was Punkitititi, she Schabla Pumfa, the servant, Sagadarata, and the dog, Schamanuzky.[30] Later, Mozart populated his opera *The Magic Flute* with similar imaginary characters such as Papageno and Papagena. When Mozart created his imaginary world en route to Prague, he was not four or six but thirty-one! When he created the childlike kingdom of *The Magic Flute* in 1791, he had only a few months yet to live.

AT THE 2015 GENIUS GALA AT LIBERTY SCIENCE CENTER IN NEW Jersey, Amazon's Jeff Bezos explained youthful creativity in these words: "You have to have a certain childlike ability to not be trapped by your expertise. And that fresh look, that beginner's mind, once you're an expert, is unbelievably hard to maintain. But great inventors are always looking. They have a certain divine discontent. They may have seen something a thousand times and still, it occurs to them that that thing, even though they're accustomed to it, could be improved."[31] To encourage "a beginner's mind," tech companies such as Amazon, Apple, and Google have built their own "creativity zones." Amazon has a Wi-Fi-enhanced bird's nest in a "tree house"; Pixar has wooden huts and caves that serve as meeting rooms; and Google has a beach volleyball court and a pink-flamingo-covered dinosaur. In fact, the Liberty Science Center itself is not a museum of science and technology but rather a gigantic play space in which you can dig for dinosaur bones, build a Lego city, explore your way through a Disney-based jungle, or fashion a cave out of sponge blocks. Kids are welcome, too.

"Every child is born blessed with a vivid imagination," Walt Disney said. "But just as a muscle grows flabby with disuse, so the bright imagination of a child pales in later years if he ceases to exercise it." But why does the imaginative capacity of the human spirit pale as it morphs from childhood to adulthood, from the world of the imagination to that of adult reality, as Kanye West suggests? As we grow up, we become responsible for our own survival in real terms, putting food on the table, and so on. Many animals display playful flexibility during childhood but then follow rigidly programmed patterns as adults. Neoteny saves us.

Neoteny is a term coined by evolutionary biologists to explain the human capacity to perpetuate juvenile characteristics, such as curiosity, play, and imagination, into adult life.[32] In a 1979 article in *Natural History* titled "A Biological Homage to Mickey Mouse," Harvard's Stephen Jay Gould observed that "Humans are neotenic. We have evolved by retaining to adulthood the originally juvenile features of our ancestors. . . . We have very long periods of gestation, markedly extended childhoods, and the longest life span of any mammal. The morphological features of eternal youth have served us well."[33] A childlike "what-if" imagination is one of the things that makes us human. It accounts for our discoveries and innovations in art, science, and social organization. It allows us to see the world of the future. As the eternal child Albert Einstein said in 1929, "I am enough of the artist to draw freely upon my imagination. Imagination is more important than knowledge. Knowledge is limited. Imagination encircles the world."[34] Although we owe human progress to neoteny, this specialized term is unfamiliar to many of us, and certainly to my spellchecker. Neoteny: the retention of juvenile traits in human adults, a species-preserving habit so deeply engrained as to be almost entirely hidden.

IN SUM, WHAT CAN WE CONCLUDE FROM THIS FORAY INTO THE minds of childlike geniuses over the centuries? That the least helpful thing we can say to our children, as well as to ourselves, is "Grow up!" Children's bedtime stories, fairy tales with genies and godmothers, play toys and puppets, tree forts and dollhouses, recess, camps outside of school and home, and imaginary friends; adult play/work spaces, creative retreats, comedy hours, and the injunction to "go play with this idea"—these things allow us to retain or recapture our creative minds. The poet Charles Baudelaire got it right when he observed in 1863, "Genius is only childhood recovered at will."[35]

CHAPTER 5

DEVELOP A LUST FOR LEARNING

Queen Elizabeth I (1533–1603) of England had the finest traditional education that a king's money could buy. While her father, Henry VIII, was sending Anne Boleyn and his subsequent wives to the chopping block, he provided his children with the best private tutors, knowing that someday one of them, even a girl, might rule. Elizabeth, his youngest child, received a classical education that was typical for a Renaissance humanist prince but exceedingly rare for a woman at the time. Elizabeth not only studied history, philosophy, and ancient literature but also read the early Church fathers, the Greek New Testament, and the Latin writings of Reformation theologians. Her tutor, the Oxford don Roger Ascham, said of his star pupil when Elizabeth was only seventeen, "The constitution of her mind is exempt from female weakness [!], and she is endued with a masculine power of application. No apprehension can be quicker than hers, no memory more retentive. French and Italian she speaks like English; Latin, with fluency, propriety and judgement; she also spoke Greek with me, frequently, willingly, and moderately well."[1]

But Elizabeth's education did not stop when her tuition with Ascham ended; even after she became queen in 1558, Elizabeth remained an autodidact for life. As she once wrote to her step-mother Queen Katherine Parr, "The wit of a man, or woman, wax[es] dull and unapt to do or understand anything perfectly, unless it be always occupied upon some manner of study."[2] Having set three hours of reading daily as her standard, Elizabeth was able to remind Parliament on March 29, 1585, "I must yield this to be true: that I suppose few (that be no professors) have read more."[3] Said her contemporary William Camden, "She informed her minde with most apt documents and instructions, and daily studied and applied good letters, not for pomp but for practice of love and virtue insomuch as she was a miracle for learning among the Princes of her Time."[4]

Indeed, Elizabeth was a miracle of learning. But what practical good did all her learning avail her? It gave her power. As one of Elizabeth's courtiers, Francis Bacon, famously declared, perhaps with Elizabeth in mind, "Knowledge is power." Learned Elizabeth had earned a standing equal or superior to that of the all-male diplomatic corps of the day. Her fluency in Latin, French, and Italian enabled her to speak with foreign envoys (and understand them while they spoke with one another) as well as read letters from abroad without the need for interpreters. When, in 1597, a Polish ambassador attempted to upstage the queen by speaking in Latin, she cut him off, issuing a wholly extemporized harangue in that language. Then she turned her back on the unfortunate emissary and said to her courtiers with false humility, "My lords, I have been forced this day to scour up my rusty old Latin."[5]

Having acquired power and authority through learning, Elizabeth had no intention of relinquishing it. As her personal motto, she chose the Latin *Video et taceo* ("I see all and say nothing"). The huge imbalance between what Elizabeth had in her head and what she publicly said worked to her advantage in all things politic. Compare Elizabeth's approach to the current British and American heads of state Boris Johnson and Donald Trump, who blast out impetuous tweets daily. By knowing all and saying nothing, Elizabeth ruled for forty-four years, at the time the longest reign of any English monarch, laid the foundations of the British Empire, and gave her name to an entire epoch, the Elizabethan era. Having judicious control of everything she had put into her head allowed genius Elizabeth to keep it attached and to keep her nation on course.

CALL IT A LUST FOR LEARNING, A PASSION TO KNOW, OR A POWERful curiosity—it's all the same impulse, and we all have it, albeit to varying degrees. Although invisible and immeasurable, curiosity is an essential part of each person's personality, and it is inextricably intertwined with other personal traits, particularly with passion. For geniuses, more than the rest of us, the desire to understand is tantamount to an itch. Great minds are annoyed by a mysterious problem and want a solution. "They experience a 'divine discontent,' as Jeff Bezos called it," between what is and what might be—and they act. Marie Curie, as we will see, was driven to solve the mystery of radiation in pitchblende. Albert Einstein felt impelled by the mystery of the compass needle that would not move. Ignaz Semmelweis (1818–1865) was curious about a discrepancy in mortality rates in a Viennese maternity hospital and discovered the virtues of handwashing. Curious people want to bring comfort to a discomfort; there is a disjunction between what they see and what they know—and they feel compelled to reconcile the two.

With varying degrees of frequency and intensity, we all want to know what we don't. Experts in the psychology of education and marketing try to capitalize on this deep-seated human desire. Sigmund Freud, when hunting for mushrooms with his children and finding a prize specimen, did not exclaim, "Look, there it is!" Rather, he put his hat over it and let the children uncover the secret themselves. Freud intuited what more recent psychologists demonstrated in a 2006 study: "When asked to recall the information they had learned, subjects were far better at remembering those items about which they had expressed surprise." Children remember more when they discover things themselves.[6] Perhaps the way to learn is not to be taught, but to be curious.

Leonardo da Vinci has been called "the most relentlessly curious man in history."[7] That's hyperbole, perhaps, but Leonardo asked a lot of questions, both of others and of himself. Consider, for example, a single day's "to-do" list that he wrote while in Milan around 1495.[8]

- Calculate the measurement of Milan and its suburbs.
- Find a book describing Milan and its churches, which is to be had at the stationer's on the way to Cordusio.
- Discover the measurement of the Corte Vecchia [old courtyard of the duke's palace].
- Ask the Master of Arithmetic [Luca Pacioli] to show you how to square a triangle.
- Ask Benedetto Portinari [a Florentine merchant passing through Milan] by what means they go on ice at Flanders?
- Draw Milan.
- Ask Maestro Antonio how mortars are positioned on bastions by day or night.
- Examine the crossbow of Maestro Gianetto.
- Find a Master of Hydraulics and get him to tell you how to repair a lock, canal and mill, in the Lombard manner.
- Ask about the measurement of the sun, promised me by Maestro Giovanni Francese.

Leonardo's questions extend to many fields: urban planning, hydraulics, drawing, archery and warfare, astronomy, mathematics, and even ice skating. How many of those subjects had he studied in school? None, for Leonardo was of illegitimate birth and thus barred from the only system of formal education then available, that of the Roman Catholic Church. He had received no instruction in Latin or Greek, the learned languages of the day, and accordingly later said of himself, "I am a *uomo senza lettere*"[9]—an unlettered man. Thus Leonardo belongs to the first of two types of curious individuals: those who learn experientially and those who learn vicariously by reading—in other words, those who do or discover and those who read about what others have done or discovered.

Leonardo was a doer. He painted, of course, but he also went into the mountains to examine rocks and fossils and to the tidal marshes to look at the wings and flying habits of dragonflies. He took apart machines to see how they worked and took apart humans to the same end. He recorded all of his discoveries in what amounted to about thirteen thousand pages of notes and drawings.

What made Leonardo so curious? Among the earliest attempts to explain his inquisitiveness was a theory advanced in 1910 by the genius Sigmund Freud. Strange as it may seem today, Freud attributed Leonardo's curiosity to the fact that he was apparently gay, which had "caused him to sublimate his libido into the urge to know."[10] Freud believed he saw physical evidence of Leonardo's gayness in the androgynous faces Leonardo depicted in some of his paintings, most notably his *St. John the Baptist* (Figure 5.1), as well as in the artist's handwriting.

Many geniuses throughout history have been left-handed,[11] and Leonardo may have been the most famous "lefty" of them all. But Leonardo had another oddity in his script: he wrote almost everything backward. Of course, there is a simple explanation for this: For a left-handed person, writing backward (right to left) removes the possibility that the writer's hand will pass through and smudge the ink.

But Freud saw more than a practical explanation: Leonardo's backward drawing was a mark of "secretive behavior," a sign of his repressed sexuality in a less-than-open society. By means of such coded writing Leonardo might remain private, an enigma as to his thoughts and desires. Freud's conclusion: "The sublimated libido reinforces curiosity and the powerful investigation impulse. . . . Investigation becomes to some extent compulsive

FIGURE 5.1: The face in Leonardo's *St. John the Baptist* (1513–1516): male or female? (Musée du Louvre, Paris).

and substitutive of sexual activity."[12] In brief: curiosity can manifest as a substitute for sex.

Though all of this may seem far-fetched, Leonardo himself remarked in his *Codex Atlanticus*, "Intellectual passion drives out sensuality."[13] Is homosexual passion really a spur of curiosity and ultimately creativity, as Freud suggests? Not according to a 2013 report in *The International Journal of Psychological Studies* that summed up current research on the matter in these terms: "The present findings were compatible with previous studies that homosexuals are no more or less creative."[14] Although the life experiences of gay individuals may open up new vantage points of otherness, homosexuals are apparently no more or less likely to be curious—and become creative geniuses—than are heterosexuals.

TO CREATE HIS FAMOUS PAINTINGS, INCLUDING THE *MONA LISA*, the inquisitive Leonardo seems to have taken a step backward and asked, "What is it that I am painting, and how does this living organism work?" These questions he pursued by picking up not a brush to paint but a knife to cut. To satisfy his curiosity about anatomy, Leonardo dissected dead pigs, dogs, horses, and oxen, and also humans, including a two-year-old child.

Dissection of humans in this or any day requires courage—a combination of passion and a tolerance for risk. And Leonardo had courage in abundance, as his early biographer Vasari noted in several places in his *The Lives of the Most Eminent Painters, Sculptors, and Architects* (1550).[15] To begin with, where to obtain human cadavers? In an era in which Church authorities still considered dissection heresy, Leonardo did not explicitly identify his sources, though we know that at least one came from the hospital of Santa Maria Novella in Florence.[16]

Once Leonardo had obtained the bodies, things only got worse. The weather in Milan and Florence can be hot. To peel back layers of skin and lift up tendons, some degree of firmness and integrity of the tissue must be present. Without refrigeration and air-conditioning, once living tissue degenerates and approaches liquid form. Leonardo's dissections seem to have been done under the secrecy of night, as he reported to his readers in these words:

But though possessed of an interest in the subject, you may be deterred by natural repugnance, or, if this does not restrain you, then perhaps by the fear of passing the night hours in the company of these corpses, quartered and flayed and horrible to behold; and if this does not deter you then perhaps you may lack the skill in drawing essential for such representation; and even if you possess this skill it may not be combined with a knowledge of perspective, while if it is so combined, you may not be versed in the methods of geometrical demonstration or the method of estimating the forces and strength of muscles, or perhaps you may be found wanting in patience so that you will not be diligent.[17]

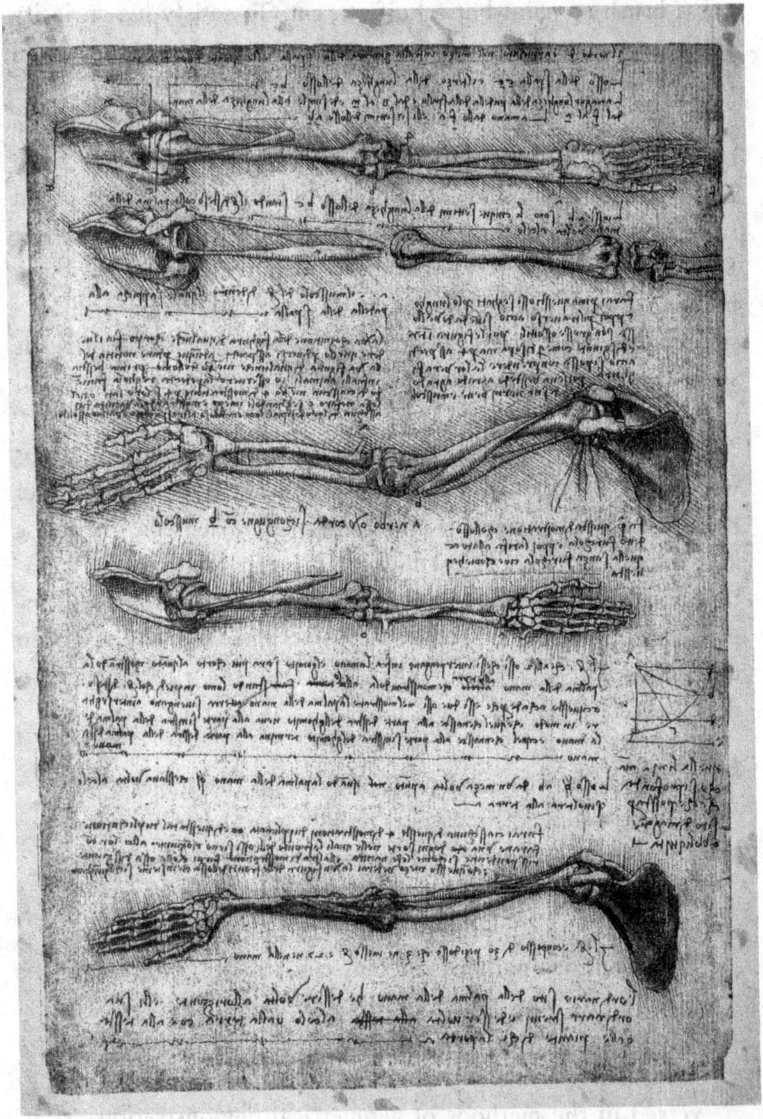

FIGURE 5.2: Leonardo's drawing of the bones, muscles, and tendons of the hand, arm, and shoulder. The text is a beautifully clear Italian, written backward (Royal Collection Trust, Windsor Castle).

And then there would have been the stench. But Leonardo was not dissuaded from the task at hand. Did he even notice? Possibly not, for Vasari reports that as a prank Leonardo once affixed to a shield the dead bodies of several ferocious creatures that soon stunk to the high heavens. The stench went unnoticed by the creator.

This raises the question: When a genius is in the height of passionate investigation, does he or she notice discomfort? Michelangelo didn't bewail his fate as he reached up for four years, sixteen hours a day, during his "agony" beneath the ceiling of the Sistine Chapel in the Vatican. Isaac Newton seems not to have complained when he stuck a large needle into his eye and wiggled it around to measure the effect on his perception of color. Nikola Tesla soldiered on after more than once shocking himself with high-voltage electric current. Do the fires of creative curiosity drive away pain?

Having persevered, what did Leonardo learn as a result of his many dissections? Nothing less than the structure of human anatomy understood in modern terms. He was the first to identify the condition we now call arteriosclerosis. He was the first to recognize that seeing is the process of light being dispersed on the whole of the retina, not on a single point of the eye. He was the first to discover that the heart has four chambers, not two. And he was the first to demonstrate that blood swirling as vortices at the base of the aorta forces a closing of the aortic valve—something not verified in published medical journals until 1968.[18] And so it goes. Eventually, 450 years after his death, medical science caught up with the genius of Leonardo, with the advent of machines for computerized axial tomography (CAT) and magnetic resonance imaging (MRI) that could see inside the body without cutting it open. But even today, some physicians prefer to use copies of Leonardo's handwritten drawings (Figure 5.2), rather than the computer-generated images in medical textbooks, believing that the master's crosshatched shadings more clearly reveal the functional processes within the body.[19] Leonardo's curiosity taught him how to paint the muscles in Mona Lisa's smile,[20] but it also led him to discoveries far beyond the world of art.

When Leonardo breathed his last at the age of sixty-seven, his legacy consisted of fewer than twenty-five finished paintings.[21] What he left behind in abundance, by contrast, were his voluminous notes and 100,000 sketches and preliminary drawings. Why so few paintings from arguably the greatest artist of all time? Because once he had figured out how to do something, his curiosity drove him on to the next project. He had a greater desire to learn than he did to finish.

MOST OF US DO NOT DISSECT ANIMALS OR DIVERT STREAMS, AS DID Leonardo, to satisfy our curiosity. Most of us learn vicariously by reading, and we do so for at least three reasons: (1) to acquire information that can lead to knowledge, wisdom, authority, and power; (2) to expand our life experiences, thereby gaining insight into human behavior without having emotional skin in the game; and (3) to find role models by which to set our own moral compass.

One genius who has changed the lives of millions is Oprah Winfrey. As a TV reporter and talk show host, Oprah's curiosity and desire to learn were amply demonstrated in the course of the thirty-seven thousand interviews she conducted. No less impactful on her TV audience was Oprah's Book Club, which caused people who had not picked up a book since high school to do so. As a child, Winfrey had to fight so as to learn. "You're nothing but a something-something bookworm," she has recalled her mother yelling as she grabbed the book from her daughter's hand. "Get your butt outside! You think you're better than the other kids. And I'm not taking you to no library!"[22]

The great-great-granddaughter of a slave, Winfrey was born to a young single mother, was moved from home to home, was sexually molested in her childhood and early teens, and had a child out of wedlock at age fourteen. "I went back to school after the baby died," she recalled, "thinking that I had been given a second chance in life. I threw myself into books. I threw myself into books about troubled women, Helen Keller and Anne Frank. I read about Eleanor Roosevelt."[23]

From poverty Winfrey rose to become a media mogul and the first African American billionaire. How did she do it? By continually working to improve herself, and others, through reading. Nobel Prize winner Toni Morrison said about Winfrey, "I have very seldom seen a home with so many books—all kinds of books, handled and read books. She's a genuine reader, not a decorative one. She's a carnivorous reader."[24] In 2017, Winfrey spoke of the importance of reading and education but never once mentioned learning in the context of a school, a college, or a university. "[It] matters because it's an open door to a real life, and you can't get through this life without it and succeed. It's an open door to discovery and wonder and fascination and figuring out who you are, why you're here, and what you came to do. It's an invitation to life, and it feeds you forever."[25]

LIKE OPRAH WINFREY, BENJAMIN FRANKLIN WAS A LIFETIME learner, both a reader and a doer. In his autobiography (1771), Franklin confessed that he was born a bibliophile: "From my infancy I was passionately fond of reading, and all the little money that came into my hands was laid out in the purchasing of books. I was very fond of voyages. My first acquisition was Bunyan's works in separate little volumes."[26] In 1727, Franklin formed the Junto Club, a group of twelve tradesmen who met each Friday to discuss issues of morality, philosophy, and science. Eventually, Franklin accumulated 4,276 books, one of the largest libraries, public or private, in the American colonies.[27]

John Bunyan's *Pilgrim's Progress,* Daniel Defoe's *An Essay upon Projects,* and Plutarch's *Lives of the Noble Greeks and Romans* were Franklin's early companions. Later, "ashamed of my ignorance in figures which I had twice failed in learning when at school," he worked through all of *Cocker's Arithmetick* (first edition London, 1677) and taught himself a bit of geometry as an aid to celestial navigation. To make himself a man of the world, Franklin learned to speak French and Italian and obtained a reading knowledge of Spanish and Latin. He found time for such self-improvement mostly on Sundays, when he determined that the traditional Christian devotional hours would be better spent in solitary learning than "in the common attendance on public worship."[28] A latter-day genius, Bill Gates, said much the same in 1997: "Just in terms of allocation of time resources, religion is not very efficient. There's a lot more I could be doing on a Sunday morning."[29]

At age forty-two, Ben Franklin retired from his profession as newspaper and magazine publisher to the American colonies to pursue other interests. His aim now was to satisfy his insatiable scientific curiosity. What caused a high-pitched violin to break a glass? Why does electricity go through water but not wood? Such questions then fell under the heading of natural philosophy, what we today call physics. (The term "scientist" was not coined until 1833.) "When I disengaged myself from private business, I flattered myself that, by the sufficient tho' moderate fortune I had acquired, I had secured leisure during the rest of my life for philosophical studies and amusements."[30] Never mind that he knew only shopkeeper's math and no physics. Again, curious Ben would teach himself what he needed.

Franklin's curiosity about electrical science was pricked by a serendipitous event. In 1746, a traveling lecturer, Archibald Spencer of Edinburgh, arrived in Philadelphia and demonstrated the effects of static electricity.[31] Intrigued, Franklin purchased Spencer's electricity-generating devices on the spot, began to read about electricity, and started to experiment, mostly for fun. As he said of this exploration, "I never was before engaged in any study that so totally engrossed my attention and my time as this has lately done, what with making experiments when I can be alone, and repeating them to my friends and acquaintances, who . . . come continually in crowds to see them."[32] In one such experiment before a crowd, Franklin attempted to kill (and cook) a Christmas turkey by means of electrocution. In the excitement of the moment, he forgot to don his insulated shoes and nearly electrocuted himself.[33]

Between 1746 and 1750, Franklin shifted from performing parlor tricks to seriously investigating electricity. In 1752, he boldly flew a kite in an electrical storm. When lightning struck it, a line carried the charge down to a set of keys that jangled, just as they might if connected to an electrical charge emanating from a Leyden-jar battery on the ground. That was dangerous business: indeed, the next year the German physicist Georg Wilhelm Richmann electrocuted himself when trying to duplicate Franklin's experiment.[34] But Franklin had proved that lightning in the sky and electricity on earth are one and the same, that lightning moves from ground to cloud with as much intensity as from sky to earth, and that electricity is neither an ether nor a fluid but rather a force that, like gravity, pervades all nature. In recognition, he was awarded not only honorary degrees by Yale and Harvard but also the eighteenth-century equivalent of the Nobel Prize in Physics, the Copley Medal of the Royal Society (of London). Inquisitive to the end and even beyond, Franklin wrote to a friend in 1786 that he had experienced much of his world but was now "feeling a growing curiosity to see the next."[35] Four years later, his wish was granted.

THE SCIENTIST-INVENTOR NIKOLA TESLA (1856–1943) ALSO HAD a lust to learn about electricity. The results of his pursuits led to the universal adoption of alternating current, the system still in use today, as well as the induction motor, a device still used to power much of the world. The honorific eponym of the carmaker Tesla, he was a visionary who foresaw solar heating, X-rays, the radio and MRI machine, robots and drones, cell phones, and the internet. Like Franklin before him, Tesla was a passionate bibliophile from his earliest days, as he wrote in his autobiography.

FIGURE 5.3: Nikola Tesla in his Colorado Springs lab, 1899 (Francesco Bianchetti, Corbis).

My father had a large library and whenever I could manage to, I tried to satisfy my passion for reading. He did not permit it and would fly into a rage when he caught me in the act. He hid the candles when he found that I was reading in secret—he did not want me to spoil my eyes. But I obtained tallow, made the wicking and cast the sticks into tin forms, and every night I could cover the keyhole and the cracks in the door and read, often til dawn.[36]

In addition to studying physics, math, and electrical engineering, mostly on his own, Tesla drank in philosophy and literature. He claimed to have read all of the multiple volumes of Voltaire as well as committed to memory Goethe's *Faust* and several Serbian epics—feats possible owing to his photographic memory.

If a picture is worth a thousand words, at least that many might be written about the accompanying photograph (Figure 5.3). It shows Nikola Tesla in his laboratory in 1899, impeccably dressed, with starched collar and polished shoes. In his hands he holds a book, a copy of Rogerio Boscovich's *Theoria philosophiae naturalis* (1758).[37] Tesla reads, oblivious to the swirls of electricity bolting around him. He created these "electrostatic thrusts," as he called them, by means of "Tesla coils" built in a specially constructed laboratory in Colorado Springs, Colorado.[38]

Tesla's ultimate aim was to create a new electrical "world system" that could transport not only raw electricity but also information and pleasure of all sorts (news, stock quotes, music, and phone calls) instantly and without wires around the globe. Needless to say, the experiments he did with blasts of high-voltage electricity in his lab were dangerous.[39] The photo that we see here has actually been "Photoshopped" by Tesla, who superimposed an image of waves of electricity on top of a simple one of himself sitting. The result was an act of self-promotion intended to impress prospective investors and the general public alike. In the midst of the storm is the image that Tesla wished to create of himself: a genius quietly reading.

THE MODERN GENIUS ELON MUSK, THE CURRENT CEO OF TESLA— the name was chosen not by Musk but by the company's founder— has also been a voracious reader since childhood. The driving force behind not only an electric car company but also SolarCity, Hyperloop, and SpaceX, young Musk always had a book in hand. Said his brother, Kimbal, "It was not unusual for him to read ten hours a day. If it was the weekend, he could go through two books in a day." Musk himself recounts how around the age of ten, "I ran out of books at the school library [in Pretoria, South Africa] and the neighborhood library. This is maybe the third or fourth grade. I tried to convince the librarian to order books for me. So then, I started to read the *Encyclopaedia Britannica*. That was so helpful. You don't know what you don't know. You realize there are all these things out there."[40]

So from childhood Musk read "from when I woke up until when I went to sleep." Eventually, he read so much that he seemed to know everything. Musk's mother recalled that whenever her daughter, Tosca, had a question, she'd say, "Well, go ask genius boy."[41] When asked how he had learned enough "rocket science" to help draft the booster designs for his aerospace company (SpaceX), he answered very quietly, "I read a lot of books."[42] Musk's aim is to get to Mars.

WAS ELON MUSK BORN CURIOUS, OR IS HIS CURIOSITY AN ACQUIRED trait, or some of both? The psychologist Susan Engel, the author of *The Hungry Mind: The Origins of Curiosity in Childhood* (2015), stated that curiosity, like intelligence, is mostly innate and a stable part of one's personality: "From birth some children may be more likely to explore novel spaces, objects, and even people."[43] Yet in a 2010 survey of all fifty U.S. states, researchers seeking to identify the catalyst of "giftedness" among children found that psychologists in forty-five of the states tested for a high IQ but only three for motivational curiosity.[44] Which is more essential to greatness, intelligence or curiosity?

Eleanor Roosevelt would have said curiosity. As she declared in 1934, "I think, at a child's birth, if a mother could ask a fairy godmother to endow it with the most useful gift, that gift would be curiosity."[45] Indeed, recent research has linked curiosity to happiness, satisfying relationships, increased personal growth, increased meaning in life, and increased creativity.[46] Moreover, curiosity may play a role in the very survival of our species, as Jeff Bezos suggested in a 2014 interview on Business Insider: "I think it's probably a survival skill that we're curious and like to explore. Our ancestors, who were incurious and failed to explore, probably didn't live as long as the ones who were looking over the next mountain range to see if there were more sources of food and better climates and so on and so on."[47] Like Musk with his SpaceX program, Bezos, via his Blue Origin private space company, is looking with curious eyes over to the next planet.

As to the incurious of this world: perhaps they did not begin life that way. Many evolutionary psychologists believe that humans are born curious but lose their innate inquisitiveness over time.[48] But a childlike curiosity seems to always accompany a genius. As Albert Einstein said of himself in his later years, "I have no special talents. I am only passionately curious."[49]

As a child, Albert Einstein was intrigued by mechanical gadgets, toy steam engines and puzzles in particular. He also played with a set of tiny stone building blocks (the predecessors of today's Legos), and he would arrange the pieces to conform to a visual concept in his mind. (Einstein's set survives and was for sale in 2017 at Seth Kaller, Inc., for $160,000.) Einstein later recalled how at age four or five a compass caught his attention, and he became transfixed by the way the needle would remain north pointing rather than move as he turned it. "I can still remember—or at least I believe I can remember—that this experience made a deep and lasting impression on me. Something deeply hidden had to be behind things."[50] We have all puzzled at the immobile compass needle, but only one of us followed his curiosity to arrive at a Theory of Special Relativity.

When he was ten, Einstein got his hands on a series of short "popular science" volumes entitled *People's Books on Natural Science* (*Naturwissenschaftliche Volksbücher*, 1880) by Aaron

Bernstein, which he read "with breathless attention."[51] Posed within were questions to which the curious Albert wanted answers: What is time? What is the speed of light? Is anything faster? Bernstein asked his reader to imagine a speeding train and a bullet shot through one side of a train car; the path of the bullet would appear curved inside the train as it raced forward. Einstein, when later working on his Theory of General Relativity and curvilinear space-time, asked his reader to imagine an elevator ascending rapidly but with a pinhole on one side allowing for the intrusion of a beam of light; by the time the light reached the other side of the lift, it would appear to be a descending arc. Said a family friend, Max Talmey, of Einstein's youth, "In all those years, I never saw him reading any light literature. Nor did I ever see him in the company of schoolmates or other boys his age."[52]

Alone, Einstein educated himself. At the age of twelve, he taught himself algebra and Euclidean geometry, and shortly thereafter integral and differential calculus. After he entered college, the self-schooling continued. The Polytechnic Institute in Zurich did not teach him what he was passionate to learn: cutting-edge physics. Thus Einstein, on his own, studied the electromagnetic equations of James Clerk Maxwell, the molecular structure of gases propounded by Ludwig Boltzmann, and the atomistic electric charges described by Hendrik Lorentz. After college, Einstein and two colleagues formed a club, the Olympia Academy, collectively to educate themselves, just as Franklin had done 170 years earlier with his Junto Club. Together Einstein's group read and discussed, among other works, Miguel de Cervantes' *Don Quixote*, David Hume's *A Treatise of Human Nature*, and Baruch Spinoza's *Ethics*. Einstein's disappointing experience in college later caused him to say, "It is, in fact, nothing short of a miracle that the modern methods of instruction have not yet entirely strangled the holy curiosity of inquiry."[53] Mark Twain is believed to have once said, "I have never let my schooling interfere with my education." Einstein seems to have riffed on that idea when he observed with irony, "Education is that which remains, if one has forgotten everything he learned in school."[54]

EINSTEIN SHOULD NOT HAVE EXPECTED OTHERWISE. MOST SCHOOLS— even top-flight colleges and universities—don't explicitly teach the most important thing to learn in life: how to become a lifetime learner. Thus emblazoned over the entry arch to every academic institution should be these words: *Discipule: disce te ipse docere* ("Student: learn to teach thyself").[55] Students may receive information and learn methodologies in school, but the game changers of this world acquire the vast majority of what they know over time and on their own. Perhaps the science fiction writer Isaac Asimov got close to the truth when he said in 1974, "Self-education is, I firmly believe, the only kind of education there is."[56]

SHAKESPEARE WAS ONCE CHASTISED BY HIS CONTEMPORARY BEN Jonson for having "little Latin and less Greek"—but at least the Bard had acquired *some* Latin and Greek. Mozart and Michael Faraday never had any formal schooling. Abraham Lincoln had a total of fewer than twelve months. Leonardo became the foremost medical scientist of his day without training in medical science. Michelangelo, Franklin, Beethoven, Edison, and Picasso never went beyond a bit of primary school. Elizabeth I and Virginia Woolf were homeschooled. Einstein left high school but after a year returned to prep for college. Tesla abandoned university after a year and a half and never returned.

To be sure, most dropouts do not become geniuses or success stories. But prominent among the dropout titans of recent history are Bill Gates (Harvard), Steve Jobs (Reed College), Mark Zuckerberg (Harvard), Elon Musk (Stanford), Bob Dylan (University of Minnesota), Lady Gaga (New York University), and Oprah Winfrey (Tennessee State). Jack Ma never went to college, and neither did Richard Branson, who dropped out of high school at age fifteen. Creative force Kanye West dropped out of Chicago State University at age twenty to pursue a musical career; six years later he released his first album to great critical acclaim and commercial success: *The College Dropout* (2004). The point is not to encourage dropping out but rather to observe that these transformative figures were somehow able to learn what they needed to know. Here successful people and geniuses share a common trait: most are lifelong learning addicts. It's a good habit to have.

Finally, how might we nongeniuses cultivate a lust for learning beyond the obvious acts of reading, attending lectures, or finding a challenging vacation venue for next year? Here are some everyday ideas.

- Be open to new and unfamiliar experiences: Push yourself to do something that scares you. Let yourself get lost while wandering in a new city; you'll see a lot of places you didn't know existed.
- Be fearless: When in a new town, don't call for an Uber—walk or take public transportation; you'll learn about geography, history, and the local culture.
- Ask questions: When you stand in the "presenter mode" (as teacher, parent, or corporate leader), use the Socratic method. And when you are in the role of student or employee, don't be afraid to reveal what you don't know—instead, ask!
- Once you ask, *listen* carefully to the answer; you'll learn something. Here we might all learn from a negative example: geniuses are generally *not* good listeners because they are usually too obsessed with their own vision of the world. Savvy successful people, however, know how to listen.

A WISE PERSON ONCE OBSERVED, "EDUCATION IS WASTED ON THE young." But education doesn't have to go only to the young. Today, young and old alike can learn independently, as the world has learned during the COVID-19 shutdown of 2020. Online Tech Ed platforms—such as Coursera (Yale and other universities), edX (Harvard and MIT), and Stanford Online—offer nearly one thousand high-quality courses to the general public, and most are entirely free. My own online Yale course, Introduction to Classical Music, now has more than 150,000 learners, and the median age of the participants is forty-four. Adult book clubs are similarly thriving, in part because it has never been easier to get access to just about any book that you might want to read, delivered in one day or even instantly by downloading an e-book to your Kindle, Nook, or iPad. "No professor has read more," said Queen Elizabeth; "I ran out of books in the school library," said Musk; "It's an invitation to life, and it feeds you forever," said Winfrey, in reference to reading and education. With modern technology at hand, the opportunity to self-educate, anywhere at anytime, is more robust and more diverse than ever. Compared to the geniuses of yore, we have it easy.

CHAPTER 6

FIND YOUR MISSING PIECE

Be passionate. Do what you love," Katie Couric told graduating students at Williams College in 2007. "If you really want to fly, first harness your power to your passion," urged Oprah Winfrey at Stanford University in 2008. "Follow your passion, stay true to yourself," said Ellen DeGeneres at Tulane University in 2009. "Will inertia be your guide, or will you follow your passions?" asked Jeff Bezos at Princeton University in 2010. Year after year, we hear this message delivered to wide-eyed graduates. Idealistic nonsense? But consider this: Plato emphasized the power of passion as far back as 380 B.C.: "the true lover of knowledge . . . soars with undiminished and unwearied passion until he grasps the essential nature of things" (*Republic*, 490A), as did Shakespeare in 1595 in *Romeo and Juliet* and van Gogh in a letter of October 2, 1884—"I'd prefer to die of passion than of boredom"—so maybe there is something to the valedictory imperative "Follow your passion."

Before we can follow our passion, of course, we have to find it, a process that can occur quickly or take almost a lifetime. Picasso, Einstein, and Mozart knew by the age of five that their life's passion would be for drawing, science, and music, respectively. But as Vincent van Gogh wrote to his brother Theo in

1880, "[A man] does not always know what he can do, but he nevertheless instinctively feels, I am good for something! . . . There is something inside me, but what can it be?"[1] Van Gogh tried various things before he found his passion. Only after pursuing careers as a gallery dealer, a teacher, a bookseller, and a street minister did he turn to art at age twenty-nine. His fellow painter Paul Gauguin spent six years as a seaman and then eleven as a stockbroker before painting became his sole passion at age thirty-four. Grandma Moses (1860–1961) didn't take up painting until she was seventy-six.

Sigmund Freud was once asked by a patient, "What are the most important things in life?" to which he replied "*Lieben und arbeiten*" ("To love and to work").[2] He might have combined the two into "a labor of love," for that is where most people, including great athletes, find their passion. In an interview explaining his 2018 documentary *In Search of Greatness*, the filmmaker Gabe Polsky concluded that the single most important driver of great athletes is the joy they experience. "If you find the thing that gives you the most amount of fun in your sport, there is a chance that you'll be great at it because it doesn't become work anymore. It becomes a joy. You can become obsessed in that joy."[3] As Confucius is reputed to have said some 2,500 years ago, "Find a job you love and you will never have to work a day in your life."

I USED TO LOVE READING THE STORIES OF SHEL SILVERSTEIN TO MY children. Silverstein began as a tough-talking Korean War veteran who drew cartoons for *Playboy* and wrote short stories, film scripts, novels, and country music songs. Belatedly, he turned to writing children's poems and stories with phenomenal success, selling more than 20 million books. Genius Silverstein didn't find his passion until later in life. As he told *Publishers Weekly* in 1975:

When I was a kid—12, 14, around there—I would much rather have been a good baseball player or a hit with the girls. But I couldn't play ball, I couldn't dance. Luckily, the girls didn't want me; not much I could do about that. So, I started to draw and to write. I was also lucky that I didn't have anybody to copy, be impressed by. I had developed my own style, I was creating before I knew there was a Thurber, a Benchley, a Price and a Steinberg. I never saw their work till I was around 30. By the time I got to where I was attracting girls, I was already into work, and it was more important to me. Not that I wouldn't rather make love, but the work has become a habit.[4]

Silverstein's children's book *The Missing Piece* is a commentary on his own passionate habit of working. The story centers on a circular humanoid that is missing a wedge-shaped piece of itself. The circle feels unfulfilled and sets out on a grand adventure to find its missing piece. Merrily rolling along, it sings, "Oh I'm lookin' for my missin' piece/I'm lookin' for my missin' piece/ Hi-dee-ho, here I go/Lookin' for my missin' piece." Eventually the circle finds its missing piece, and it fits perfectly. But then it realizes that the happiness resided in the looking, not in the accomplishment. So the circle gently puts the piece down and begins searching again.

Silverstein's fable brings us to another story of passion, happiness, and the quest for a missing piece: Marie Curie and the discovery of radium.

WHAT WERE THE CHANCES THAT A YOUNG WOMAN WORKING AS A nanny in rural Poland, with no formal education beyond the age of fifteen, would go on to win the Nobel Prize in Physics? Slim to none. But Maria Skłodowska (1867–1934), known as Marie Curie after her marriage to Pierre Curie, was that genius from nowhere. Only Curie's passion—and perseverance—explain the otherwise inexplicable.

Around the age of twenty, Curie left behind her interest in

literature and sociology and found her passion in math and physics. In 1891 she emigrated to France to attend the Faculté des Sciences of the Sorbonne to study graduate-level physics, having intensely self-educated until she was capable of passing the school's entrance exam. She had no undergraduate diploma, was a foreigner, and was one of only 23 women among an entering class of 1,825.[5]

And Curie had almost no money. Still, she was happy during her student days of deprivation:

> The room I lived in was in a garret, very cold in winter, for it was insufficiently heated by a small stove which often lacked coal. . . . In the same room I prepared my meals with the aid of an alcohol lamp and a few kitchen utensils. These meals were often reduced to bread with a cup of chocolate, eggs or fruit. I had no help in housekeeping and I myself carried the little coal I used up the six flights.
>
> This life, painful from certain points of view, had, for all that, a real charm for me. It gave me a very precious sense of liberty and independence. Unknown in Paris, I was lost in the great city, but the feeling of living there alone, taking care of myself without any aid, did not at all depress me. If sometimes I felt lonesome, my usual state of mind was one of calm and great moral satisfaction.[6]

But Curie's years of satisfying deprivation were not over. They were to be followed by ten years of painstaking research in what she would come to refer to as the "miserable old shed."[7] In 1897, having completed master's degrees in both physics and math, Curie began research for a doctorate under the direction of her new husband, the physicist Pierre Curie. The subject of her dissertation was Becquerel rays, the high-energy waves emitted by uranium salts, discovered by Henri Becquerel in 1896. At a critical juncture in her research, Curie experienced not a sudden "aha" moment but rather a "my, that's strange" insight: subtracting the energy of uranium from uranium ore still did not account for the powerful radiation emanating therefrom. As she said to her sister at the time, "You know, Bronya, the radiation that I couldn't explain comes from a new chemical element. The element is there and I've got to find it."[8] Thus Marie Curie went in search of her missing piece. Ultimately she found it deep inside pitchblende, the residue left after the extrusion of uranium from uranium ore.

Over the years Curie processed approximately eight tons of pitchblende in the shed that served as her makeshift laboratory. Situated in Paris just south of the Panthéon, where she is now enshrined, the outbuilding had once been used as a dissection room by the Faculté de Médecine but had been abandoned even by the cadavers. In that shed, which lacked proper heating and electricity, and in an adjoining yard, Curie first boiled the pitchblende in large vats, separated its components through fractional crystallization, and finally measured the minute amounts of radioactive material down to a thousandth of a milligram. By assiduously testing and eliminating each element within the ore, one by one, she worked her way down to just two radioactive suspects. She named the first "polonium" after her native country. Yet even polonium was not the answer; the missing piece was far more radioactive. By 1902, Curie had it and could hold it in her hand, or at least in her glass test tube. Eventually she distilled the eight tons of pitchblende down to just one small gram of deadly pure radium.

Many of us keep our passions—reading, painting, or travel—to ourselves, and they don't impact the world at large. If we are passionate and exceptionally talented at things of interest to others, such as singing on TV or throwing a football, the result may be instant celebrity. If our passions drive us in ways that ultimately change society, that change is a mark of genius. What followed Marie Curie's discovery of radium was public recognition of her genius, in this case two Nobel Prizes, one in physics (1903) for the discovery of radioactivity, and one in chemistry (1911) for isolating radium. Curie had discovered two new elements (polonium and radium), coined the term "radioactivity," and shown that radium could be used to destroy deadly tumors—still the basis of radiation oncology today. Ironically, and through the law of unintended consequences, her discovery of radium also led in 1939 to the beginning of the construction of an atomic bomb.

Extracting radium from pitchblende presumably was not fun—but then that depends on your definition of fun. Marie Curie worked in her leaky shed, where, as she said, "the heat was suffocating in summer, and the bitter cold of winter was only a little lessened by the iron stove."[9] Here she experienced "irritating gases" and radium burns on her hands and fingers that made touching objects thereafter painful. "Sometimes I had to spend a whole day," she said, "stirring a boiling mass [of pitchblende] with a heavy iron rod nearly as large as myself." The isolation of radium took years, and Marie's husband, Pierre, was ready to quit.[10] But Marie just stirred on, oblivious to the pain and suffering. Had her passion for research anesthetized her against pain? As she later said, "It was in this miserable old shed that we passed the best and happiest years of our life, devoting our entire days to our work."[11] Curie's experience calls to mind the original Latin root of the word "passion": *passio,* which means "pain." "Passion is the bridge that takes you from pain to change," Frida Kahlo reminds us.[12]

Ultimately, Curie's passion killed her. She carried bits of radium around in her pockets. Radioactive elements and gases permeated her shed and her research papers; the documents are preserved today at the Bibliothèque Nationale in Paris, encased in lead boxes to protect future generations from radiation exposure. For amusement, she and Pierre enjoyed sitting exposed to radium in the dark, entranced by its lava lamp–like luminous effects. Only now do we know what she helped us discover: that atomic radiation can kill both malignant *and* healthy cells. Curie understood some of the pernicious effects of that "evil," as she called it, but she took almost no safety precautions until the 1920s. She died at age sixty-six of aplastic anemia, a rare disease in which the bone marrow and the blood-generating cells therein have been damaged. Her daughter, Irène Joliot-Curie, also won a Nobel Prize for her work with radium and similarly died of leukemia, she at age fifty-eight. A deadly passion, indeed.

THE PHILOSOPHER JOHN STUART MILL OBSERVED IN HIS AUTOBIOGRAPHY that happiness is something that happens to us while we are pursuing some other purpose; it approaches us stealthily and sideways, "like a crab."[13] Marie Curie came to realize that she had been happiest while boiling pitchblende in a shed. In *The World as Will and Idea* (1818), the philosopher Arthur Schopenhauer connected passionate distraction to genius: "Genius is the power of leaving one's own interests, wishes, and aims entirely out of sight, thus of entirely renouncing one's own personality for a time."[14] In his book *Flow: The Psychology of Optimal Experience* (1990) the psychologist Mihaly Csikszentmihalyi called this transcendent state simply that: "flow." All creative individuals—composers, painters, writers, coders, architects, lawyers, and chefs—experience a flow state when looking for that missing piece. Happiness sneaks up on us like a crab. Time flies by—we forget our emails, forget lunch.

LOUISA MAY ALCOTT CALLED HER TRANSCENDENT STATE NOT A flow or a zone but a vortex. Alcott wrote the two-volume novel *Little Women* (1868) in a burst of little more than four months, aiming for a chapter a day.[15] Scholars uniformly classify *Little Women* as an autobiographical novel. When we read "Jo" or "she" below, it is Alcott herself revealing what passion looks like.

Every few weeks she would shut herself up in her room, put on her scribbling suit, and "fall into a vortex," as she expressed it, writing away at her novel with all her heart and soul, for till that was finished she could find no peace. . . . [Her family would occasionally pop in their heads to ask] "Does genius burn, Jo?" . . .

She did not think herself a genius by any means, but when the writing fit came on, she gave herself up to it with entire abandon, and led a blissful life, unconscious of want, care, or bad weather, while she sat safe and happy in an imaginary world, full of friends almost as real and dear to her as any in the flesh. Sleep forsook her eyes, meals stood untasted, day and night were all too short to enjoy the happiness which blessed her only at such times, and made these hours worth living, even if they bore no other fruit. The divine afflatus usually lasted a week or two, and then she emerged from her "vortex," hungry, sleepy, cross, or despondent.[16]

"The happiness which blessed her only at such times" was all consuming. While working on *Little Women,* Alcott said, "I am so full of my work I can't stop to eat or sleep, or for anything but a daily run."[17]

PASSION, DETERMINATION, GRIT, COMPULSION, OR OBSESSION— each word has a nuanced meaning. Together they span the gamut from positive to negative. Where on the spectrum does a positive passion turn to the dark side of obsession? The former impels and can be self-regulated; the latter compels and can't be. One is considered healthy; the other isn't. Marie Curie knowingly played with dangerous radium. In 1962, Andy Warhol created thirteen different renderings of the sex symbol Marilyn Monroe, then reproduced 250 lithographs of each. In 1964, he made even more, larger images of her. Passion or obsession?

"GENIUSES ARE VERY PECULIAR," SAID THE RENOWNED ECONOMIST John Maynard Keynes in 1946 in an essay honoring Isaac Newton.[18] Newton was indeed peculiar. As a student and then a fellow at Trinity College, Cambridge, he would stay in his rooms for days on end, obsessing over a problem, eating little, and even then usually standing up so as not to break "the flow."[19] On the occasions when Newton did dine in the hall, he most often sat by himself, the other fellows having learned to leave him to his solitary thinking. While returning to his chambers, Newton might stop and draw diagrams with a stick on the gravel path. Such obsessive concentration was part of his persona, and ultimately it led to a new understanding of the mechanical workings of the universe and his reputation today as the greatest physicist the world has ever known.[20]

But hidden from view, at least until his complete papers came to light in 1936, is Newton the alchemist.[21] Newton's missing piece, it turns out, was made of gold. During his lifetime, Newton filled twice as many notebooks with thoughts about alchemy and the occult than those dealing with math or physics. Of the 1,752 volumes in his personal library, 170 were devoted to the subject of what we would today call occult magic.[22] Granted, in Newton's day, little was known about the process by which one metal could be transmuted into another, and thus the line between true chemistry and the pseudoscience of alchemy was not clearly drawn.[23] Newton's observations on what holds a substance together, or tears it apart, might be said to distantly prefigure the field of quantum physics. But most of Newton's readings about chemical transmutation focused on "the philosopher's stone"—a secret material believed to cure illness and turn lead into gold. In his own words, he intended to find out "whether I know enough to make a mercury which will grow hot with gold."[24] For twenty years, Newton, like Curie, toiled away at a furnace in a shed that served as a laboratory, his next to his quarters in Trinity College, Cambridge.

Liberation came in 1700 when Newton's passion for metals, as well as his reputation as a physicist, caused King William III to appoint him warden of the Mint. Now guardian of the royal currency, Newton abandoned almost all scientific pursuits and relocated to a large house in London. There he relentlessly chased after those who might debase the king's money, causing a number of men to be hanged for counterfeiting.[25] As to his own miraculous piece of gold, Newton never found it.

So Newton went on one last search: he wanted to determine when the world would end. John Conduitt, the husband of Newton's niece and ward Catherine, stated that he "saw [Newton] in his last days working in near darkness on an obsessional history of the world—he wrote at least a dozen drafts—*The Chronology of Ancient Kingdoms Amended*. He measured the reigns of kings and the generations of Noah, used astronomical calculations to date the sailing of the Argonauts, and declared the ancient kingdoms to be hundreds of years younger than generally supposed."[26] Ultimately, Newton identified the year of the second coming of Christ and the end of the world as we know it: 2060.

AS THE STORIES OF NEWTON'S FOOL'S GOLD AND DOOMSDAY PREdiction suggest, passion may sometimes lead the genius astray. Beethoven was eager to write his populist "Wellington's Victory," or "The Battle Symphony" (1813) for the popular acclaim it would bring, but today the piece sounds trite and is rarely performed; undeterred, however, Beethoven went on to compose his magisterial Ninth Symphony with its beloved "Ode to Joy." Steve Jobs was so enthusiastic in 1983 about the new computer he was developing that he gave it the same name as his daughter, Lisa; it flopped, but Jobs went on to create the Mac computer, the iPad, and the iPhone. In the 1920s, George Herman "Babe" Ruth remade the way American baseball is played with his eye-popping home runs. On September 30, 1927, he set a Major League Baseball record that would stand for thirty-four years when he hit his sixtieth home run of the season, and in the course of his career he would hit 714 home runs total, long a U.S. record. Ruth also struck out 1,330 times, proving that even a genius doesn't always hit the target. But homer or whiff, the Babe kept swinging for the fences.

CHARLES DARWIN WAS DRIVEN BY A PASSION FOR THE NATURAL world. Initially, as the beneficiary of an inheritance, the well-to-do Darwin seemed passionate only about shooting birds and collecting insects. In the pursuit of the latter, he did things that at first seem bizarre but that in retrospect, for a naturalist, may be taken as early marks of genius.

As a young man, Darwin developed an obsession for beetles. "I employed a labourer," he said, "to scrape, during the winter, moss off old trees and place it in a large bag, and likewise to collect the rubbish at the bottom of the barges in which reeds are brought in from the fens, and thus I got some very rare species."[27] If that didn't produce enough missing pieces, Darwin would take matters into his own hands. He once buried a snake in order to dig it up again in a few weeks, expecting to find some flesh-eating insects therein.[28] Sometimes he was too successful, as he recounted in his autobiography: "I will give a proof of my zeal: one day, on tearing off some old bark, I saw two rare beetles, and seized one in each hand; then I saw a third and new kind, which I could not bear to lose, so that I popped the one which I held in my right hand in my mouth."[29] So what motivated Darwin? Curiosity, of course, but eventually something else: the need for self-esteem.

A less-than-stellar student, Darwin washed out of the medical program at the University of Edinburgh in 1827 before moving on the next year to the University of Cambridge, where he seems to have majored in drinking, gambling, hunting, and shooting.[30] Exasperated by his son's poor school record and desultory ways, Darwin's father, Robert, once barked at him, "You care for nothing but shooting, dogs, and rat-catching, and you will be a disgrace to yourself & all your family."[31] Eventually, Robert paid for Charles to embark on the ship HMS *Beagle* and what would prove to be a five-year expedition around the world. The voyage of the *Beagle* provided the context in which took shape Darwin's own quest for a truly big missing piece: a scientifically rigorous explanation as to why and how species survive and evolve over time.

When Darwin returned to England in 1836, he focused on issues of evolution with an intensity that made him a workaholic to the day he died. Candidly listing his strengths and weaknesses in his autobiography, Darwin said this about his passion: "Far more important [than his capacity for observation], my love of natural sciences has been steady and ardent. This pure love has, however, been much aided by the ambition to be esteemed by my fellow naturalists."[32] Thus Darwin had been born with a love for nature, but he had also developed a desire to prove himself the equal of the scientific superiors he had failed to impress at Edinburgh and Cambridge, and possibly of his father as well. Call it a chip on his shoulder or making up for lost time—here Darwin sounds like filmmaker Orson Welles, who said, "I've spent most of my mature life trying to prove that I'm not irresponsible."[33]

ASKED IN 1903 ABOUT THE SOURCE OF HIS GENIUS, THOMAS EDISON replied, "Genius is one percent inspiration and ninety-nine percent perspiration."[34] Over time, the ratios had changed—"Two percent is genius and 98 per cent is hard work," he had said in 1898—but the message is consistent: Thomas Edison worked hard. According to his lab assistant Edward Johnson, Edison averaged eighteen hours a day at his desk: "He does not go home for days, either to eat or sleep," even though his house was only a few steps away.[35] In 1912, at age sixty-five, Edison invented and had installed in his office a punch-in-and-out time clock, so that he, the boss, could calculate the number of hours he worked each week. For Edison, like Elon Musk, it was a badge of honor to outstrip, even humble, his own workers. At the end of a week, he would call in reporters to broadcast the self-aggrandizing news: that he had worked twice as many hours as his employees.[36]

What drove Edison's passion? He had, even more than Darwin, a competitive ego. "I don't care so much about making my fortune," he said in 1878, "as I do for getting ahead of the other fellows";[37] and similarly in 1898, "If you want to succeed, get some enemies."[38] Edison did care about money, and he had plenty of enemies, George Westinghouse and J. P. Morgan among them. Although Edison directed a scientific team in his research lab, when he applied for a patent, his name alone appeared on the application. Other great inventors, Nikola Tesla and Frank Sprague, for example, left Edison's employment after less than a year; they had their own passions and egos. But Edison persevered with relentless independence. Over the course of his life Edison said several times in several different ways, "I have not failed. I have just found 10,000 ways that won't work."[39] But Edison found 1,093 ways that did—1,093 missing pieces. That is the number of patents he successfully registered, still a U.S. record.

"People should pursue what they're passionate about. That will make them happier than pretty much anything else," said Elon Musk in 2014.[40] Some passions spring from love for other people and some from the pursuit of a simple amusement or a game, such as playing golf or following a favorite sports team. Some passions are driven by envy (wanting to have the biggest house) or greed (wanting to make the next billion). Some people are passionate about employing their gifts to the fullest and about doing a good job at whatever job they do. But rarely do such passions lead to genius. What results from everyday passions may be unique, but it is not transformative.

Genius springs from a different impetus. Reviewing the geniuses in this book reveals a trait common to all: geniuses cannot accept the world as described to them. Each sees a world asunder and cannot rest until things are put right. Thus, ask yourself: Do you see something to which the rest of the world is oblivious? Does this blind spot annoy you? Do you believe that you are the only person on the planet who could possibly fix the problem, and do you feel that you cannot possibly rest until you do so? If you answer these questions affirmatively, you have found your passion and perhaps your genius.

But once you've found your passion, be careful. "The secret of life," the sculptor Henry Moore said, "is to have a task, something you devote your entire life to, something you bring everything to, every minute of every day for the rest of your life. And the most important thing is, it must be something you cannot possibly do."[41] Moore and Shel Silverstein got it right: unalloyed passion is essential to happiness and human progress. The missing piece, however, is really only fool's gold.

CHAPTER 7

LEVERAGE YOUR DIFFERENCE

O n the night of December 23, 1888, in Arles, France, Vincent van Gogh, enraged that fellow painter and possibly romantic partner Paul Gauguin was about to leave him, took a razor and sliced off his left ear—not just a part but all of it.[1] With severed lobe in hand, van Gogh then walked to a nearby brothel and presented the trophy to a young prostitute, Gabrielle Berlatier. Authorities quickly apprehended the self-assailant and placed him in a mental hospital.

The story of van Gogh mutilating his ear is well known, and immortalized in the artist's famous *Self-Portrait with Bandaged Ear and Pipe* (1889). We associate van Gogh with mental instability and wild behavior, and we project those qualities onto his art. Did van Gogh really paint his hallucinations? Similarly, did the eccentric and half-crazy Beethoven really compose sounds he couldn't hear? Simple anecdotes may help us understand complex issues. But are these tales of "mad geniuses" accurate representations? Or have they been exaggerated because we love a good story? Is there a greater incidence of insanity and suicide among geniuses, or do a few notoriously disturbed creators distort our view?

SINCE THE ANCIENT GREEKS, THE LINE BETWEEN GENIUS AND IN-sanity has been seen as hazy. Plato referred to genius as a "divine mania."[2] His pupil Aristotle linked creativity to insanity when he said, "There is no great genius without a touch of madness."[3] The seventeenth-century poet John Dryden voiced this same senti-ment by rhyming, "Great wits are sure to madness near allied/ And thin partitions do their bounds divide."[4] Having been called insane, Edgar Allan Poe responded, "Men have called me mad; but the question is not yet settled, whether madness is or is not the loftiest intelligence—whether much that is glorious—where all that is profound—does not spring from disease of thought."[5] "You're mad, bonkers, completely off your head," said Charles Dodgson's Alice in *Alice in Wonderland,* "But I'll tell you a se-cret. All the best people are."[6] And the comedian Robin Williams brought this ancient trope of the mad genius into modern times when he said wistfully, "You are only given a little spot of mad-ness, and if you lose that, you are nothing."[7]

Although psychologists have debated the relationship be-tween genius and mental illness for more than a century, there is still no unanimity of opinion. As early as 1891, the Italian criminologist Dr. Cesare Lombroso, in his book *The Man of Ge-nius,* posited a link among heredity, mental disorder, degeneracy, and criminal behavior, associating all with genius.[8] "Genius is just one of many forms of insanity," he said. More recently, the psychiatrists Kay Redfield Jamison and others have associated il-lustrious creators with identifiable mental disorders, as classified by the authoritative *Diagnostic and Statistical Manual of Mental Disorders (DSM).*[9] Rates of unbalance, it seems, can be minutely quantified. Jamison's conclusions regarding poets, drawn from her 1989 study of forty-seven "eminent British writers and art-ists," is typical of the statistical approach: "A comparison with rates of manic-depressive illness in the general population (1 per-cent), cyclothymic (1 to 2 percent), and major depressive disor-der (5 percent) shows that these British poets were thirty times more likely to suffer from manic-depressive illness, ten to twenty times more likely to be cyclothymic or have other milder forms of manic-depressive illness, more than five times as likely to commit suicide, and at least twenty times more likely to have been committed to an asylum or madhouse."[10] Scientists, according to one study, had the lowest prevalence of psychopathology (a 17.8 percent increase above the general public), and the rate increased steadily through composers, politicians, and artists, with the highest prevalence present in writers (46 percent) and, again, poets (80 percent).[11] The greater incidence among artists may confirm a saying attributed to the rapper Kanye West: "Great art comes from great pain."[12]

Pain, however, is no guarantee of great art. Many individuals have great psychic pain but no art (or science) to show for it. Conversely, many individuals generate great art or science without pain. Bach, Brahms, Stravinsky, and McCartney come to mind among well-integrated composers; Faraday, James Maxwell, and Einstein likewise among scientists. For every certifiably insane Bobby Fischer, there is a seemingly normal Magnus Carlsen; for every van Gogh there is a Matisse.

Taking a very unscientific look at genius and mental disorder, what do the nearly one hundred luminaries considered in this book tell us? At least a third of the group—a high percentage—were or are seriously affected by mood disorders. Hildegard of Bingen, Newton, Beethoven, Tesla, Yayoi Kusama, van Gogh, Woolf, Hemingway, Dickens, Rowling, Plath, and Picasso, among others, displayed some form of affective disorder. Geniuses don't have a habit of being unbalanced, but they do have a proclivity to it. Mathematicians and scientists, according to the experts, experience less psychic disorder than artists, possibly because they deal in logical precepts and rational limits rather than boundless emotive expressions.[13] An orderly, step-by-step protocol often plays out within the lines of the scientific method as well as in solving a mathematical equation.

The Nobel Prize–winning economist and mathematician John Nash, the subject of the film *A Beautiful Mind*, was an exception to the "sane scientist" rule. A schizophrenic since his late teens, Nash told the *Yale Economic Review* in 2008, "[Creative insight] is something of a mystery. It's a special area where smart thinking and crazy thinking can be related. If you're going to develop exceptional ideas, it requires a type of thinking that is not simply practical thinking."[14] And elsewhere he stated, "The ideas that I have about the supernatural came to me in the same way that my mathematical ideas did, so I took them seriously."[15]

When Nash said these ideas "came to me in the same way," he implicitly raised an additional question: Is the creativity that is generated by the unbalanced brain coincidental or causal? In other words, is the capacity to create caused by the psychosis, or does it happen at the same time but independent of the psychosis? Vincent van Gogh provides a test case that yields no clear answer.

PHYSICIANS HAVE POSITED MORE THAN A HUNDRED THEORIES AS TO the cause of van Gogh's deranged state, among them bipolar disorder, schizophrenia, neurosyphilis, interictal dysphoric disorder, sunstroke, acute intermittent porphyria, temporal lobe epilepsy precipitated by the use of absinthe, subacute angle closure glaucoma, xanthopsia, and Ménière's disease.[16] In addition, there was a strong genetic component in the painter's mental unbalance. Vincent killed himself at thirty-seven; his younger brother Theo became deranged and died in a psychiatric hospital at age thirty-three, six months after Vincent; their younger brother Cornelius died, apparently of his own hand, also at thirty-three; and a sister, Wilhelmina, spent forty years of her life in a mental institution, where she died in 1941 at age seventy-nine.[17]

Van Gogh understood that he was often mad. "Either lock me up in a madhouse straightaway, I won't resist if I'm wrong, or let me work with all my strength," he wrote Theo on January 28, 1889.[18] Both came to pass. In May of that year, van Gogh entered an asylum in Saint-Rémy, France, and was assigned to two rooms with bars on the windows, one of which he used as a

studio. During the next year, he produced some of his most beloved creations, including *Irises,* as he saw them in the courtyard
at Saint-Rémy, and *The Starry Night,* painted while looking out
his sanatorium window. His final work, *Tree Roots,* done after his
release, "Is one of those paintings," said the art historian Nienke
Bakker, "in which you can feel van Gogh's sometimes tortured
mental state."[19]

But the question remains: Was Vincent van Gogh a genius
because he was mad (did madness shape his visionary art), or was
he a genius who just happened also to be mad? All of the pecu-
liarities of van Gogh's style—his theory about painting, color,
and perspective, his swirling textures and shimmering lights—
were carefully explained in his letters to his brother Theo long
before they were fully executed on canvas later in his life.[20] The
exclusive use of yellow, the intense reds and greens together, the
twining of bicolor striated brushstrokes were all part of a radically new but wholly rational aesthetic.[21] In van Gogh's case,
mental disintegration and artistic production may have been two
separate, albeit collateral, parts of his life experience. When he
was sane, van Gogh knew exactly what he was doing.

Most important, van Gogh also knew when he was sane and
when he was not. When impaired he did not paint, as he said
on July 6, 1882: "As a patient you are not free to work as one
should, and not up to it either."[22] Hallucinations may or may not
have been a source of artistic material for him, but they were
certainly a frightful experience to be avoided. To do so, and to
stay alive, van Gogh painted. As he said in 1882, "Yes, I can understand why there are people who jump into the water . . . [but
I] thought it much the better to get ahold of myself and seek a
medicine in work";[23] and in 1883, "Work is the only remedy. If
that does not help, one breaks down."[24] Van Gogh's cry for survival, as he emphasized in his letters in many ways many times:
"I must paint."

And so he painted, manically producing nearly a hundred and
fifty works during his last year. Eventually, toggling between mania

and depression, insanity and lucidity, and asylum and outside world, even painting was not enough. On the morning of July 27, 1890, van Gogh wandered off into a field near the Oise River north of Paris and shot himself in the stomach with a revolver.

ON THE MORNING OF MARCH 28, 1941, VIRGINIA WOOLF, AGE fifty-nine, filled her pockets with rocks and walked into the Ouse River north of London, to the same fatal end. Woolf's mental unbalance met the clinical criteria for both schizophrenia and bipolar disorder.[25] As her nephew Quentin Bell wrote, "This was one of the difficulties of living with Virginia; her imagination was furnished with an accelerator and no brakes; it flew rapidly ahead, parting company with reality."[26] Leonard Woolf, Virginia's long-supportive husband, concurred: "In the manic stage she was extremely excited; the mind raced; she talked volubly and, at the height of the attack, incoherently; she had delusions and heard voices, for instance she told me that in her second attack she heard the birds in the garden outside her window talking Greek; she was violent with the nurses. In her third attack, which began in 1914, this stage lasted for several months and ended by her falling into a coma for two days."[27] Earlier, in 1904, Woolf had thrown herself out a window but had survived.

Where did Woolf get the ideas for her introspective novels? Herman Melville acquired "deep background" for *Moby-Dick* while sailing on a whaling boat in the South Seas, and Ernest Hemingway similarly got journalistic "context" as a reporter on the front lines during World Wars I and II. Some writers are keen observers of the everyday. Some rely heavily on their own vivid but rational imagination—Shakespeare seems to have had both a keen eye *and* an expansive imagination. Occasionally, a writer will journey deep into her own psychotic mind.

In the most self-revelatory of her novels, *Mrs. Dalloway*, Woolf transfers to her characters her own experiences, both real and hallucinatory. Mrs. Dalloway is the sane, conventional Virginia; Peter Walsh serves as her hypomanic alter ego; and Septimus Warren Smith portrays her psychotic doppelganger who hears birds singing in Greek, comes to think that the staff wishes to harm him, and escapes by jumping out a window to his death. "As an experience," Woolf said, "madness is terrific I can assure you, and not to be sniffed at; and in its lava I still find most of the things I write about."[28]

Writing was how Woolf exorcised her demons—the demons of madness that drove her genius. Most patients talk to their psychiatrist as part of the "talking cure," but Woolf, acting as her own psychiatrist, simply wrote. In an essay of 1931, she demonstrated through her writing the connection between a psychotic experience and self-therapy and thereby eliminated a threatening alter ego. "I discovered that if I were going to review books I should need to do battle with a certain phantom. . . . It was she who used to come between me and my paper when I was writing reviews. It was she who bothered me and wasted my time and so tormented me that at last I killed her. . . . I turned upon her and caught her by the throat. I did my best to kill her. . . . I took up the inkpot and flung it at her. She died hard."[29]

Like many manic-depressives, Woolf toggled between highs and lows and the balanced (euthymic) state in between. As she once wrote about coming down from manic to normal, "I saw myself, my brilliancy, genius, charm, [and] beauty diminish and disappear. One is in truth rather an elderly dowdy fussy ugly incompetent woman, vain, chattering & futile."[30] But only in this latter, normal state, when her discord could synthesize into a coherent narrative stream, was Woolf stable enough to write. This she realized one night in June 1933 while driving through the London suburb in which she lived: "I thought, driving through Richmond last night, something very profound about the synthesis of my being: how only writing composes it: how nothing makes a whole unless I am writing."[31] One of the hidden habits of some geniuses is the capacity to step over into an imaginary world and then come back. Woolf could do this—until she couldn't.

THE CONTEMPORARY ARTIST YAYOI KUSAMA (B. 1929) IS STILL toggling back and forth between the Seiwa Psychiatric Hospital in Tokyo, Japan, where she has lived since 1977, and the world outside. Named one of *Time*'s 100 most influential people in 2016 and arguably among the world's best-known living artists, Kusama still follows the same obsessive-compulsive regime: "Across the street from the hospital I built a studio, and this is where I work each day, commuting back and forth between the two buildings. Life in the hospital follows a fixed schedule. I retire at nine o'clock at night and wake up the next morning in time for a blood test at seven. At ten o'clock each morning I go to my studio and work until six or seven in the evening."[32] Elsewhere in her autobiography she added, "I fluctuate between the two extremes: the sense of fulfilment an artist gets from creating, and the fierce inner tension that fuels the creativity . . . between feelings of reality and unreality."[33]

Kusama has been experiencing unreality since she was a child. She described the sort of psychotic occurrence that came to mark her stay in New York City (1957–1973) as a young adult:

I often suffered episodes of severe neurosis. I would cover a canvas with nets, then continue painting them on the table, on the floor, and finally on my own body. As I repeated this process over and over again, the nets began to expand to infinity. I forgot about myself as they enveloped me, clinging to my arms and legs and clothes and filling the entire room. I woke one morning to find the nets I had painted the previous day stuck to the windows. Marveling at this, I went to touch them, and they crawled on and into the skin of my hands. My heart began racing. In the throes of a full-blown panic attack I called an

Figure 7.1: Yayoi Kusama photographed in the room installation titled *With All My Love for the Tulips, I Pray Forever* at the exhibition *Eternity of Eternal Eternity* (City Museum of Art, Matsumoto Nagano, Japan).

ambulance, which rushed me to Bellevue Hospital. Unfortunately this sort of thing began to happen with some regularity. . . . But I just kept painting like mad.[34]

Moving on from infinity nets, Kusama obsessively painted infinities of polka dots (see Figure 7.1) or some other quickly reproducible fixation. Critics have dubbed her "The High Priestess of Polka Dots" and "The First Obsessional Artist." She herself has labeled her work "psychosomatic art"—art arising from psychosis. Her aim? To remove the obsessional disorder from which she suffers and thereby allow her spirit (and that of the viewer) to transcend into an infinite, undifferentiated "vertigo of nothingness." "My art," she says, "originates from hallucinations only I can see. I translate the hallucinations and obsessional images that plague me into sculptures and paintings. All my works in pastels are the products of obsessional neurosis and are therefore inextricably connected to my disease. . . . By translating hallucinations and fear of hallucinations into paintings, I have been trying to cure my disease."[35] And in her autobiography, she wrote, "You might therefore say that my painting originated in a primal, intuitive way that had little to do with the notion of 'art.'"[36]

As the examples of Vincent van Gogh, Virginia Woolf, and Yayoi Kusama show with increasing certainty, mental "disorder" can not only disable but also enable. Creative expression can protect and heal the psyche, and from that process of personal survival emerges a work of art. A creator can impose upon a reader, viewer, or listener his or her life experiences. The artist says, "I see it, I feel it, I want you to see and feel it as well, and when you do, I and you will be more in infinite harmony within ourselves individually and with each other." Below are the declarations of a few exceptional people for whom a mental "imbalance" was the driver of their art.

Vincent van Gogh: "I must paint."

Virginia Woolf: "I write to stabilize myself."

Yayoi Kusama: "Art is a release as well as a treatment."

Pablo Picasso: "[*Les Demoiselles d'Avignon*] was my first canvas of exorcism."

Anne Sexton: "Poetry led me by the hand out of madness."

Winston Churchill: "Painting came to my rescue at a most trying time."

Martha Graham: "When I stopped dancing I lost my will to live."

Robert Lowell: "[I'd] escape into writing and be healed."

Chuck Close: "Painting saved me."

Amy Winehouse: "I write songs because I'm fucked up in the head and need to get something good out of something bad."[37]

Every human needs an activity with a salutary forward trajectory. Even if what you are creating is insignificant to others, thinking that it is important can be a lifesaver.

IN A DESPONDENT LETTER WRITTEN IN 1803, CALLED THE HEILIgenstadt Testament after the Vienna suburb in which it was written, the then-suicidal Ludwig van Beethoven (1770–1827) explained why he had decided not to end his life: "It was only *my art* that held me back. It seemed to me impossible to leave the world until I had brought forth all that I felt was within me. So I endured this wretched existence."[38] That was not the only time Beethoven had contemplated taking his own life. In 1811, for example, he had gone missing for three days in the woods and had been found in a ditch by the wife of another musician. Beethoven had confessed to her that he "wanted to let himself die of starvation."[39] Beethoven had a lot wrong with him. He suffered from bipolar disorder, paranoia, long-term gastrointestinal disease, and lead poisoning and was a functioning alcoholic.[40] The disability that we remember him for today, however, is deafness.

Beethoven began to have a ringing in his ears (tinnitus) and increased difficulty in hearing higher tones during the 1790s, when he was in his twenties. In 1801, he wrote to a friend, "My ears continue to hum and buzz day and night. . . . In the theater I have to place myself quite close to the orchestra, lean against the railings, to understand the actors. . . . Sometimes, too, I scarcely hear those who are speaking softly, I hear the tones, but not the words."[41] By 1814, Beethoven no longer appeared in public as a performer. Yet not until 1817, when he was forty-seven, did his deafness become so extreme that he could no longer hear music at all. When he died, an autopsy revealed that his auditory nerves were "shriveled and destitute of neurina; the accompanying arteries were dilated to more than the size of a crow quill and cartilaginous."[42]

Two points provide context: First, Beethoven continued to hear, albeit with greatly diminished capacity, throughout the decade 1803 to 1813, during which years he wrote the music that is most beloved by concertgoers today: his most popular symphonies, concertos, and piano sonatas; the notion of "deaf Beethoven," therefore, is not entirely accurate but is dependent on the time in question. Second, many gifted composers, best exemplified by Mozart, have the ability to create music without external sound, composing by means of an "inner ear"; Beethoven, too, had the capacity to hear music in his head, make written sketches, and finish the final score writing at a desk without the aid of a sound-making instrument.

But a disability can make a difference. The process that made Beethoven's music the stuff of the ages was, in part, his response to a "deficit." Ironically, the "deaf" Beethoven's contribution to music history was that he discovered musical sound. That is to say, his music privileges not so much the musical idea but rather the sound of that idea repeated again and again. Beethoven created his unique music by setting a chord, melodic phrase, or rhythm into place and simply repeating it over and over, increasing the volume and often raising the pitch with each iteration. Reducing music into its basic elements and then insistently pushing them forward in a growing tidal wave of sound gave unprecedented power to Beethoven's music: "I cannot hear, I cannot hear, I cannot hear. LOUDER!" he seemed to say.

The hearing impaired often "hear" only vibrations—poundings of the earth—when they experience music. Is that why so many of Beethoven's compositions are stylized dances (music reduced to basic pulsations)? Perhaps the best way to experience dancing Beethoven and the vibrating earth is to listen to the first movement of his Symphony No. 7, where the composer repeats the same motif fifty-seven times in succession. Most telling are the beautifully strange textures and abstract dislocations—call it extreme interiority—to be found in the now completely deaf Beethoven's last quartets and piano sonatas.[43] "Deafness did not impair and indeed may even have heightened his abilities as a composer," concluded Beethoven expert Maynard Solomon.[44] Indeed, to a degree, Beethoven's genius rests in the sounds his disability forced him to hear internally and then transmit to paper.

WHICH ARTIST FACES A GREATER CHALLENGE, THE COMPOSER WHO cannot hear or the painter who cannot see? The painter Chuck Close (b. 1940) is unable to recognize friends, family members, or acquaintances no matter how many times they meet. In addition

FIGURE 7.2: Chuck Close's 2006 portrait of Bill Clinton is an assemblage of 676 individual diamonds, which reflects Close's artistic response to his disability, known as prosopagnosia (gift of Ian and Annette Cumming, National Gallery, Washington, D.C.).

to dyslexia and other cognitive impairments, Close suffers from "face blindness," a disability to which neurologists have given the clinical name prosopagnosia.[45] Face blindness results from a disorder of the fusiform face area within the fusiform gyrus of the temporal lobe, which links the neural pathways related to visual recognition.[46] As the Nobel Prize–winning neurologist Eric Kandel said to Close in an interview, "You are the only face-blind artist in the history of Western art who has chosen to do portraits."[47]

Chuck Close cannot recognize faces in part because he cannot conceptualize three-dimensional images, but he can do so if the subject is two-dimensional. To create a portrait, Close takes a photograph of a face and then divides the two-dimensional image into a myriad of small incremental units, each of which he paints separately in a distinctive manner. For a portrait of his friend Bill Clinton (2006; Figure 7.2), Close created an assemblage of 676 individual diamonds. What resulted was something akin to an atomization of the face, a disassemblage that causes us to realize that a person—and every potential genius—is a composite of countless small elements that may or may not come together. Close points specifically to Clinton's disassembled teeth: "Each tooth was separate, and I had to smoosh them together so they look like teeth."[48] Forced to see the world in a different way, the prosopagnosiac Chuck Close improvised his way to a solution. Close's portrait of Clinton today hangs in the National Portrait Gallery in Washington, D.C., both a president and a disability memorialized.

If the portraitist Chuck Close cannot remember faces, the artist Stephen Wiltshire sees and remembers everything. Wiltshire has an eidetic, or photographic, memory. He can look at a cityscape or scene in London, New York, Rome, Dubai, or Tokyo just once, for twenty minutes or so, and later meticulously replicate what he has seen in every detail. His drawings, which may take hours to generate, sell in his London gallery for tens of thousands of pounds.

Is Stephen Wiltshire a genius? Impressive as his feats of memory are, he is not. An autistic savant, Wiltshire has the capacity to process visual information at computerlike speed, but he possesses the general cognitive development of a five-year-old.[49] Wilshire paints exactly what he sees; no more, no less. What about other so-called savant geniuses: the calculating wonder Kim Peek, the inspiration of the Oscar-winning film *Rain Man* (1988), and the musical prodigy Derek Paravicini, who can play back any piece note for note after just one hearing? Lightning-fast processing is one thing; originality is another. By hand painting each of his incremental units and assembling them in a unique way, Chuck Close adds value to his portraits; Stephen Wiltshire and Derek Paravicini merely replicate existing things. As the neurologist Oliver Sacks has pointed out with regard to Wiltshire and other autistic savants, true art must involve a personal process in which the creator takes the borrowed material, "places it in relation to oneself and expresses it in a new way, one's own."[50]

"FOR SUCCESS IN SCIENCE AND ART A DASH OF AUTISM IS ESSENtial," said Hans Asperger, after whom Asperger's syndrome is named.[51] A dash of autism may be needed, but so, too, is a large dollop of imagination, the ability to visualize and make new connections. Isaac Newton, who saw relationships across the galaxy, Srinivasa Ramanujan (1887–1920), who solved mathematical problems previously thought unsolvable, and Alan Turing (1912–1954), who played a key role in developing modern computing as well as decoding the Nazi Enigma machine—all were said to manifest symptoms of autism spectrum disorder, but all additionally possessed expansive imaginations. The latter two geniuses have been popularized in recent films, Ramanujan in *The Man Who Knew Infinity* (2015) and Turing in *The Imitation Game* (2014). Yet among recent public figures exhibiting extreme ability and disability, no one had a crazier, more cosmic imagination than the late comedian Robin Williams.

To say that Robin Williams's frame of reference was wide-ranging does his mind a disservice. Once, after riffing on ways of defusing terrorists from the Near East, he quickly pivoted to the United States and added, "If you are ever in Amish country and you see a man with a gun buried in a horse's ass, that's a mechanic, not a terrorist."[52] Williams had a mind that moved with lightning speed. Billy Crystal once said of his friend, "If I was fast tonight, he'd be faster." And James Lipton introduced Williams on *Inside the Actors Studio* by asking, "How do you explain the mental reflexes that you deploy with such awesome speed? Are you thinking faster than the rest of us? What the hell is going on?"[53] The answer, perhaps, is attention deficit disorder (ADD).[54]

"I'd try to have a conversation with Robin," said drama school classmate Joel Blum, "and it would go okay for about ten seconds. And then he would go into a character voice, he would do a bit. He would almost literally bounce off the walls with craziness. And then he would be gone."[55] Although never officially diagnosed with attention deficit disorder, in Williams's case numerous mental health observers suspected as much.[56] Many people with ADD are also known to have highly active imaginations, allowing for special creative gifts.[57] They are also prone to developing Lewy body dementia (LBD),[58] a disease that manifests in an abnormal buildup of neurochemical proteins in the brain. Williams suffered from LBD, and it likely hastened his death by suicide at age sixty-three. In many cases, accompanying both ADD and LBD is depression. Despondency, however, may be the source of black humor, giving rise, ironically, to a therapeutic good joke. "I should, many a good day, have blown my brains out," said Lord Byron, "but for the recollection that it would have given such pleasure to my mother-in-law."[59]

Gallows humor, a tragic sense of irony—so many minds of genius have possessed it. The deeper the pit, the more humor is needed to dig out. The depressive comedian Jonathan Winters, a mentor to Williams, once said, "I need that pain—whatever it is—to call upon it from time to time, no matter how bad it was."[60] "Isn't it funny," Williams himself observed, "how I can bring great happiness to all these people, but not to myself."[61] Williams's own dark thoughts gave rise to bright laughter with toss-offs such as "In Texas there are so many electric chairs, even Santa Claus has one. And they give you an alcohol swab on your arm before administering a lethal injection. That way you don't get an infection."[62] Williams saw it coming: "That's what is exciting: the idea of exploratory activity. This is what we are dealing with as artists, comedians, actors. You are going to come to the edge and look over, and sometimes you are going to step over the edge, and then you are going to come back, hopefully."[63]

DID ADD EMPOWER THE LIGHTNING-FAST CONNECTIONS ROBIN Williams made in the service of comedy? Chuck Close had prosopagnosia, which necessitated a "workaround," one that opened a new direction for modern art. Stephen Hawking had ALS and, according to his friend Nobel laureate Kip Thorne, "had to learn an entirely new way" to progress as a physicist.[64] British scientists have attributed Isaac Newton's extraordinary capacity to concentrate, as well as Andy Warhol's propensity to produce repetitive images, to Asperger's syndrome.[65] Asperger's was added to the *DSM* in 1995 but then removed in 2013 and reclassified within the diagnostic category of autism spectrum disorder. Times and cultures change. So do our attitudes about genius and perceived disabilities.

IN APRIL 2015, JOSEPH STRAUS, DISTINGUISHED PROFESSOR AT THE Graduate Center of the City University of New York, came to my Yale "genius course" to speak on autism. Straus has written a book on the subject of disability (*Extraordinary Measures: Disability in Music*, 2011), drawn to that subject by the fact that his older son is autistic. At the end of his lucid presentation, Straus and the assembly of about eighty students engaged in an increasingly heated discussion. Many in the audience were psychology or neurobiology majors; several had had summer internships in labs where NIH money was supporting autism research. They were all keen to learn about recent advances in finding a "cure" for autism.

Straus would have none of it. He and his wife had spent much of their lives accommodating and embracing the human potential of their son in all its diversity and fullness. "For the autistic person," Straus said, "the special interests or skills arise not in spite of the autism but precisely because of it: autism enables the skill. Disability is a difference, not a deficit that requires medical professionals to remediate, normalize, or cure." When class time ran out, only one conclusion could be agreed upon by both sides: here was an urgent ethical dilemma relevant to millions. Would we want to eliminate autism, or any disability, if we could? Are not these "other" psychological profiles merely alternative modes of intelligence that might lead to genius?[66]

Martin Luther King, Jr., valorized the unbalanced when he said, "Human salvation lies in the hands of the creatively maladjusted."[67] Geniuses need to create, and we need them to do so. Similarly, many neurological differences prove to be hidden enablers of genius. Rather than thinking of them as insurmountable barriers or disabilities, we might view them as opportunities from which original thinking can emerge.

Were Beethoven alive today, surgery could ameliorate, if not eliminate, the inner-ear otosclerosis from which he suffered. Psychoanalysis and antidepressants might have helped Woolf go on writing, but at what cost? Kusama tried the "talking cure" of Freudian psychoanalysis for six years, but her art suffered. "Ideas stopped coming out no matter what I painted or drew," she said, "because everything was coming out of my mouth."[68] Robin Williams knew he would never be balanced and doubted that he wanted to be, for fear of losing his comedic genius. "Then you're fucking dead, okay!" he said.[69] Scientists may one day discover a way to eliminate or radically reduce such "dis-ablers" as deafness, autism, Asperger's, OCD, and ADD. But can this really be considered progress if it means no more "Ode to Joy," no more theory of gravity, no more *Starry Night* on my coffee mug, no more laugh-till-you-cry jokes? You make the call.

A final point: We often think of the genius as a star who flames brilliantly but burns out quickly. Taking van Gogh as an archetype, we imagine a suicidal crazy man who dies young, in his case at age thirty-seven. But van Gogh was an outlier. Although his single, sensational life makes for a compelling story, it obscures the fact that geniuses have a habit of living long lives.

We may debate who the greatest geniuses are among painters, scientists, or classical musicians—it depends, again, on your values and cultural perspective. But to make a simple point regarding longevity, I conducted a very unscientific study. I went to Google and searched for "the ten greatest classical composers," which gave me a list of names including Beethoven, Mozart, Bach, Richard Wagner, and Pyotr Tchaikovsky. For those ten musical geniuses I computed that the average life span was 51.4 years. Moving on to painters, my Google search identified Picasso, Leonardo, van Gogh, Michelangelo, Warhol, Kahlo, and others, and their average life span was 67.2 years. Those famous painters lived, on average, thirty years beyond van Gogh. When I did the same calculation for the scientists—Newton, Galileo, Einstein, Curie, Hawking, Tesla, and their colleagues—I found an average life span of 75.3 years. To put these numbers into context, almost all those geniuses were born before the general use of antibiotics (1940) when life spans were much shorter; the life span of the general population for white males, adjusting for infant mortality, was approximately 35 years in 1750, 40 years in 1830, and 47 years in 1900. Thus, according to these rough calculations, many geniuses seem to live perhaps as much as a decade longer than the general populace. These numbers call into question an old Latin proverb, *Dum spiro, spero*—"while I breathe, I hope." Our geniuses suggest reality is the reverse, *Dum spero, spiro*—"while I hope, I breathe." Why?

Why do optimists live on average a decade longer than pessimists? This according to a 2019 Harvard–Boston University study published in *Proceedings of the National Academy of Sciences*.[70] "When individuals were compared based on their initial levels of optimism, the researchers found that the most optimistic men and women demonstrated, on average, an 11 to 15 percent longer lifespan, and had 50–70 percent greater odds of reaching 85 years old compared to the least optimistic groups."[71] Although the physiology of the "why" remains unknown, the important fact becomes clear: optimists, like geniuses, live longer.

But geniuses—the creatively maladjusted—*are* mainly optimists. As Facebook's Mark Zuckerberg said in 2017, "Optimists tend to be successful, and pessimists tend to be right. . . . If you think that something's going to be terrible and it's going to fail, then you're going to look for the data points that prove you right. And you'll find them. That's what pessimists do. . . . But if you think that something is possible, then you're going to try to find a way to make it work."[72] Finding that "way to make it work" is the genius's mission, passion, perhaps compulsive obsession. Genius or plodder, we all need a mission that we think we can accomplish. No matter how "crazy" or "maladjusted" it may seem, simply having that mission helps keep us alive.

CHAPTER 8

REBELS, MISFITS, AND TROUBLEMAKERS

> Here's to the crazy ones, the misfits, the rebels, the trou-
> blemakers, the round pegs in the square holes . . . the ones
> who see things differently—they're not fond of rules. . . .
> You can quote them, disagree with them, glorify or vilify
> them, but the only thing you can't do is ignore them be-
> cause they change things . . . they push the human race
> forward, and while some may see them as the crazy ones,
> we see genius, because the ones who are crazy enough to
> think that they can change the world are the ones who do.

With the words of this 1997 TV commercial, "Think Different," genius Steve Jobs initiated what would prove to be the turn-
around of his then-floundering Apple Computer, Inc. Millions
watched the original broadcasts of that commercial, which ran
from 1997 to 2002, as actor Richard Dreyfus did the voice-over
(originally it was to have been Jobs himself) and photographs of
many of the iconic geniuses of the twentieth century appeared on
the screen: Albert Einstein, Bob Dylan, Martin Luther King, Jr.,
John Lennon, Thomas Edison, Muhammad Ali, Mahatma Gandhi, Amelia Earhart, Martha Graham, Jim Henson, Pablo Picasso,
and Frank Lloyd Wright. Accompanied by slow, quasi-religious

music, the message sounds less like a sales pitch and more like a hymn to one of our most cherished beliefs: that the rebellious genius makes our world a better place. In this context, "crazy," "troublemaker," and "misfit" sound like compliments. These geniuses are our friends, our heroes, our contemporary deities.

As a culture, we honor the rebellious genius because he or she has the capacity to make us see the world differently. What conformists do we remember? Without rebellion against the status quo, there is no genius. Not every rebel is a genius, of course, because not every disruptive idea proves to be a bright one. The rebellious Icarus flew too close to the sun, and how well did that turn out? The genius, however, has a habit not only of rebelling but also of getting things right.

But the genius isn't always universally beloved. Socrates was a man so dangerous that the citizens of Athens forced him to drink poison. Martin Luther and Galileo Galilei were subjected to house arrest. Nelson Mandela, Martin Luther King, Jr., and Mahatma Gandhi were imprisoned. Joan of Arc was burned at the stake. Even the benign Impressionist painters were at first reviled and exiled to a *salon des refusés*. According to the historian John Waller, Vincent van Gogh, Albert Einstein, Winston Churchill, and Jesus Christ were just a few visionaries who experienced periods of public exile, real or figurative.[1] Societal change requires time and a willingness to accept modification. Only over time can the crazy notion become the new norm.

Sometimes acceptance is long in coming. For millennia a few scientists at different times argued that the sun, not the earth, was the center of the galaxy; but only in 1820 did that belief become officially accepted by the Church of Rome.[2] Around 1796, Edward Jenner took pus from cowpox-infected cows and injected it into humans; some families, including the Mozarts, refused to be vaccinated and suffered the consequences, but by 1980, smallpox had been eradicated. Einstein's Theory of General Relativity was proved in 1919, but it took exactly a century before visual collaboration of a corollary of that theory was offered: the existence of black holes.[3] By contrast, the ascension of Martin Luther King, Jr., from prisoner to civil rights icon on the National Mall in Washington, D.C., required mere decades. Why does it take so long? Because the rest of us don't like disruptive ideas and the rebels who bring them.

"When a true genius appears in the world," said Jonathan Swift in 1728, "you may know him by this sign: that the dunces are all in confederacy against him."[4] So why do we dunces all align against the genius, at least at first? It's because geniuses are troublemakers, and troublemakers make things difficult for the rest of us. They make us uncomfortable. They force us to change. And change requires work. When offered a choice between a creative new idea and a practical old one, most people choose the practical old one, judging by the results of a test published in 2011 in *Psychological Science*.[5] The status quo is our default mode. Even teachers professing a professional responsibility to urge students to be creative nonetheless find creative students a disruptive nuisance in the classroom.[6] "Whatever else they may say," wrote Amanda Ripley, the author of *The Smartest Kids in the World: And How They Got That Way*, "most teachers do not in fact appreciate creativity and critical thinking in their own students. [There are legions of] stories of small geniuses being kicked out of places of learning."[7]

IN 1632, GALILEO GALILEI CASTIGATED POPE URBAN VIII BY REpeatedly referring to him as "the Simpleton."[8] Urban couldn't abide the radical notion that the earth revolved around the sun, and Galileo couldn't abide Urban's ignorance. But put yourself into Urban's red shoes. All empirical evidence suggests that the sun rises in the east, moves across the sky, and sets in the west; indeed, the Bible affirms this in sixty-seven places.[9] I don't feel myself whizzing through space at 500,000 miles per hour, and neither did Pope Urban. Yet Galileo, using the new 30× magnification telescope he had invented, could see the planet Jupiter as well as four moons orbiting it. Then he thought analogously: If Jupiter spins around the sun with its four moons, might not earth with its single moon likewise be doing the same?

Nicolaus Copernicus (1473–1543) had suggested as much but hedged his bet (and saved his life) by stating that his heliocentric worldview was only a conceptual model. He had reason to be cautious: the Inquisition was in full force, and it employed torture and execution to combat heresy. One of his disciples, the philosopher Giordano Bruno, was burned at the stake in 1600 for teaching Copernican unorthodoxy. Galileo, however, went further than Copernicus both in speech and in print: Copernican theory, he said, was more than mere hypothesis, it was reality. Appearing before the Inquisition in Rome in 1616, Galileo recanted—for a while. Then, in 1632, he published his *Dialogue Concerning the Two Chief World Systems,* which offered a full endorsement of the Copernican model supported by additional evidence. So again, in January 1633, Galileo went to Rome to explain himself before the Inquisition.

To us, this aspect of astrophysics might seem distant from daily life, but to the existing Church of Rome, the matter was deadly serious. In the premodern Christian view, earth was the center of the cosmos and Rome its spiritual epicenter. Above the earthly endpoint was Heaven with the saints and angels; below was Hell with sinners and devils. Galileo's contention that the earth was flying through space and was in fact merely one among many planets, and the sun merely one among many stars, was blasphemy. Instead of occupying a central and immovable position in the cosmos, earth, the Church, and all Christian eschatology would now be relegated to a fast-moving sideshow. Instead of a divine plan, reality might be something closer to a mysterious accident. Revolutionary stuff, indeed!

Faced with the prospect of being burned at the stake for preaching false doctrine, Galileo cut a plea bargain with the Inquisition.[10] He agreed to plead guilty to having unwittingly given the impression that his writings supported the notion of a helio-centric solar system, and Church authorities would subject him to no more than house arrest for the remainder of his life, which proved to be eight years. But as the rebel Galileo walked away from the bench at the end of his trial, he was said to have mut-tered, *"E pur si muove"*—"And yet (the earth) still moves."

It sounds obvious enough today: the earth revolves around the sun. But even today some of us don't seem to be willing to yield in the face of overwhelming scientific evidence. In 1953, the researcher Jonas Salk announced the development of a vac-cine against polio, but some African countries are still reluctant to distribute it. In 1961, John Enders discovered a vaccination against measles, yet some people still refuse to accept it, just as they refuse to allow their children to be vaccinated against diph-theria, tetanus, and pertussis, as well as human papillomavirus. A preponderance of scientists argues that both wildfires and ocean storms of ever-increasing intensity are linked to global warming, but climate change deniers gainsay a causal connection. Some world leaders initially denied the science pointing to a COVID-19 pandemic. What is it that *all* of us believe today that some genius will disprove tomorrow?

TODAY WE USE THE WORD "PROTESTANT" WITHOUT MUCH THOUGHT: "A Protestant is a Christian who is not Catholic," one might very loosely say. But strictly speaking, the original Protestants, relying on written scripture, were those offering witness (*pro* + *testa-mentum*) in support of a rebellious notion: that religion could be structured according to a new system, one different from that of the Church of Rome. Similarly, we generally assume that a "protester" is an antagonist, someone marching and chant-ing to change the status quo, as the antiwar protesters did against the Vietnam War in the 1960s or as those protesting President Trump's border wall and anti-immigrant policies are doing today.

Martin Luther (1483–1546) was both a Protestant and a protester, professing a new religion and protesting against the old; and if there was ever a genius who wrought change, it was Luther.

By the end of his life, Martin Luther had created a new religion with its own theology and liturgy, instituted clerical marriage, set into motion the dissolution of monastic orders, made northern Europe financially independent from the south, and fostered an environment in which individualistic capitalism and the seeds of democracy could take root. The power structure that had run top down—from pope to prelate (episcopal) to presbyter (priest) to parishioner—was reversed, now bubbling up from parishioners to the leaders they chose. Arguably more than any other single individual, Martin Luther opened the door leading from theocracy to democracy and from the medieval world to the modern.

It all began at the front door of the humble castle church in Wittenberg, Germany. There, on October 31, 1517, Martin Luther nailed his famous Ninety-Five Theses—ninety-five complaints about the actions of the pope generally and specifically about the papal practice of selling indulgences.[11] "As soon as the coin in the coffer rings/The soul from purgatory springs"[12] was the sales jingle used by collection agents sent from Rome to offer everlasting spiritual grace in exchange for German money. Thus Luther's rebellion was as much economic as it was religious, and only because Luther was supported by a few German princes with similar beliefs was he able to escape an ecclesiastical court in 1518 and then a secular one in 1521.[13] One papal emissary declared, "In three weeks I will throw the heretic into the fire!"[14] Holy Roman Emperor Charles V ordered Luther's arrest, but he slipped away. Luther would go on to spend the remaining years of his life in protective custody in pro-Lutheran towns and fortresses. He was driven by his conscience and a willingness to risk death to profess what he believed. At the end of the published account of his defense in Worms, Luther issued this famous declaration: "I cannot and will not retract anything, since it is neither safe nor right to go against conscience. I cannot do otherwise. Here I stand. God help me. Amen."[15]

WHAT OTHER DISRUPTORS HAD THE COURAGE OF THEIR CONVICTIONS? When others doubted, Christopher Columbus sailed west to reach the Far East, Karl Marx and Friedrich Engels wrote *The Communist Manifesto,* and Gustave Eiffel built his tower. Charles Darwin understood that man had not been created on the sixth day by God but had gradually descended from less developed primates; the Book of Genesis, he concluded, was at best a metaphor.[16] Nikola Tesla came to America in 1884 to work for Thomas Edison but soon walked away from his boss because he believed that his own system of alternating current, not Edison's direct current, would illuminate the world. In a radio broadcast in 1953, Albert Einstein thanked those who had given him an award for "nonconformity in scientific matters" with these words: "It gives me great pleasure to see the stubbornness of an incorrigible nonconformist warmly acclaimed."[17] Each of these geniuses rebelled against conventional wisdom. But what impulse causes such rebellion?

In a word: discontent. As previously noted, the genius sees things that others do not and becomes excited or alarmed, or both. Louis Pasteur was alarmed at the number of people dying from contaminated milk and developed the process of pasteurization to exterminate the germs. Tim Berners-Lee saw disjointed local networks and fashioned them into the World Wide Web. Jeff Bezos looked at user traffic data on that Web and became excited by the prospect of profitably disrupting traditional commerce. Steve Jobs was annoyed that all mainframe and home computers were in metal frames: "I got a bug up my rear that I wanted the computer in a plastic case," he recalled in 1997.[18] Elon Musk was alarmed by the dangers of fossil fuels and by global warming, and thus were born Tesla, SolarCity, and SpaceX.

Andy Warhol seemed discontent with just about everything.

He rejected his birth name (changing it from Warhola to Warhol), the sexual preference his parents expected of him, his real hair (he wore a wig), and his nose (he had rhinoplasty). Leaving his native Pittsburgh in 1949, he moved to New York to work as a commercial graphic artist. There he experienced a disconnect between the "old masters" art that dominated the established museums and galleries of Manhattan and the blatantly commercial values that drove the business world.

Why did the visual arts have to be about context, symbolism, meaning, and painterly technique? Warhol asked. Those were all implicit issues of past art. Warhol changed the art world by putting his finger on the obsessions of modern society: its narcissism, exhibitionism, commercialism, and superficiality. Those mindsets he turned into visual images that could be immediately recognized and enjoyed for the moment. Everyday commercial objects, such as a Coke bottle, a Campbell's soup can, and a Brillo box, as well as bankable celebrities, such as Marilyn Monroe, Marlon Brando, Mao Zedong, and Elvis Presley, might remind us of the vibrancy of the here and now. In the spirit of commercial industry, Warhol built an artistic studio he called "The Factory." As the Factory became a mecca for the cultural elite during the 1960s, Warhol aggressively pushed to see, and be seen with, every avant-garde celebrity in New York, eventually garnering camp nicknames such as "the pope of pop" and "Drella," a contraction of Dracula and Cinderella.[19]

But as with many troublemaking innovators, Warhol's creative vision wasn't immediately appreciated. At the 1964 New York World's Fair, he caused a scandal when he installed a commissioned work in the New York State Pavilion: thirteen neatly arranged mug shots of America's most wanted gangsters. Governor Nelson Rockefeller was irate; he ordered Warhol to remove the piece, and within days the criminals disappeared behind a coat of silver paint. In 1962, Warhol mounted his first exhibition, at the Ferus Gallery in Los Angeles, and offered for sale images of thirty-two Campbell's soup cans (one for each flavor) at the price of $300 each. None sold, so gallery owner Irving Blum bought all of them for $1,000 and then mounted them together. In 1996, Blum sold Warhol's *32 Campbell's Soup Cans* to the Museum of Modern Art in New York for $15 million.[20] In little more than thirty years, the son of an immigrant steelworker had gone from rebellious iconoclast to establishment icon, recognized as second only to Picasso among influential twentieth-century artists.[21]

IN AN ESSAY TITLED "WHY INDIVIDUALS REJECT CREATIVITY," Berkeley psychologist Barry Staw provided a short list of character traits common to rebellious innovators. According to Staw, "Creatives are nonconformists. They are willing to defy convention and even authority to explore new ideas and to get to the truth. Creatives are persistent. They don't give up when they get frustrated or rebuffed by a problem, they keep at it. Creatives are flexible. They are able to reformulate a problem when facing failure rather than just give up or continue down the same path." But above all else, Staw emphasized, creative types are risk takers. "They are willing to take their chances on an unproven solution rather than go with the tried and true."[22]

ALL GENIUSES TAKE RISKS. IN 1891, MARIE CURIE LEFT POLAND IN a fourth-class railroad car with little money and fewer prospects. Between 1927 and 1947, the revolutionary Mao Zedong fought the better equipped army of Nationalist general Chiang Kai-shek before achieving victory and establishing the People's Republic of China. In 1988, the author Salman Rushdie published *The Satanic Verses,* knowing that it might be interpreted as blasphemy against Allah; the supreme leader of Iran placed a *fatwa* on Rushdie's head, thereby encouraging Muslims worldwide to assassinate him. In 1994, Jeff Bezos quit his job, cashed in all he had, and borrowed from friends and family to start Amazon. Steve Jobs once said, "You've got to be willing to crash and burn."[23]

If, in 1870, had you asked someone in the southern town of Cambridge, Maryland, "Is Harriet Tubman a genius?" the response would likely have been "No, she is a troublemaker and a rebel." Tubman, who had been born a slave in Dorchester County, Maryland, and escaped to Philadelphia, had rebelled against the legal system of the rebels of the Confederacy during the Civil War.[24] Again, most rebels are not geniuses, because ultimately their ideas prove useless to society. Had you asked the same question of northerners in 1870, most would likely have responded, "Who?" Few knew that the diminutive Tubman had helped build the Underground Railroad, leading thirteen rescue missions from Philadelphia into enemy territory in Maryland and liberating more than seventy slaves. She also served, gun in hand, as a leader of a successful military assault in South Carolina, freeing 750 additional slaves. When Tubman died at the age of ninety-one in 1913, one of the few mentions of her passing was an obituary in the *New York Times,* a mere four sentences in length.[25]

Times have changed. Since 1913, shifting societal values have elevated the rebel Tubman to the stature of American hero and genius, and she was most recently the subject of an acclaimed motion picture (*Harriet,* 2019). In 2016, the administration of President Barack Obama conceived a plan to replace Alexander Hamilton with Tubman on the ten-dollar bill.[26] But the growing fame of Lin-Manuel Miranda's *Hamilton* had increased the recognition of the father of the Federal Reserve System, so Tubman was redeployed to replace the "populist" slaveholder President Andrew Jackson on the twenty-dollar bill. But then U.S. voters elected the "populist" Donald Trump president. Trump promptly put a portrait of Jackson next to him in the Oval Office and put the plan to place Tubman on the twenty-dollar bill on hold. As political winds shift and societal values change, just who merits the designation "genius" changes as well. Incessantly society moves the hidden target. The rebellious Tubman shot her arrows 160 years ago, but only gradually did the public begin to move the target (toward racial justice and gender equality) into a position that would allow her ultimately to score a bull's-eye; only now do most Americans perceive her as a role model of courageous action in the face of overwhelming odds.

SOME GENIUSES TAKE SMALL RISKS TO PROVOKE US. ON SUNDAY, March 13, 2005, a hooded figure carrying a shopping bag walked into the Museum of Modern Art in New York, past sleepy guards, and up to the third floor where Andy Warhol's iconic *32 Campbell's Soup Cans* is displayed. Removing from the bag a three-color image the same size and shape as one of Warhol's cans, the outsider quickly affixed his own painting, *Soup Can* (Tesco Value Cream of Tomato Soup), to the wall. Three hours later, security guards arrived, but by then the vandal had slipped away, apparently exiting through the gift shop.[27] It turned out that the drive-by installation had been perpetrated by the well-unknown street artist Banksy, who had pulled off similar capers elsewhere. In 2004, at the Museum of Natural History in New York, he disguised himself as a museum worker and placed on display a stuffed rat with the title *Banksus Militus Ratus;* and that same year at the Louvre, he installed his own reproduction of the *Mona Lisa,* her face replaced by a mysterious Mickey Mouse smile.[28] We don't know Banksy's real name or much about his identity, though theories abound. The anonymous artist has made a name for himself as a "vandal" engaged in outsider street art, causing *Time* magazine to rank him, in 2010, among the world's one hundred most influential people.

Thirteen years after the soup can prank, on October 5, 2018, an auctioneer at Sotheby's in London banged down a gavel to signal the final bid on a copy of Banksy's most famous work, *Girl with a Balloon;* the price, $1.04 million. Rebellious street art had been co-opted and tamed by the establishment, or so it seemed. After the sale, as the painting was being removed from the wall, it self-destructed. Banksy had rigged the frame to shred the work on signal. The $1.04 million was reduced to zero, a real discount. Andy Warhol did the unconventional to make art the equivalent of commerce. Banksy takes risks to reveal the truth as it appears to him: much of modern art is worthless—or shouldn't have a price.

TOLERANCE OF RISK IS A HABIT OF GENIUS, AND SO IS RESILIENCE. Consider Frida Kahlo's 1944 painting *The Broken Column* (Figure 8.1). It shows a woman (Kahlo herself) wearing a medical corset of the sort used to hold a spine together. In the painting a broken Ionic column represents a fractured spinal cord, and the fissures in the desolate landscape suggest a broken, lonely world. Across the woman's body are affixed nails of the sort used to symbolize the passion and pain of Jesus; they extend down through her right leg but not the left. Tears stream from her eyes, but her face shows resoluteness, even defiance.

At age six, Frida Kahlo contracted polio, leaving her with a shortened right leg and eventual scoliosis. At age eighteen, she was riding in a bus that was struck by a streetcar. Several people were killed, and Kahlo was left with broken ribs, two broken legs, a broken collarbone, and an iron handrail protruding from her pelvis.[29] She spent three months in bed recovering, and for the rest of her life she had to wear medical corsets of various kinds: plaster, metal, and leather, the last depicted in *The Broken Column*. During her forced immobility, Kahlo changed from occasional sketch artist to serious painter, reaching up to an easel that her father had constructed above her bed. By the 1940s, she could neither stand nor sit without pain, and a series of spinal fusions and grafts was undertaken, with limited success, in hospitals in New York and Mexico City. In August 1953, the pain in her right leg became so unbearable that her leg had to be amputated below the knee.[30] But she persevered, sometimes from a wheelchair and sometimes from a hospital bed.[31] "The pain is not part of the life but can be converted into life itself," she

FIGURE 8.1: *The Broken Column* (1944) depicts the physical and psychological pain through which the Mexican artist Frida Kahlo persevered (Museo Dolores Olmedo, Mexico City).

said.[32] Other geniuses—Chuck Close (spinal artery collapse), John Milton (blindness), Beethoven (deafness), and Stephen Hawking (ALS), for example—persevered in the face of physical obstacles, but perhaps none showed resilience of this magnitude. Said Kahlo, "I am not sick. I am broken. But I am happy to be alive as long as I can paint."[33]

ADVERSITY CAN STIFFEN RESOLVE, AND FAILURE CAN BECOME OPportunity. As Oprah Winfrey said in a Harvard commencement speech in 2013, "There is no such thing as failure. Failure is just life trying to move us in another direction."[34] Geniuses don't set out to fail, but most do at some point, some spectacularly. In 1891, Thomas Edison tried to mine and process high-grade iron ore in New Jersey and to that end built a processing plant; when cheap ore was discovered in Minnesota, the plant was torn down. When Edison was working to devise a better telephone transmitter, he needed just the right material in the diaphragm to convert sound waves into electric impulses. The list of candidates he tried included glass, mica, hard rubber, aluminum foil, parchment, pitch, leather, chamois, cloth, silk, gelatin, ivory, birch bark, rawhide, pig's bladder, fish guts, and a $5 bill.[35] "Negative results are just what I want," he said. "They are just as valuable to me as positive results."[36] In 1901, Nikola Tesla thought he could beam pure electricity from his broadcast tower in Wardenclyffe, NY; he couldn't, and in 1917 the tower was sold for scrap. George Balanchine needed four attempts to launch a successful ballet company in New York, and Elon Musk needed five to launch a rocket from earth and safely return it. "If things are not failing, you are not innovating enough," he said in 2015.[37] Jeff Bezos seems to invite failure at Amazon; as he wrote to shareholders in 2019, "Amazon will be experimenting at the right scale for a company of our size if we occasionally have multibillion-dollar failures."[38] Steve Jobs failed colossally in 2004. "I'm the only person I know," he said, "to have lost a quarter of a billion dollars in one year. . . . It's very character-building."[39]

THE WRITER J. K. ROWLING KNOWS FAILURE FIRSTHAND. "A MERE seven years after my graduation day," she wrote in 2008, "I had failed on an epic scale. An exceptionally short-lived marriage had imploded, and I was jobless, a lone parent, and as poor as it is possible to be in modern Britain, without being homeless. The fears that my parents had had for me, and that I had had for myself, had both come to pass, and by every usual standard, I was the biggest failure I knew."[40] Ironically, in Rowling's eyes a modicum of success would have worked against her genius. "Had I really succeeded at anything else, I might never have found the determination to succeed in the one arena where I believed I truly belonged. I was set free, because my greatest fear had been realized, and I was still alive. . . . And so rock bottom became the solid foundation on which I rebuilt my life. . . . The knowledge that you have emerged wiser and stronger from setbacks means that you are, ever after, secure in your ability to survive. You will never truly know yourself, or the strength of your relationships, until both have been tested by adversity."[41]

Stephen King's novel *Carrie,* the first of his books to be published, was rejected by thirty publishers before finally being acquired by Doubleday for an advance of $2,500. As of 2018, King had published eighty-three novels with a total of 350 million copies sold, and from them he earns approximately $40 million annually in royalties. Theodor Seuss Geisel similarly experienced approximately thirty "no's" for his first children's book, *And to Think That I Saw It on Mulberry Street.* A chance encounter with a Dartmouth classmate brought about its publication in 1937, and thereafter followed sales of approximately 600 million books by "Dr. Seuss." Rowling's first Harry Potter novel was rejected by a dozen publishers before being picked up by Bloomsbury in London for an advance of £1,500 ($2,200) in 1996. Rowling's books have gone on to sell more than 500 million copies. Yet even Bloomsbury editor Barry Cunningham had his doubts, saying to Rowling at the time, "You'll never make any money out of children's books, Jo."[42]

Add to that these excerpts from rejection letters sent to the following now-famous American writers:[43]

> To Herman Melville, regarding *Moby-Dick* (1851): "First we must ask, does it have to be about a whale?"

> To Louisa May Alcott, regarding *Little Women* (1868–1869): "Stick to teaching."

> To Joseph Heller, who named his book *Catch-22* (1961) after receiving twenty-two rejections: "Apparently the author intends it to be funny."

> To Ernest Hemingway, regarding *The Sun Also Rises* (1926): "I wouldn't be surprised to hear that you had penned this entire story locked up at the club, ink in one hand, brandy in the other. Your bombastic, dipsomaniac, where-to-now characters had me reaching for my own glass of brandy."

> And finally, to F. Scott Fitzgerald, regarding *The Great Gatsby* (1925): "You'd have a decent book if you would get rid of that Gatsby character."

As can be seen by the subsequent publication dates for each of these works, those brilliant authors were resilient and self-confident. Follow their lead. If you are a creative type or an entrepreneur bent on change, develop a thick skin, understand that rejection is part of the process, and be prepared to be misunderstood for a long time. Relish the outsider status that attends contrarian thinking, as did Galileo, Warhol, and Banksy. Finally, remember the fierce determination of Vincent van Gogh: in January 1886, the director of the Antwerp Academy of Art, Karel Verlat, gazed upon van Gogh's unconventional work and judged it "putrefaction," sending the pupil back to the beginning class.[44]

Van Gogh ignored Director Verlat's rules and went on to paint now-iconic, paradigm-shifting works such as *Sunflowers* and *The Starry Night*. The genius meets any setback with disbelief: surely the judge, the critic, or the evidence is wrong; surely the solution is just around the corner.

AS A CHILD GROWING UP IN POST–WORLD WAR II AMERICA, I spent my days building tree forts, exploring sewers, and teaching myself to ride a bike that another kid had left in the street—all of that unsupervised. Today things are different. Modern terms abound to describe the current trend toward parental over-involvement, including "helicopter mom," "snowplow dad," and "bubble-wrapped kid."[45] The social environment has shifted from laissez-faire parenting to intense parental control. In 2019, the aforementioned college admissions scandal known as "Operation Varsity Blues" revealed that thirty-three parents, including prom-inent businesspeople and well-known actors, had been charged with bribing college officials, often to inflate their kids' entrance exam scores and help them gain admission to prestigious col-leges. Not genius. Those parents viewed exposing their children to risk and failure as a hardship to be avoided, rather than seeing them as life experiences from which much can be learned and resilience born.

How do we reconcile the images of fearless, independent-thinking, risk-taking, resilient heroes in this chapter with the way we are rearing our children today? We can't. Statistics show that children and college students are becoming more anxious, fear-ful, and risk averse,[46] even though our city streets, according to the Bureau of Justice Statistics, are much safer than they were thirty years ago.[47] Parents and "concerned citizens" are more in-clined to hover, and parents are being arrested for letting their children walk to the park alone.[48] A 2019 study in the journal *Nature Human Behaviour* suggested the downside of such overregu-lation: put a rat into a maze and give it an electric shock along one path; eventually the rat will find a safe path through the maze and always adhere to it, thereafter exploring no other; but it will never learn whether the risk taking is still there or how to cope.[49] Fortunately, a few educators and parents are pushing back with "dangerous" playgrounds that encourage creativity and risk and the "free-range parenting" movement.[50] Want to raise a bold, brilliant, original thinker? Permit your children to explore alone, take risks, and experience failure. Let them have fun and break the rules once in a while. It's more work, worry, and pain for parents, yes, but the ultimate outcome will be better. As Steve Jobs once wondered, "Why join the navy when you can be a pirate?"

CHAPTER 9

BE THE FOX

We all know Aesop's fable "The Tortoise and the Hare" in which a hare begins with a natural advantage but fails to live up to his potential. But Aesop has another lesser-known parable called "The Fox and the Hedgehog," the point of which is this: "The fox knows many small things, while the hedgehog knows one big thing." As the restless fox roots about exploring a multitude of possibilities, the immobile hedgehog rolls himself up in a single big idea. The story suggests two contrasting cognitive styles. Foxes have different strategies for different problems; they are curious and comfortable with nuance, and they can live with contradictions. Hedgehogs, on the other hand, focus on one big problem, and they reduce it to a quest for a single overarching solution.

In 1779, the English man of letters Samuel Johnson formulated the issue this way: "The true genius is a mind of large general powers, accidentally determined to some particular direction."[1] Indeed, broad thinking and narrow thinking are not mutually exclusive. But which will lead you to a breakthrough, going a thousand miles wide or going a thousand miles deep? Which are you innately, the fox or the hedgehog? The point of this chapter is to suggest that if you want to embrace a hidden habit of genius, be the fox.

Like the fox, geniuses roam widely and are curious in random and sometimes uncontrolled ways. Often their natural inquisitiveness is stronger than their self-discipline, pushing them beyond the borders of their primary area of interest. "It is easy," said the Renaissance man Leonardo da Vinci, "to make oneself universal" (*Facile cosa è farsi universale*).[2] It is if you have that polymath's far-ranging genius. "My curiosity is interfering with my work!" Einstein lamented in 1915 while trying to finalize his Theory of General Relativity.[3] Similarly, as he moves among his electric cars, rocket ships, Hyperloop, solar energy panels, and interest in artificial intelligence, Elon Musk sometimes has difficulty staying "on task." But this sort of restless searching changes the world.

To illustrate the benefits of cross-border thinking, I start with two very different foxes, one seemingly outrageous, the other staid: Lady Gaga and Ben Franklin.

My name is Stefani Joanne Angelina Germanotta. I am an Italian-American. I was not born hot, like my mother would have you believe. I, over time, read so many books, watched so many movies, did so much art, met so many sculptors, filmmakers, poets, musicians, sidewalk artists that I invented something that was much stronger than I ever could [have] been on my own.[4]

Those were Lady Gaga's opening remarks at a 2015 awards banquet for the arts-education nonprofit Americans for the Arts. Like Mozart, Stefani Germanotta started keyboard lessons at age four and practiced hard to become a skilled classical pianist. In high school she acted in plays and sang with a jazz band and the school chorus. She was an excellent student but not popular. "For a little while," she has said, "I thought girls were just jealous, which is why they were mean to me. Maybe they were jealous of my fearlessness."[5] "Fearless" is a word frequently used to describe her and other cross-border raiders.

At age seventeen Stefani Germanotta gained early admittance to the prestigious Tisch School of the Arts at New York University. There she studied not only music but also art history and dramatic writing, yet she dropped out after a year to pursue a career as a songwriter and performance artist. To earn money, she moonlighted as a go-go dancer in Lower East Side bars. Around that time Stefani Germanotta became Lady Gaga, her stage name reportedly inspired by the Queen song "Radio Ga Ga," which gave her a new identity. Unlike pop "cover" artists, Lady Gaga is an original creator and one who integrates many arts. "It's all about everything all together—performance art, pop performance art, fashion," she has said.[6] Her innovative 2017 Super Bowl halftime performance had 150 million viewers, the largest live audience in TV history. She has won nine Grammys. In 2019, she was nominated for an Academy Award for best actress, and she won the Academy Award for best original song—the first time someone has been recognized in two such disparate categories. Composer, choreographer, cosmetics creator (Haus of Gaga), fashion designer, actress, record producer, philanthropist, and social activist, Lady Gaga is a transformative pop artist whose shape-shifting and range echo those of Andy Warhol. As she says, "I'm not one icon. I'm every icon. I'm an icon that is made out of all the colors on the palette at every time. I have no restrictions. No restrictions."[7]

WHO COULD BE MORE DIFFERENT FROM THE FORMER LATE-NIGHT burlesque performer Lady Gaga than the "early to bed, early to rise" Ben Franklin? But Franklin, too, was a polymath with an extraordinary range. Every oddity that Franklin experienced became an object of inquiry: Why does a whirlwind swirl? Why does it take twice as long to sail from London to Philadelphia as it does to sail back? Why does a high-pitched violin sound cause a glass to break? For the curious Franklin, an explanation always lurked beneath the surface. But not too far beneath! A typical fox, Franklin saw no point in digging deep just for the sake of depth. Although he explored a diverse array of interests—physics, astronomy, botany, meteorology, oceanography, and politics—he wanted his pursuits to have practical value, and he ultimately arrived at insights with useful purposes. Here are just a few things his roving mind conceived.

The Franklin stove: A metal-lined fireplace that produced more heat and less smoke than an ordinary fireplace.

Bifocals: Why carry two pairs of glasses if one will do?

The lightning rod: Protects a building (and its occupants) by channeling electricity around it.

The glass harmonica: Both Mozart and Beethoven wrote music for his novel three-octave instrument.

Swimming flippers: Undoubtedly one of his most fun and enduring inventions.

The long arm (or grabber): Designed for those who need to reach high places or who can't bend over.

Medical catheter: The first flexible urinary catheter used in America.

Franklin Gothic type: Named in 1902 to commemorate a font style created by Franklin in 1726.

Daylight saving time: Sets the clock later in the "long days" and thereby, by making sunset later, saves on candles or electricity.

Franklin phonetic alphabet: An alternative alphabet that removed c, j, q, w, x, and y but added four new consonants and two new vowels so as to bring consistency to spelling in the English language.

The gulf stream: Explained the more rapid return voyage to England and the need to sail south when heading west, as well as European winters that are milder than those in the Western Hemisphere.

The public library: Franklin established the first lending library in America, located in Philadelphia.

An extraordinary range of interests! And consider Franklin's curriculum for the new University of Pennsylvania, which he established in 1749. Whereas Harvard and Yale aimed to graduate clergymen and mandated the study of Latin, Greek, and Hebrew, Franklin thought in terms of worldly entrepreneurs. He required his students to be exposed to "every Thing that is useful" because "Art is long and their Time is short."[8] Faculty appointments assured that priority was given to physics, engineering, and economics, as well as accounting and farming. French, Spanish, and German were also required, because they would be of use in the business world. What Franklin was advocating in 1749 was a general education curriculum with a smattering of preprofessional courses. Franklin's educational model has since been adopted by many U.S. schools and colleges, setting the precedent for what we now call a liberal arts education, in which "liberal" means a widely ranging curriculum that frees the student from too-early preprofessional specialization.

The movers and shakers of the world seem to embrace a diverse range of skills, perspectives, and habits of mind. Alibaba founder Jack Ma recalls saying to his son in 2015, "You don't need to be in the top three in your class, being in the middle is fine, so long as your grades aren't too bad. Only this kind of person [a middle-of-the-road student] has enough free time to learn other skills."⁹ The tech entrepreneur Mark Cuban said in a 2017 interview on Business Insider, "I personally think there's going to be a greater demand in 10 years for liberal arts majors than there were for programming majors and maybe even engineering, because when the data is all being spit out for you, options are being spit out for you, you need a different perspective in order to have a different view of the data."¹⁰ Lin-Manuel Miranda earned a liberal arts degree, with a theater studies major, at Wesleyan University and then got a job as a seventh-grade English teacher. While on vacation in 2008, he read Ron Chernow's exhaustive biography of Alexander Hamilton. The combination of his interest in the theater and his interest in political history led to the creation of *Hamilton,* during the writing of which he said, "I have a lot of apps open in my brain right now."¹¹ The more broadly based the information in mind, the more likely that disparate ideas are combined.

POLYMATHS HAVE BEEN COMBINING DISPARATE THINGS TO CREATE transformative new ones for millennia. The ancient Egyptians combined the head of a human and the body of a lion to fashion the Sphinx. Archimedes combined a screw and a pipe to produce the Archimedes screw, a machine that can lift water to higher ground, enabling either irrigation or flood relief. Johannes Gutenberg looked at the block-letter stamps used in printing and at a wine press and created the printing press, arguably the most important invention between the wheel and the computer. Cyrus McCormick saw a scythe and a comb and invented the reaper for harvesting crops. Samuel F. B. Morse knew how to send electrical signals over short distances, but seeing teams of relay horses gave him the idea for periodic signal boosters and an effective system of telegraphy. Vincent van Gogh grew up in Holland among textile weavers and throughout his life carried with him a box full of two-colored skeins of wool; about 1885, he thought of combining the striated pairs with the brushstrokes in his paintings, and the result was the ball-like, two-tone swirls we see in works such as *The Starry Night* (1889).

Ordinary mortals combine things, too. George de Mestral (1907–1990), for example, invented Velcro when he realized that the burrs that got stuck to his clothing on a hunting trip could be combined with a new synthetic fiber to form the hook-and-eye material we today call Velcro. Art Fry (b. 1931), an employee at 3M, saw the adhesive capacity of Scotch tape and the usefulness of bookmarkers in his hymnal; one day he put them together and voilà!: the Post-it Note. Lonnie Johnson (b. 1949), who worked at the Jet Propulsion Laboratory in Pasadena, needed to design a new heat pump, one that would use water rather than freon; he saw a squirt gun in a swimming pool in his native Alabama and put the squirt gun together with the heat pump. The result: the Super Soaker, today among the bestselling toys in the world. Keep your eyes open.

What enables diverse ideas to coalesce into something original? In 2019, Amazon's Jeff Bezos commented that in the business world, "The outsized discoveries—the 'non-linear' ones—are highly likely to require wandering."[12] Tim Berners-Lee (b. 1955), the self-effacing genius behind the World Wide Web, describes the creative process in these words: "Half-formed ideas, they float around. They come from different places, and the mind has got this wonderful way of somehow just shoveling them around until one day they fit."[13] The creative mind does not run along a straight track but rather jumps frenetically in a game of conceptual hopscotch. The more squares in play and the greater the distances, the greater the potential for a combinatorial insight that generates an exceptionally original idea. As Albert Einstein said to a friend in 1901, "It is a glorious feeling to discover the unity of a set of phenomena that seem at first to be completely separate."[14] The writer Vladimir Nabokov saw this as an act of genius, writing in 1974 that genius is "seeing things others don't see. Or rather the invisible link between things."[15] Combine things.

IN AN INTERVIEW IN *WIRED* IN 1996, STEVE JOBS SAID, "CREATIVity is just connecting things. When you ask creative people how they did something, they feel a little guilty because they didn't really *do* it, they just *saw* something. It seemed obvious to them after a while. That's because they were able to connect experiences they've had and synthesize new things."[16] Although Jobs dropped out of Reed College, he stayed around long enough to audit courses of special interest, including one in calligraphy taught by a Trappist monk. That experience would lead him to pay close attention to the fonts used on the first Macintosh computers, which subsequently became the classical fonts on every Apple computer.[17] In 2007, Jobs implemented his most transformative—and profitable—idea when he combined Apple's mobile music player (iPod) with its new telephone (iPhone). Up to that point the two functions had resided in entirely different bodies. Eventually, Apple created a device that combined camera, calculator, voice recorder, alarm clock, email, news, GPS navigation, music, and—oh, yes—a telephone.

Apple Inc. was founded in a garage in California in 1976 by two guys named Steve: Jobs and Wozniak. Wozniak fashioned the innards of the first Apple computers: hardware, circuit board, and operating system—technical things that Jobs did not fully understand. Jobs focused on the externals: functionality, the user's experience, and interconnectivity with other devices. It was Jobs who saw the broader picture—that the future in computing would rest with the company that could combine software design with the production of computer hardware. Wozniak was the hedgehog; Jobs was the fox.[18] For years the two made a great team. But which genius do we remember today?

As Jobs suggested, most invention comes from observing disparate things and seeing an unexpected relationship between them. We do this in science when we use equations such as $E = MC^2$, for example; and in poetry and everyday speech when we use metaphor and simile. Aristotle considered a metaphor to be something extraordinary: "This alone cannot be imparted by another; it is the mark of genius, for to make good metaphors implies an eye for resemblances."[19] Professor Dedre Gentner of Northwestern University, an expert in analogical thinking, says this about analogies: "Our ability to think relationally is one of the reasons we're running the planet."[20]

Sometimes beneficial relationships exist that we don't see or fully understand. For example, experts have observed that a broad-based precollege education in art and music will lead to higher scores in standardized tests of math and verbal skills.[21] But why? In the case of math and music, at least, there is a hidden connection. Math is patterns of numbers, and, if we look more deeply, music is as well. Music has two primary elements: sound and duration. Pitches and harmonies are measured in precise vibrations (sound waves) per second, and rhythms are set by proportional durations written in time signatures such as 4/4. We all respond to mathematically organized pitch patterns when we enjoy a pleasing melody and to durational patterns when we dance to a consistent beat in exercise class. Music and math are logic-based processes that produce aesthetic satisfaction,[22] and many great minds have linked the two. Leonardo da Vinci was a professional-level musician on the *viola da braccio,* and Galileo, the son of a world-famous music theorist, played the difficult lute. Edward Teller, the "father of the hydrogen bomb," was an excellent violinist and Werner Heisenberg, a Nobel Prize winner who gave us the first formulation of quantum mechanics, a skilled pianist. Max Planck, likewise a Nobel laureate in physics, wrote songs and operas. Albert Einstein, the personification of genius, said that had he not become a physicist, he would have become a musician.[23] His favorite composer was Wolfgang Amadeus Mozart.

Who knew that Mozart was a mathematician? Mozart began to study math around age four, about the time that he first engaged with music.[24] His sister, Nannerl, recounted, "In these years he was eager to learn, and whatever his father wrote out for him he pursued immediately with the greatest energy to the point that he would forget about everything else, even music. For example, when he learned arithmetic, he covered table, chairs, walls, indeed the entire floor with numbers."[25] By the time he was a young adult, Mozart had become fascinated with number theory, numerical riddles and puzzles, and gambling. About age twenty-four, he acquired a copy of Joseph Spengler's *Anfangs-gründe der Rechenkunst und Algebra* (*Fundamentals of Arithmetic and Algebra*, third edition, 1779) and began a program of self-study, paying special attention to the section "Relationships and Proportions."

Figure 9.1 is just one of many of Mozart's musical sketches in which his desire to work with numerical patterns eclipsed his desire to compose music. Look carefully, and bear with me for a moment. Mozart selected five numbers: 2, 3, 5, 6, and 28. From those he took all three-number combinations (2, 3, and 5 or 3, 5, and 6, for example) and placed them in a column to the right side of the page, identifying the column with the Italian abbreviation *tern*, which stands for *ternario*, or "group of three." Then he did the same with all possible two-number combinations (again, ten are possible). He called the process *amb*, short for the Italian *ambedue*, meaning "both." At some point Mozart looked over his two columns and, working in a way akin to that of a modern number theorist, had an insight: the sum of all possible ten *pairs* of numbers (176) taken from a five-number set is equal to four times the sum of the five numbers within the set (2 + 3 + 5 + 6 + 28 = 44), and the sum of all ten *three*-number possibilities within the set of five (264) is six times the sum of the five numbers of the set. This is true for any set of five numbers (try it). But Mozart wasn't finished; he began to play with retrograding patterns of numbers: 1936:484:1936 and 44:176:264:484:264:176:44. As his obsessive calculations show, Mozart was deeply interested in numerical relationships. Not coincidentally, listeners over the centuries have commented on the "perfect proportions" in Mozart's music, Einstein calling them "a reflection of the inner beauty of the universe."[26] Here the observation of Berkeley psychologist

FIGURE 9.1: While working out an erudite three-voice fugue during 1782, Mozart broke off to engage in mathematical computations (Mozart, Skb 1782j, recto, National Library, Vienna).

Donald MacKinnon can be applied to the arts as well as the sciences: "Some of the most creative scientific achievements have been accomplished by men who, trained in one field, enter upon another."[27] You need to cross-train.

Pablo Picasso, another brilliant polymath, famously said, "I do not borrow, I steal!" And like the thieving fox, Picasso "stole"

FIGURE 9.2: Pablo Picasso, *Les Demoiselles d'Avignon* (1907), a thunder-bolt of modernism wrought in part by the artist's exposure to African masks and in part by a new awareness of the art of Paul Cézanne (Museum of Modern Art, New York).

from everywhere, taking from seventeenth-century old masters as well as from the junkyard. He would combine an idea in his head with an image or object he saw to create something radically new. An old bicycle seat and handlebars might be combined with a childhood memory of a bullfight to form a modernist sculpture. Picasso's mind was energized by external appropriation, and what he stole, he did not intend to return.

Picasso's *Les Demoiselles d'Avignon* (1907; Figure 9.2) is arguably the most important painting of the twentieth century, the first work of Cubism and the opening salvo in the onslaught of modern art. In *Les Demoiselles*, two new external experiences combined in Picasso's mind. First, in 1907, Picasso confronted the work of Paul Cézanne (1839–1906) in a retrospective exhibition of that artist at the Petit Palais in Paris; there he saw a new kind of painting, one that exploited simple forms, two-dimensional planes, and geometric shapes. Later that same year, Picasso discovered African masks at the musty Museum of Ethnography at the Trocadéro, across the Seine from the Eiffel Tower.[28] The exposure to Cézanne brought a new awareness of the power of pure form in art. The African masks did the same but added an element of primal terror. Seeing the masks was a defining moment for Picasso: "I understood why I was a painter. All alone in that awful museum, with the masks, the redskin dolls, the dusty mannequins—*Les Demoiselles d'Avignon* must have come to me that day."[29] Picasso combined those two visual elements with his own psychic intensity and thereby changed the course of art history.

But wait a minute: Isn't "stealing" things, as did Picasso, illegal? Not if you combine the object with original material of your own and thereby create something new and transformative. Picasso put real newspapers and other copyrighted objects into his collage art, and no one sued. Warhol incorporated images of Elizabeth Taylor, Marlon Brando, Elvis, Marilyn, and Ma into his art, and they didn't go to court to stop him. You, too, can be a creative fox. Just be sure that, pursuant to the Fair Use Doctrine of the 1976 Copyright Law of the United States, you are repurposing and transforming the "stolen" work for social or cultural benefit.[30]

CHARLES DARWIN WAS TOO MUCH OF A GENTLEMAN TO STEAL ANYthing. But he did combine two disparate theories circulating in the early nineteenth century: the transmutational theory of evolution and the Malthusian theory of population. Transmutation, as propounded by Darwin's grandfather Erasmus Darwin (1731–1802) and more clearly by the French biologist Jean-Baptiste Lamarck (1744–1829), held that species evolved over time as they adapted to local environments, then passed their *acquired* traits on to the next generation;[31] Malthusian population theory posited that humans would grow in uncontrollable numbers unless limited by the "beneficial" effects of famine, disease, and war. Charles Darwin had studied the writings of his grandfather and of Lamarck both before and during college in Edinburgh. But not until after his voyage on the *Beagle* (1831–1836) around the Galápagos Islands did he happen to read Thomas Malthus's *An Essay on the Principle of Population*. At that point, genius Darwin appears to have experienced a combinative "eureka" moment.[32]

> In October 1838, that is fifteen months after I had begun my systematic enquiry, I happened to read for amusement Malthus on *Population,* and being well prepared to appreciate the struggle for existence which everywhere goes on from long-continued observation of the habits of animals and plants, it at once struck me that under these circumstances favourable variations would tend to be preserved, and unfavourable ones to be destroyed. The result of this would be the formation of a new species. Here, then, I had at last got a theory by which to work.[33]

That theory, of course, was what we now call Darwinian evolution, one based on a genetic advantage, or "natural selection."[34] No theory was more potentially explosive for both science and theology than Darwin's "brutalist" model: that only those animals lucky enough to have the right genes for a particular environment will survive. Yet for another twenty years, Darwin continued to verify and fine-tune his big idea. Finally, in 1859, he came forth with *On the Origin of Species*.

So what does this make Darwin, fox or hedgehog? Presumably the latter: Darwin relentlessly pursued one great big idea, maybe the biggest of them all. But recall Jeff Bezos's observation that creative ideas come from "wandering." Possibly no Victorian had wandered more and seen more things than Charles Darwin had. In 1831, he left the comparative comfort of England on the *Beagle* for uncharted territories, eventually circumnavigating the globe. But unlike the sailors on the *Beagle,* he got off the ship to make land excursions across the plains of Patagonia, into the Amazon rain forest, and up the rocks of the Andes, during which time he saw, ate, and was bitten by almost every species imaginable. In fact, during his five-year voyage "on" the *Beagle,* he spent two-thirds of his time on land, prowling around like a fox.[35] By the end, he had become a pluralist—a zoologist, botanist, geologist, and paleontologist of the first order. Darwin was a fox in hedgehog's clothing.

SOMETIMES A FOX FALLS INTO A HEDGEHOG'S HOLE. THAT HAP-pened to the far-ranging Thomas Edison while he was looking to build out an electrical system to connect and supply power to all of North America. Having invented a long-burning light bulb in 1879, Edison now needed wall sockets and circuits, power lines, transformers, and power generators to light those bulbs.[36] But which mode of electrical current to use, direct or alternating? DC is good for lower voltages and short distances, AC for high voltages and long distances. Edison, fresh off the success of the light bulb, bet the farm on DC. In February 1881, he left his rural Menlo Park research lab and moved his family and the manufacturing center of Edison Electric to lower Manhattan. There his men tunneled deep beneath the streets to lay conduits for DC current (Figure 9.3).

But Edison had blundered. DC is not an effective means by which to wire a large city or a nation because it requires expensive generators to create new current about every half mile, depending

the Electrical Tubes

FIGURE 9.3: Detail from an illustration from the June 21, 1882, *Harper's Weekly* captioned "The electric light in houses—laying the tubes for wires in the streets of New York." Edison chose to bury the wires underground rather than string them on poles.

on the load. To build out his capital-intensive DC system, Edison needed money and decided to sell progressively larger amounts of his Edison Electric stock to J. P. Morgan and his partners, who, within a decade, had ousted Edison and turned Edison Electric first into Edison General Electric and then simply into General Electric.[37] With Edison no longer in control, J. P. Morgan and General Electric switched to AC.

Tunnel vision is often the result of "sunk cost syndrome." Edison had gone so deeply, and at such expense, into a single solution that it seemed impossible to admit defeat and change course. The problem for a genius like Edison is to recognize the moment at which grit and perseverance must yield to common sense. But the foxy Edison had more than one interest. He would go on to make a commercial success out of an array of diverse practical products, not only the light bulb, phonograph, and motion picture but also the public address system, hearing aid, talking doll, and even the prefabricated cement house.

THE OVERCONFIDENCE OF THE EXPERT, ALONG WITH THE SUNK cost syndrome, had caused the Wizard of Menlo Park to fail in this case by ignoring other possible solutions. "Cognitive entrenchment can limit creative problem solving if the expert fails to look beyond his existing schemas for new ways to tackle a challenge," said David Robson in his 2019 book, *The Intelligence Trap: Why Smart People Make Dumb Mistakes.*[38] The hedgehog can't see the forest for the trees. On the other hand, often the fox roots around so brazenly that he doesn't see the danger in the forest. How many times have you said to yourself, "If only I'd known what I was getting into, I wouldn't have gone there!" The creativity specialist Donald MacKinnon explained why lack of expertise can be a good thing: "The expert, all too often, 'knows' both on theoretical grounds and on the basis of empirical findings that certain things are not so or just cannot be done. The naive novice ventures what the expert would never attempt, and often enough succeeds."[39] MacKinnon's exhortation: Don't be the blinkered hedgehog. Do what the farsighted fox Nikola Tesla urged: have the boldness of ignorance.[40]

Economists such as the Nobel Prize–winning Daniel Kahneman (*Thinking, Fast and Slow*) and Philip Tetlock (*Superforecasting: The Art and Science of Prediction*) agree. They point out that narrowly focused experts, no matter how famous, do less well than wide-ranging generalists when it comes to predicting the future and solving the problems of tomorrow.[41] Tetlock's work inspired a four-year competition between teams of U.S. intelligence analysts demonstrating that widely read foreign language–speaking generalists make better predictions than do narrow experts in matters of world affairs.[42] Recent studies have also shown that Nobel Prize–winning scientists were nearly three times as likely to engage in a fine arts activity as were their less distinguished colleagues, with music being the most frequently chosen pursuit.[43] Similarly, they are twenty-two times as likely to get engaged in amateur performance activities, such as acting, dancing, or doing magic.

U.S. politicians, however, are slow to get the message, at least with regard to education. Governors and state legislatures are linking education to "employability," as reported in articles such as "A Rising Call to Promote STEM Education and Cut Liberal Arts Spending."[44] Some colleges are doing away with majors in classics and art history.[45] Even liberal president Barack Obama recently took a jab at the "useless" liberal arts.[46]

The geniuses of this chapter, however, teach a different lesson. They instruct us to wander widely, combine things, cross-train, be fearless, keep our eyes open, avoid sunk cost syndrome, and have the boldness of ignorance. They also implicitly caution us against thinking that education must lead immediately to that job of a lifetime. In the 1920s, a tech engineer's "half-life of knowledge" was thirty-five years; in the 1960s, it was a decade; and today it is five years at most.[47] The lesson for all of us is: stay nimble. Educators in the Tech Ed field are coming to believe that as we move from job to job, now at the rate of one new position every five years, what will be needed is access to college-level short courses across a wide range of subjects over the duration of a lifetime, the "sixty-year curriculum," as it is called.[48]

In 2011, Steve Jobs said that for technology to be truly brilliant, it must be coupled with artistry. "It's in Apple's DNA that technology alone is not enough," he said. "It's technology married with liberal arts, married with the humanities, that yields the results that make our hearts sing."[49] Thus, aspirational young people majoring in the STEM fields would do well to heed the advice of the Nobel laureate/violinist Albert Einstein, who, in a talk in 1950, disparaged specialization and concluded, "Every serious

scientific worker is painfully conscious of this involuntary relega-
tion to an ever-narrowing sphere of knowledge, which threatens
to deprive the investigator of his broad horizon and degrades
him to the level of a mechanic."[50] We all need hedgehogs to fix the
things we dearly love, but to create a new and improved world,
better call Mr. Fox.

CHAPTER 10

THINK OPPOSITE

To discover the East, Christopher Columbus sailed west. To inoculate people against smallpox, Edward Jenner injected them with pox. Instead of luring the customer to the goods, Jeff Bezos brings the goods to the customer. According to Isaac Newton's Third Law of Motion, "For every action there is an opposite and equal reaction." Shakespeare's Hamlet said, "I must be cruel only to be kind."

The above contrarian insights exemplify the process of "thinking opposite," an age-old strategy deeply embedded in the arts and sciences, as well as in industry. If you want to better understand an object or concept, conceive of the opposite. If you want to understand how a machine was put together, disassemble it. If you want to achieve a particular result, define the end goal and then fashion a line of development leading back to the beginning. The practical advantages of oppositional thinking are at least four: first, it allows us to see solutions to problems that we would otherwise not see; second, it makes us more mentally flexible and imaginative; third, it teaches us to be comfortable with ambiguity and paradox; and finally, it often makes us laugh, a sure sign of happiness.

A talent for seeing the importance of opposites is a hidden

habit of genius, particularly in science and industry. Why does lightning strike? Because negative and positive charges in the air and ground race to join from opposite directions, as Ben Franklin knew. Why does an airplane go up? Because the wings of a flying plane pull the air above them down, forcing the air below and the plane to go up, as the Wright brothers demonstrated. How can we understand the moment of the "Big Bang" in astrophysics? Play the universe backward until it shrinks into a single incomprehensibly dense atom, as Stephen Hawking suggested.

In 1953, in the famous Cavendish Laboratory at Cambridge University, the team of James Watson and Francis Crick discovered the structure of deoxyribonucleic acid (DNA), the building block of all living things. Their insight involved understanding the principle of opposites. Within each strand of DNA lies hidden a palindrome of molecules. For example:

XXGATCXXXXXGATCXX—
XXCTAGXXXXXXCTAGXX

Together the sequence goes forward and backward. Every living organism has genes with a retrograding pattern. If, as cells multiply, they do not replicate the palindromic process precisely, malignancy or other defects may develop. Understanding this is an important part of today's biomedical research and genetic engineering. The discovery of the structure of DNA won Watson, Crick, and their colleague Maurice Wilkins a Nobel Prize in Chemistry in 1962.

Occasionally, oppositional thinking is just child's play. When, in 1785, mathematical genius Johann Carl Friedrich Gauss was eight, his teacher asked him to solve the following problem, just to keep the precocious child occupied for a while: "What is the sum of all the numbers from one to a hundred?" Immediately Gauss came back with the answer: 5,050. Instead of wasting time adding all the numbers, he had a contrarian insight: fifty is the midpoint, and the extremes balance against each other; the sequence of numbers 1, 2, 3, 4, 5, and so on, up to 50, could be set as a palindrome against itself. For those of us who are not geniuses, let's reduce the problem down from one hundred to just nine numbers. This will enable us to see the insight Gauss experienced; he visualized a reverse pattern that would quickly lead to the solution. In our scheme nine numbers can be set backward against themselves:

$$1 + 2 + 3 + 4 + 5 + 6 + 7 + 8 + 9 \longrightarrow$$
$$9 + 8 + 7 + 6 + 5 + 4 + 3 + 2 + 1 \longleftarrow$$

Adding vertically, these produce a series of 9 10's, or 9 × 10 = 90. We've doubled the numbers (added a second row that goes backward), so now we have to divide by two to get the answer: 45. Brilliant! But then, thinking inductively, Gauss saw that this procedure could be the basis of a formula for any such problem: Total number $T = N(N + 1) \div 2$. Try it by using your own sequence of consecutive numbers. Gauss's backward insight demonstrated how "thinking opposite" can save a mathematician time.

Making a rocket booster go up and come back down can save an industrialist money. In 2011, Elon Musk's SpaceX and the National Aeronautics and Space Administration, formerly frenemies, formed a partnership.[1] Henceforth, Musk's rockets would provide transportation for NASA, taking cargo and astronauts into space. SpaceX had become the dominant force in space transportation by showing that a rocket booster might go round-trip—into space and back down safely to be reused—thereby reducing the cost of each launch by up to 80 percent.[2] It took Musk five tries, but he did it. As he said in a 2013 TED Talk, "Physics is really figuring out how to discover new things that are counter intuitive."[3]

THINKING OPPOSITE, OR IN CONTRARY MOTION, CAN ALSO PROVIDE structure in the arts. The composer Johann Sebastian Bach saw how a tune could go round-trip, thereby pleasing a king. In 1747,

FIGURE 10.1: A twenty-bar melody Mozart wrote in a sketchbook (Sk 1772o) at the age of sixteen when he was learning the art of counterpoint. He wrote only the melody (top part) but indicated by the context that it should be played backward against itself.

Bach journeyed from Leipzig to Berlin to meet the music-loving King Frederick the Great, who handed Bach a melody and asked him to improvise on it. Bach returned home, cogitated, and then responded with *The Musical Offering,* in the course of which he turned the royal melody on its head in musical inversion (notes that went up now go down to the same degree) and then employed retrograde motion (pitches of the melody going forward are now made to go backward). Franz Joseph Haydn, Mozart, Beethoven, Franz Schubert, Igor Stravinsky, and Arnold Schoenberg used the same retrograding gambit.

Mozart, whose nickname for himself was Trazom, loved creative palindromes. In one case, he fashioned a melody that might go in opposite directions simultaneously, as shown in Figure 10.1. Sometimes he incorporated this oppositional process in a finished composition, but most often he made use of it in his practice sketches. In those he employed oppositional thinking to develop his craft and expand his imagination.

For Mozart, as for us, thinking in opposites is a challenge that can lead to a better outcome. To play a scale in a sonata smoothly, instrumentalists are instructed to practice the scale with exaggerated syncopation. To be a lethal striker in soccer (football), the naturally right-footed kicker is instructed to practice continually with the left. Leonardo da Vinci taught himself how to write both backward and forward, which improved his skill as a draftsman. All such contrarian exercises improve physical flexibility as they promote neuroplasticity.

Leonardo da Vinci belonged to the 10 percent of the general population that is left-handed.[4] Within the 100,000 sketches he drew rests evidence that he, too, recognized the creative value of "thinking opposite." His sketches for his famous painting *The Virgin and Child with St. Anne,* one of four superb Leonardo works in the Louvre, offer a case in point.[5] Around 1478–1480, he imagined two versions of the scene he wanted to create: Virgin and child with a lamb (the cat was a placeholder for the lamb). One faces right (Figure 10.2A), the other left (Figure 10.2B), in near mirror image. In the left-facing composition a second female head appears. About a decade later, a more finished right-facing version appears, but now with the second head (St. Anne) in near mirror image of the Virgin's (Figure 10.3A). The two stare lovingly at each other. In the finished painting of ca. 1503 (Figure 10.3B), St. Anne's head is now in alignment with the Virgin's, but the figures of the Christ Child and the lamb are turned 180 degrees. No viewer standing in the Louvre before Leonardo's masterpiece would realize that this final version of it was the product of a twenty-year struggle regarding figures in dramatic opposition. Here the process of "thinking opposite," essential though it is, remains entirely hidden.

FIGURES 10.2A AND B:
A: Leonardo da Vinci's
drawing *Virgin and Child
with Cat*, ca. 1478 (Department of Prints and
Drawings, British Museum, London). B: His
later drawing *Virgin
and Child with Cat*, ca.
1480 (British Museum,
London).

FIGURES 10.3A AND B: A: Leonardo's cartoon (finished drawing), ca. 1499 (National Gallery, London). B: His painting *The Virgin and Child with St. Anne*, ca. 1503 (Musée du Louvre, Paris).

Walk from *The Virgin and Child* seventy-five feet northwest in the Louvre, and you will arrive at the world's most famous painting: Leonardo's *Mona Lisa*. It, too, involves a reversal of thinking, but of an even more subtle type. Before the arrival of Leonardo, late-medieval and early-Renaissance painting had been either religious or historical in theme. A painting depicted Christian dogma or left a visual record of reigning kings and queens, and it did so by means of symbols: a dove to announce the coming Christ or a crown to suggest a king. The message in a painting was conveyed from painter to viewer, and the viewer could take it or leave it, believe it or not believe it. In traditional symbolic painting, communication went only one way.

With Leonardo's *Mona Lisa,* painting took a quantum turn. The lines of communication are reversed. Instead of the artist telling us something, the lady in this painting wants to engage in a dialogue with the viewer. Her question, in the form of her quizzical smile, is a provocation. Here painting ceases to be monodirectional dogma and becomes bidirectional engagement. To understand the *Mona Lisa,* we must accept that the meaning of a painting may not rest in the work itself as much as it does in the viewer. Art historians call this "reverse perspective."

Psychologists define the term "reverse psychology" as a strategy by which saying one thing is designed to produce the opposite effect. Writers sometimes employ "reverse chronology" as a storytelling technique, and they have done so for dramatic effect as far back as Virgil's *Aeneid*. The composer Richard Wagner used reverse chronology when crafting the libretto of his seventeen-hour-long musical drama *The Ring Cycle;* he began with the death of his gods and heroes (*Twilight of the Gods*), worked backward through the events of their earlier lives (*Siegfried* and *The Valkyrie*), and finally prefaced this trilogy with a context-setting preview (*Rhinegold*). George Lucas proceeded similarly in his *Star Wars* films, following up an opening trilogy with three "prequels" that went back in time. In 1922, F. Scott Fitzgerald published a short story, "The Curious Case of Benjamin Button," in which the life of the protagonist unfolds in reverse chronological order: he is born an eighty-year-old, becomes middle-aged, then becomes youthful, and then dies as a child.

"I always know the end of the mystery before I begin to write," says the bestselling murder mystery writer P. D. James.[6] Mystery writers often establish "who done it," where, and how and then go back to the beginning to lead the reader through their story. Indeed, "murder mysteries are backward creatures," wrote the mystery writer Bruce Hale in "Writing Tip: Plotting Backwards."[7] We are speaking of mystery novels here, but the principle can be widely applied. Any aspiring author might do well to ponder first: What will be the ending? Indeed, "Think backward" is good advice for anyone making a public presentation, written or spoken, be it a corporate report or a wedding speech. Look over the material, save the best and most persuasive for last, and structure everything else to lead there. Not only will the material stay "on point," but, equally important, the audience will appreciate the "big bang" conclusion.

A RAY IS, BY DEFINITION, A STRAIGHT LINE, LIKE THE FIRST FEW feet of water shot from a squirt gun. A wave is a curve, like ripples emanating from a stone tossed into a pond. If not exact opposites, "ray" and "wave" are very dissimilar. That light could be both a ray and a wave is a paradox, from the Greek *paradoxon*, "contrary opinion." "Thinking opposite" sometimes requires being comfortable with paradox.

More than once Albert Einstein wrestled with conditions that were paradoxical. In 1905, he resolved a long-standing debate between opposing theories regarding the nature of light: Is light a stream of particles (a straight line), or is it a wave? Isaac Newton had previously opted for particles; he called them "corpuscles." Newton's near contemporary Christiaan Huygens (1629–1695) argued for waves. Newton's theory seemed to prevail until James Maxwell (1831–1879) put the wave description onto more solid ground with his unified laws of electromagnetic waves (1865).[8] In 1905, Einstein showed how these oppositional theories might be reconciled, with his theory of wave-particle duality. Waves of light hit a material, which then emits a stream of photoelectrons (Einstein's photoelectric effect). "We have two contradictory pictures of reality," he said. "Separately neither of them fully explains the phenomena of light, but together they do."[9] This duality became part of quantum physics—a new orthodoxy made of paradox. In addition, the photoelectron's energy is always inversely proportional to the light's wavelength—an embedded antithesis. Illuminating the conundrum of light brought Einstein the Nobel Prize in 1921.

"When does a woman falling from a building not fall?" Answer: "When everything else is falling with her." When Albert Einstein solved that hypothetical riddle, he found the answer to another. In 1907, Einstein was vexed by the apparent opposition of two theories: Newton's theory of celestial gravity, which states that objects are pulled in a straight line to other objects, and his own Theory of Special Relativity, which states that objects are governed by the rules unique to their context. "One is dealing here," he noted, "with two fundamentally different cases, [which] was for me, unbearable."[10] Visualizing a situation in which everything was falling at once produced "the happiest thought of my life" and removed the unbearable burden. How can stasis and motion exist at one and the same time? "Because," Einstein said, "for an observer in free fall from the roof of a house there is during the fall—at least in his immediate vicinity—no gravitational field. Namely, if the observer lets go of any bodies, they remain relative to him, in a state of rest."[11] The force of gravity might be at work, but another might act with it both conterminously and equally. In the language of science, there was a "complete physical equivalence and simultaneity of the opposite effect, of a uniform gravitational field."[12] In layman's terms, forces could pull in a straight line and a curve depending on the speed of the object and the force of the gravitational field. Newton wasn't wrong, but his theory of gravity was not accurate under all circumstances. Newton's apple might fall straight down, but in Einstein's space-time it would curve. Similarly, the fact that a single atom can behave like two separate atoms under certain circumstances is the fundamental logic behind the emerging field of quantum computing and the computer of the future.[13]

"THE COLDEST WINTER I EVER SPENT," MARK TWAIN SAID, "WAS A summer in San Francisco." We were expecting Twain to elaborate on a winter experience and instead are jerked around to summer. But long before Twain's 180-degree pivot, William Shakespeare had used the same gambit in the opening lines of his play *Richard III:* "Now is the winter of our discontent, made glorious summer by this sun of York." Shakespeare fashions not only a play of opposites (winter yielding to summer) but a pun—the "sun of York" was Edward, son of the Duke of York and now the brightest sun in the York dynastic firmament. *Richard III* is a dark political tragedy, yet one full of humor owing to opposing views of Richard: the citizens see him as a malevolent force; he—being delusional—views himself as benevolent. The most famous example of Shakespeare's antipodal scenes is when the murderer Macbeth yields to the comically drunken porter. When negative and positive forces connect, drama strikes the stage like a lightning bolt.

Most of Shakespeare's poetry is built on analogies, metaphors, and similes—two related concepts joined in a pair. Poetic pairing can be all the more effective when the pair is an antithesis. To appreciate what makes genius, consider a passage spoken by Romeo in Shakespeare's *Romeo and Juliet*. Here the lover experiences a knot of contradictory feelings that come double time—fourteen in eight lines. Some might be expected: "sick health" and "cold fire"—you or I might have thought of these. But "brawling love" and "feather of lead"—there's the hidden genius!

> *Here's much to do with hate, but more with love.*
> *Why, then, O brawling love! O loving hate!*
> *O any thing, of nothing first create!*
> *O heavy lightness! Serious vanity!*
> *Mis-shapen chaos of well-seeming forms!*
> *Feather of lead, bright smoke, cold fire, sick health!*
> *Still-waking sleep, that is not what it is!*
> *This love feel I, that feel no love in this. [I love her, but*
> *she loves me not.]*

Finally, consider the staying power of Shakespeare's most succinct oxymoron, one in which he juxtaposes two opposite and incompatible existential conditions: "To be or not to be."

HENRY FORD REVOLUTIONIZED FACTORY WORK AND THE CAR INdustry when he began to mass-produce the inexpensive Model T in 1913 by means of an assembly line. A visit to a slaughterhouse in Chicago had impressed him with the speed and efficiency with which a dead steer could be disassembled to nothing, hanging from its heels and pulled along a steel chain. If disassembly might occur so quickly, he thought, could not the process be reversed in additive fashion?

The contrarian Elon Musk took the opposite approach to Ford when it came to pricing his cars. When Musk took the helm at Tesla, instead of introducing an inexpensive car and working up to expensive models, he started with the Roadster in 2011 (price $200,000), next introduced a Model X in 2015 ($80,000), and finally brought out the Model 3 in 2017 ($35,000). Thus, at the moment, Tesla is transitioning from being a high-price, low-volume company to being a low-price, high-volume one. As Musk announced loudly in a public post of 2006 titled "The Secret Tesla Motors Master Plan," his agenda was to:

Build sports car

Use that money to build an affordable car

Use *that* money to build an even more affordable car. . . .

Don't tell anyone.[14]

As a young data manager at the hedge fund D. E. Shaw & Co. during the early 1990s, Jeff Bezos was comfortable hedging a bet: correctly positioning one economic asset as a counterpoise to another. Bezos saw that internet usage was expanding at the astounding rate of 2,300 percent each year and recognized that global growth was "the big picture." The challenge was how to link it to the little guy and make money, so he went in search of a problem that he could monetize. Thinking opposite, he found one: shopping. A consumer drives around looking for things but often comes home empty-handed. Why not reverse the process, use the internet to find the goods, and have the goods go to the consumer, thereby saving time and money? He did, and today Amazon controls 40 percent of e-commerce in the United States.[15] In 2005, Bezos said, "Sometimes people see the problem and the problem is really annoying them, and they invent a solution. Sometimes you can work this from the backwards direction. And in fact in high tech I think a lot of the innovation sometimes comes from this direction. You see a new technology or there's something out there, . . . and you work backwards from a solution to find the appropriate problem."[16] Bezos's current obsession: "We have to go into space to save Earth."[17]

TO BE FUNNY, "THINK OPPOSITE." HUMOR INVOLVES IRONY, CONtradiction, or counterintuitive thinking. So does sarcasm. When we say, "Boy, *that* was smart," we actually mean the opposite. Creative comedians are philosophers who sometimes reveal the truth, as they show us, ironically, that we have the wrong target because the real one is hidden. The following shtick appears in Chris Rock's stand-up comedy special "Bigger and Blacker":

> Gun control? We need bullet control! I think every bul-
> let should cost five thousand dollars. Because if a bullet
> cost five thousand dollars, people would start to think
> before they shoot, wondering if they can afford it. . . .
> We wouldn't have any more innocent bystanders, or if we
> did, the shooters would be going around saying "Give me
> my property back!" [condensed and sanitized]

A paradox can be an oxymoron with a moral, and that is what Rock has constructed here by setting a *perceived* truth against a truth: guns don't kill, bullets do. Maybe we should just outlaw bullets. Rock has also said, "Comedy is the blues for people who can't sing." He understands that jokes explore the polar opposites of human experience and allow us to laugh along the way. As Freud argued in his *The Joke and Its Relationship to the Uncon-scious* (1905), jokes reveal the foibles, fears, and contradictions within all of us. The joke here: Freud's book on jokes is the least funny book you will ever read.

Below are some one-liners from geniuses past and present. They are funny because they involve opposites, a misunderstand-ing, a logical impossibility, or a repositioning of words.

> Shakespeare: "O villain! Thou wilt be condemned into
> everlasting redemption for this!" (*Much Ado About
> Nothing*)

> Benjamin Franklin: "If we don't all hang together we
> surely will all hang separately."

> "I probably should be proud of my humility."

Charles Darwin: "[Thomas] Carlyle silenced everyone by haranguing during the whole London dinner party on the advantages of silence."

Mark Twain: "Wagner wouldn't sound nearly so bad if it weren't for the music."

Albert Einstein: "To punish me for my contempt of authority, Fate has made me an authority."

Will Rogers (in Texas during a drought): "The Rio Grande is the only river I've ever seen that needs irrigation."

Winston Churchill: "The farther backward you look, the farther forward you can see."

Martin Luther King, Jr.: "Our scientific power has outrun our spiritual power. We have guided missiles but misguided men."

Elon Musk: "When people ask me why I started a rocket company, I say, 'I was trying to learn how to turn a large fortune into a small one.'"

"The best kind of service is no service at all."

N. C. Wyeth: "It is the hardest work in the world to try *not* to work!"

Jack Vogel: "You get what you don't pay for."

Oscar Wilde: "Work is the curse of the drinking class."

"True friends stab you in the back."

"To lose a parent is a great misfortune; to lose both looks like carelessness."

"I can resist everything except temptation."

J. K. Rowling: "We bought two hundred copies of 'The Invisible Book of Invisibility'—cost a fortune and we never found them." (*The Prisoner of Azkaban*)

Oscar Levant: "What the world needs is more geniuses with humility. There are so few of us left."

Jokes are funny, but the reason is hidden from us: it's "thinking opposite."

MANY OF THE WORLD'S GREAT RELIGIONS INVOLVE A THEOLOGY embracing a constant cycle of beginnings and endings, or an endless pull of opposing forces. In Buddhism, contrary and unified forces coexist as nirvana, the end of the cycle of rebirth, and samsara, the endless series of incarnations and reincarnations of living things.[18] Nirvana, the ultimate state, itself is both nondeath and nonlife. Within Taoism, yin and yang are opposite yet universal moral principles, operating together as a single force. The Hebrew word אמת, meaning "truth," one of the names of God in Judaism, uses the first (aleph) and last (taw) letters of the Hebrew alphabet. Satan and the angels of God do battle in Christian eschatology. *Ego sum alpha et omega,* the first and last letters of the Greek alphabet, symbolize God as described in the Book of Revelation.

Martin Luther King, Jr., was graduated from Crozer Theological Seminary in 1951 and earned a Ph.D. in theology at Boston University four years later. He knew about *alpha et omega,* beginning and end, and he employed this antithesis in his most famous speech, "I Have a Dream" (1963).

Much has been written about King's "I Have a Dream," the

defining moment of his career and a tipping point for Americans' thinking about race. The simple point here is that the rhetorical power of the speech derives from not only the relentless pursuit of a single refrain (anaphora) but also the relentless use of contradictory images (oxymoron). Rhetoric marches ahead directly, while poetry alternates between opposites.

> Now is the time to rise from the dark and desolate valley of segregation to the sunlit path of racial justice. . . .
>
> This sweltering summer of the negro's legitimate discontent will not pass until there is an invigorating autumn of freedom and equality.
>
> Nineteen sixty-three is not an end but a beginning. . . .
>
> In the process of gaining our rightful place we must not be guilty of wrongful deeds.
>
> Let us not seek to satisfy our thirst for freedom by drinking from the cup of bitterness and hatred. . . .
>
> We shall always march ahead. We cannot turn back. . . .
>
> I have a dream that one day, on the red hills of Georgia, the sons of former slaves and the sons of former slave owners will be able to sit down together at the table of brotherhood.
>
> I have a dream that one day even the state of Mississippi, a state sweltering with the heat of injustice, sweltering with the heat of oppression will be transformed into an oasis of freedom and justice. . . .
>
> I have a dream that one day every valley shall be exalted, every hill and mountain shall be made low, the rough places will be made plain and the crooked places will be made straight. . . .
>
> With this faith we will be able to transform the jangling discords of our nation into a beautiful symphony of brotherhood.[19]

In college, King encountered Indian religious beliefs and studied the life of Mahatma Gandhi, and in 1959 he went to India to learn from Gandhi's disciples about passive resistance. As the leader of the Southern Christian Leadership Conference, King then used nonviolence as a weapon against violence in the streets. The water cannon and police dogs directed against women and children in Birmingham, Alabama, had the opposite effect; they created a public backlash. In 1964, King's contrarian approach won him the Nobel Peace Prize.

IN SUM: THE GENIUSES OF THIS CHAPTER SUGGEST THAT THE MORE a person can exploit the contradictions of life, the greater his or her potential for genius. Great artists, poets, playwrights, musicians, comedians, and moralists embed oppositional forces in their work for dramatic, and sometimes comic, effect. Brilliant scientists and mathematicians seemingly do not go in search of contradictions but are comfortable when they find them. Transformative entrepreneurs look for contrarian solutions. Bach used counterpoint to fashion his greatest works. Bezos worked backward from a solution to a problem. King used oxymoronic words and vigorous inaction to change public opinion about race in the United States.

We can all employ this strategy. After telling a child a bedtime story, reverse the process and have the child tell you one—encourages visionary thinking on the part of both teller and auditor. Before launching a new company, hold a "premortem," working backward to see why the venture might fail. To write a better company report or give a better speech, look over the material and get the end in place first. Simplify your argument; less may be more. To reduce personal bias and reasoning errors when making a big decision, write a list of the pros and cons.[20] To test the validity of your position, find a devil's advocate; arguing with your spouse or partner can be a good thing and will provide an opportunity to exercise passionate restraint. To be witty in conversation, think of an opposite rejoinder. While the strategy of "thinking opposite" may go unobserved, the improved outcomes will be obvious.

CHAPTER 11

GET LUCKY

I n 1904, the genius Mark Twain published an essay titled "Saint Joan of Arc" in which he suggested how greatness had come about for this female hero as well as for other transformative minds: "When we set about accounting for a Napoleon or a Shakespeare or a Raphael or a Wagner or an Edison or other extraordinary person, we understand that the measure of his talent will not explain the whole result, nor even the largest part of it; no, it is the atmosphere in which the talent was cradled that explains; it is the training it received while it grew, the nurture it got from reading, study, example, the encouragement it gathered from self-recognition and recognition from the outside at each stage of its development: when we know all these details, then we know why the man was ready when his opportunity came."[1] For Twain, all those external "details" of genius are prerequisites of the last: opportunity. The word "opportunity" derives from the Latin *opportuna*, a favorable wind blowing toward port. The word "fortunate" descends from the Latin *fortuna*, meaning "fate" or "luck." When that lucky wind blows, it will be of greatest fortune only to those fully prepared to sail with it. Genius, greatness, and success arrive in port the same way.

A similar sentiment is conveyed more succinctly in words often attributed to the legendary golfer Gary Player: "The harder I practice, the luckier I get."[2] Who can deny that better outcomes come to the "lucky" ones who work hard, act courageously, or make bold moves? Those moves may be the result of an intelligent decision or an actual physical uprooting. Some lucky breaks attend the genius at the moment of birth; others, strangely, arrive after death. But we start at the beginning, with the lottery of birth.

For a genius, being born rich is not the same thing as being born lucky. Geniuses almost never emerge from conditions of extreme wealth. Charles Darwin, who was wholly supported as a young adult and ultimately inherited a minor fortune, may be the exception who proves the rule. Similarly, geniuses tend not to arise from the aristocracy or the political ruling class. While the genius is hell-bent on changing the world, the aristocrat most often luxuriates in the status quo. Why change anything? In truth, geniuses do not spring from either of the economic extremes of society—with extreme poverty, there is little opportunity; with great wealth, no incentive. Consider these geniuses and the professions of their fathers: Shakespeare (glove maker), Newton and Lincoln (farmers), Franklin (candle maker), Bach (town trumpeter), the Brontë sisters (village parson), Faraday (blacksmith), Edison (tavern keeper), Curie (schoolteacher), King (preacher), Morrison (welder), and Bezos (bike shop owner). With geniuses, to be born lucky is generally to be born in the middle class.

Luck, both good and bad, sometimes attends the genius postmortem, as time and events change the perception of him or her in the eyes of society. In his day, William Shakespeare was a highly successful playwright who captured the imagination of London spectators, but his audience was small. Gradually, during the eighteenth century, as English commercial influence grew, the Bard's plays were translated into French, German, and Spanish. Today his impact continues to expand, even across Asia, as English becomes the default language of the world.[3] The importance of Shakespeare, now viewed as the greatest dramatist who ever lived and a moral compass for all humanity, is partly a consequence of this latter-day linguistic expansion. In Shakespeare's time only about .8 percent of the world's population could speak English; today about 20 percent can. Shakespeare was lucky: a rising tide lifted his posthumous boat.

In the early morning of August 22, 1911, a maintenance worker, Vincenzo Peruggia, stole the *Mona Lisa* from the Louvre. The story of the heist and a photo of the painting appeared on the front page of major newspapers around the world, and an international art hunt began. "60 Detectives Seek Stolen 'Mona Lisa,'" blared the *New York Times*.[4] Even Picasso got swept up in the dragnet because antique busts stolen from the Louvre could be traced to his apartment. For a while, Peruggia hid the *Mona Lisa* under his bed. Two years later, he tried to sell it to agents of the Uffizi Gallery in Florence—not genius, for by now the entire Western world had seen the painting. The police were alerted, Peruggia was arrested, and the painting was returned to Paris. Again more photos and stories appeared in the papers. During its first two days back on display in the Louvre, more than 120,000 viewers came to have a look.[5]

The *Mona Lisa* is the one painting that almost everyone in the world can identify, but why? In part, its fame is due to the lasting impact of the art theft; it would be the most sensational news story in the West until the sinking of the *Titanic* on April 14, 1912.[6] In a broadcast commemorating the centenary of the heist, National Public Radio described this as "The Theft That Made the 'Mona Lisa' a Masterpiece." Hyperbole, perhaps, but statistical evidence supports the claim. Using collection data in the Yale University Library, I calculated the number of books and articles listed on the subject of either "Michelangelo" or "Leonardo da Vinci" prior to 1911. They skew 68 percent to 32 percent in favor of the former. But in the entries after 1911, the ratio is about fifty-fifty. Consulting standard reference works on the two artists and the number of words assigned to each, with 1911 again the tipping point, the ratios go from seven to five for Michelangelo to two to one in favor of Leonardo. If public interest be any sort of benchmark of genius, the caper of a museum worker serendipitously enhanced Leonardo's standing.

DNA HAS BEEN CALLED "THE BUILDING BLOCK OF LIFE."[7] EMBEDded in the nucleus of each cell of the human body, DNA contains hereditary traits in the form of genes, the tiniest of encryptions that drive the growth and development in each living organism. By the early 1950s, the existence of DNA had been known for nearly a century, but scientists did not yet know how DNA was structured, or, more important, how each molecule in the body was able to replicate itself and thereby build out a complete living creature. Therein lay the key to unlocking the genetic code. That key was handed to humanity on April 25, 1953, in the form of a brief scientific paper published in *Nature* titled "A Structure for Deoxyribose Nucleic Acid," the result of research by Francis Crick and James Watson, two young scientists working at the Cavendish Laboratory in Cambridge, England.[8] Who should get first billing for what was arguably the single most important scientific announcement in modern times? They flipped a coin, and precedence went to Watson.

Watson and Crick were not the only ones looking to explain life's hidden processes. In 1944, Oswald Avery had shown that DNA was the "transforming principle," the carrier of hereditary information. Coterminous with Watson and Crick, Maurice Wilkins and Rosalind Franklin were working on X-ray crystallography to generate images of a single DNA molecule. In addition, the famed chemist Linus Pauling had produced an (incorrect, as it proved) three-dimensional, three-strand model of DNA.[9] Drawing on the work of others and their own intuition, Watson and Crick had put the pieces together and built a molecular model, described in their paper, that accurately represented DNA's structure: the famed interlocking double helix. The critical piece of information contributing to Watson and Crick's insight was Rosalind Franklin's X-ray "Photograph 51" showing DNA's double-helix design. From the discovery of the structure of DNA emerged, among other things, the sequencing of the human genome, the use of genetic identification in criminal cases, and recombinant DNA research with its gene editing and therapy, all now driving a multibillion-dollar biotechnology industry. In 1962, the Nobel Committee awarded the Nobel Prize in Physiology or Medicine to Francis Crick, James Watson, and Maurice Wilkins. But what had happened to Rosalind Franklin? The answer: bad luck.

Franklin's important X-ray photographs had been stolen from her. Without permission, Franklin's supervisors had shown the images to Watson and Crick in February 1953. From the pictures the duo saw that DNA was helical in structure, its dimensions, and how many base pairs per turn it possessed.[10] Franklin had earned an undergraduate degree and a Ph.D. in chemistry from Cambridge University, perhaps the top scientific university in the world. After moving to London in 1951, she had occupied a post-doctorate research post at prestigious King's College. Franklin was highly educated, had standing in her field, and was ambitious—all prerequisites for genius. But an obstacle worked against her in that era: she was a woman. Here follows a passage regarding Franklin and her nominal supervisor, Maurice Wilkins, written by Watson.

> Maurice, a beginner in X-ray diffraction work, wanted some professional help and hoped that Rosy, a trained crystallographer, could speed up his research. Rosy, how-ever, did not see the situation this way. She claimed that she had been given DNA for her own problem and would not think of herself as Maurice's assistant.
>
> I suspect that in the beginning Maurice hoped that Rosy would calm down. Yet mere inspection suggested that she would not easily bend. By choice she did not emphasize her feminine qualities. Though her features were strong, she was not unattractive and might have been quite stunning had she taken even a mild interest in clothes. This she did

not. There was never lipstick to contrast with her straight
black hair, while at the age of thirty-one her dresses showed
all the imagination of English blue-stocking adolescents. . . .
Clearly Rosy had to go or be put in her place.[11]

Franklin refused to project feminine charms and boldly demonstrated that a woman might be a leader in the cutting-edge science of DNA. But "Rosy" wouldn't play nice with the boys, and
in the end, the boys penalized her. She was denied full honors
for what she had found—denied not merely by her male counterparts but by a fatal posthumous rule that affects only the unlucky.
The Statutes of the Nobel Foundation contain one or two
seemingly arbitrary provisions. Section 4, paragraph 1:

A prize amount may be equally divided between two
works, each of which is considered to merit a prize. If a
work that is being rewarded has been produced by two or
three persons, the prize shall be awarded to them jointly.
In no case may a prize amount be divided between more
than three persons.[12]

By no later than 1961, the Nobel Committee had recognized
the enormous implications of DNA and its double-helix structure. But to whom should the fame and glory go? Certainly to the
principal researchers Watson and Crick; possibly to Linus Pauling
for having gotten close; possibly to Maurice Wilkins as Franklin's
ersatz supervisor; or possibly, based on merit, to Franklin herself. But now read Section 4, Paragraph 2: "Work produced by
a person since deceased shall not be considered for an award.
If, however, a prizewinner dies before he has received the prize,
then the prize may be presented." Four years after her influential
work on DNA, yet four years before a Nobel Prize was awarded
in the field, Rosalind Franklin died at the age of thirty-seven of
ovarian cancer. Fame and glory denied.
To gain a better understanding of the fateful story of the dis-

covery of DNA's structure, I sat down to lunch in March 2017 with Scott Strobel, Henry Ford II Professor of Molecular Biophysics and Biochemistry at Yale and currently Yale's provost. Strobel began by pointing out to me that Watson and Crick had been lucky and Linus Pauling unlucky. Had Pauling seen Franklin's photos, the discovery might have been his. But traveling through London early in 1953 with the express aim of seeing Franklin's images, Pauling was denied a visa that would have allowed him to leave Heathrow Airport to meet her. Strobel also emphasized that the discovery of the double helix had been a team effort. As he explained it to me, "Observational science is becoming more and more complex, and no one person can control all of any one field. Increasingly, scientific discoveries are the product of communal labs. The unintended consequence is that the solitary genius is relegated to the endangered species list." As for the possibility of a future Nobel Prize being awarded for the discovery of clustered regularly interspaced short palindromic repeats (CRISPR), the exciting new field in genetic science, Strobel noted the irony: "One leading candidate is my former collaborator Jennifer Doudna at Berkeley. The problem is that there are so many candidates for the Nobel for CRISPR—at Berkeley and MIT and elsewhere—that the Nobel Committee may have trouble winnowing down to three winners. The prize for CRISPR may be delayed."[13] (On October 7, 2020, the day after the first printing of this book, Jennifer Doudna was announced as a winner of a Nobel Prize in chemistry.)

PERHAPS WE ALL MIGHT JUST AS WELL BECOME FATALISTS, SUBSCRIBing to the notion that our destiny rests posthumously in the hands of Lady Luck. The point of this chapter, however, is to suggest exactly the opposite: that although serendipity may play a role, the genius habitually makes conscious decisions that lead to significantly better outcomes.

Queen Elizabeth I was lucky in 1588 when a freak hurricane

wrecked the Spanish Armada before it could reach English shores; but for the previous thirty years her foreign policy had been one of nonengagement so as to allow the enemy to self-destruct. Wilhelm Röntgen was lucky in 1895 when he happened to leave photographic plates in his lab while experimenting with a cathode ray tube and later saw streaks of light imprinted on the plates. But as a physicist studying high-energy waves, he immediately understood what others would have missed—why the rays had been able to penetrate some objects and leave an impression of others: the phenomenon of the X-ray. Percy Spencer got lucky in 1945 when a candy bar melted in his pocket as he stood next to a magnetron. But being a trained electrical engineer, he understood the thermal power of microwaves within a metal box, soon experimented with popcorn, and then went on to patent the microwave oven. Louis Pasteur got lucky in 1879 when he accidentally left a culture being used to eradicate chicken cholera unattended for a month and then discovered, and subsequently exploited, the fact that only the "spoiled" batch proved to work as a vaccine. But as an experienced microbiologist, Pasteur had learned long before the lesson he had articulated when addressing a medical conference in Douai, France, in 1854: "In the observational sciences, luck (*le hazard*) favors only the prepared mind."[14]

FIRST CHICKENS, THEN HUMANS: ALEXANDER FLEMING'S DISCOVERY of penicillin is said to be the most famous example of "accidental genius" in medical history. But was it wholly an accident? Fleming was born the son of a farmer in rural Scotland in 1881, and at the age of thirteen he moved to London, where he eventually earned a medical degree. In 1921, he discovered the antiseptic enzyme lysozyme (from which we get the product Lysolac) and then went on to experiment with the process by which one bacterium might destroy another. Fleming had a habit of keeping a messy lab, and before leaving for a month's vacation in August 1928, he stacked, but did not clean, a set of bacteria-laden petri dishes. Upon returning, he found bacteria growing robustly in all the dishes except one. The one with little surviving bacteria, it turned out, was inhabited by a mold called *Penicillium notatum,* spores of which had blown in by accident from a neighboring lab and landed in the dish.

A colleague of mine at Yale, chemistry professor Michael McBride, once said to me, "Scientists don't have 'eureka' flashes. Rather, they experience 'My, that's strange' moments." Upon seeing the strange condition of the one petri dish, Fleming muttered, "That's funny"[15] and asked himself what was killing the bacteria, before quickly determining that it was the errant penicillin mold. He then began to speculate on the therapeutic powers of the mold, and from that lucky break emerged the miracle drug penicillin. Scientists consistently rank the discovery of penicillin among the top three medical advances in history, along with Pasteur's recognition of germs (pathogens) and Watson and Crick's discovery of the structure of DNA. With the arrival of penicillin—the first antibiotic—Western medicine entered the modern age, and countless millions of lives were saved. If genius manifests as world-changing insight, such an insight was born serendipitously in Alexander Fleming's lab. That, at least, is the story.

But the history of Alexander Fleming's fortuitous discovery of penicillin involves far more than serendipity. Winston Churchill once said of his role in World War II, "I felt as if I were walking with Destiny, and that all my past life had been but a preparation for this hour and for this trial."[16] Fleming, too, was well prepared. Unknown to him at the time, he had been training for his "lucky break" during nearly thirty years of professional activity. He had developed the observational skill and scientific knowledge to apprehend and exploit the import of what was before him. The medical historian John Waller summed it up succinctly when he said, "Fleming had the genius to see what others would have ignored."[17]

Fleming's preparation and previous breakthrough with lysozyme also gave him standing within the scientific community, meaning that others would pay attention to him. In truth, someone had already discovered the therapeutic powers of penicillin, but no one had noticed. In 1897, Ernest Duchesne (1874–1912), a student at a military university in Lyon, France, sent a thesis to the Pasteur Institute in Paris describing much of what Fleming would later discover.[18] But the twenty-three-year-old Duchesne was unlucky. He was not favored with so much as even an acknowledgment, subsequently entered the army, and died young of tuberculosis (which an antibiotic might have cured). Thirty years later, Fleming's well-earned status as a world-class bacteriologist with connections within the scientific community caused people to listen to him. Duchesne hit a hidden target—but he had no standing, so no one noticed and nothing changed.

Finally, Alexander Fleming himself did not bring the wonder drug penicillin to market; that occurred over the course of more than a decade at Oxford University and involved a team of bacteriologists led by Howard Florey. But Fleming was ambitious enough to maintain a proprietary interest in what he called "my old penicillin."[19] With the war effort in Europe ongoing, and Great Britain in need of a "magic bullet" to benefit troops and boost morale, Fleming eagerly became a poster boy for the new drug. When the Nobel Committee of medical scientists gave its award in Physiology or Medicine in 1945, it went to three people: Alexander Fleming, Howard Florey, and fellow Oxford University team member Ernst Chain.

So why do we remember only Fleming? Because the tale of a "lucky find" makes for a captivating, albeit overly simplified, story. Obviously more than luck was involved. Fleming was well prepared, he worked to maintain his image as the "great man" behind a great cause, and a conscious team effort brought his initial hopes to fruition. Thus to Louis Pasteur's boyish aphorism "Be prepared" can be added two others relevant to greatness: "Step forward" and "Don't lose what you find."

———

"FORTUNE FAVORS THE BOLD" IS A SAYING THAT IS AS OLD AS AN-
cient Rome, being ascribed variously to Pliny the Elder, Terence,
and Virgil. To be bold means to be willing to take a chance. But
what does it mean to take a chance? Does it mean that one is
willing to make a move when the outcome, although uncertain,
can be quantified—as in a fifty-fifty chance? Or does it mean simply to trust to pure serendipity—as in "That was pure chance"?
Mark Zuckerberg, the founder of Facebook, has shown himself
daunted neither by calculated risk nor by serendipity.

If genius can be measured by impact on society, then Zuckerberg can scarcely be denied the label. Granted, Zuckerberg has
recently run afoul of privacy experts, the Federal Trade Com-
mission, and the attorneys general of forty-seven U.S. states (see
also chapter 12). Nonetheless, today almost 2 billion people
spend nearly an hour each day engaged with his creation: Facebook.[20] In 2010, *Time* named Zuckerberg Person of the Year; at
age twenty-six he was at the time the second youngest person
to be so honored. Preparation—he was a computer programing
prodigy—and limitless ambition mark Zuckerberg. The risky
moves he undertook before the age of twenty-one show the extent of his capacity for bold, if sometimes illicit, initiatives.

RISKY MOVE NO. 1: HACK INTO THE HARVARD UNIVERSITY COMPUTER SYSTEM AND "BORROW" STUDENT DATA FROM FACE BOOKS.

(The name "Facebook" is derived from Harvard "face books"—
catalogues of photos of and information about each student organized by "houses," the elegant dorms in which students reside.)

On the evening of October 28, 2003, Mark Zuckerberg sat
down at his desk in Suite H33 of Kirkland House for a long night
of programming. Earlier that semester, he had created Course-
Match, which enabled Harvard students to know which courses
their friends were taking and perhaps form study groups. But
now Zuckerberg was onto something far more daring: an online

"hookup" site that would enable Harvard students to see other students and determine whether they were "hot or not." At first he even considered posting photos of students next to farm animals to invite comparisons, but then thought better of it.

To build the program, theft—or at least an unauthorized taking—was involved. Zuckerberg gained access to Harvard servers and downloaded student images and data from the house face books. To quote Ben Mezrich in *The Accidental Billionaires: The Founding of Facebook: A Tale of Sex, Money, Genius, and Betrayal,* "Sure, in a sense it was stealing—he didn't have the legal rights to those pictures, and the university certainly didn't put them up there for someone to download them. But then, if information was getable, didn't Mark have the right to get it?"[21] In the early morning hours of the twenty-ninth, Zuckerberg launched what he then called Facemash.

The impact was immediate. So many students joined Facemash that the Harvard servers began to slow down. Women's groups protested. The university demanded that Zuckerberg shut the site immediately and that he appear before the Harvard College Administrative Board, Harvard's venerable disciplinary committee. He did both. In the end, Zuckerberg was reprimanded only for hacking Harvard's computers and stealing student data.[22]

RISKY MOVE NO. 2: DOUBLE-CROSS YOUR HARVARD COMPETITORS.

The Facemash fiasco made the five-foot, seven-inch Mark Zuckerberg a big man on campus, and that development caught the attention of two bigger men, a pair of six-foot, five-inch identical twins named Tyler and Cameron Winklevoss. They were well known at Harvard for their prowess as two-man scullers, and they would go on to make the 2008 U.S. Olympic Rowing Team. But in November 2003, the Winklevoss twins had something else on their minds, plans for a new social networking site that would expand around the country: Harvard Connection. To do the last bit of programming, the twins verbally engaged Mark Zuckerberg, who agreed to work on the needed computer code and graphics. The twins and Zuckerberg met and exchanged fifty-two emails.[23] He looked at their code and gave them the impression that he would help them. But on February 4, 2004, he launched his own competing site: Thefacebook.com. Six days later Zuckerberg was again before the Harvard College Administrative Board, this time accused by the Winklevoss boys of violating the student honor code by stealing their idea. The Winklevosses' lawyers also served Zuckerberg with a cease-and-desist order, essentially charging him with theft of intellectual property. Seven months later, the duo sued Zuckerberg. They settled out of court in 2008 with the twins reportedly awarded 1.2 million shares (worth $65 million) of what was by then called "Facebook" stock.[24] Their lawyers urged them to cash out, but the twins boldly held on to the Facebook stock and eventually became billionaires themselves. They have subsequently entered a more risky venture, moving into the blockchain economy, where, as the company Gemini (Latin for twins), they intend to make Bitcoin the virtual currency of the world. As for Zuckerberg, he held on to what he founded, instituting a corporate governance structure at Facebook that ensures he can't be ousted no matter what goes wrong at the company.[25]

RISKY MOVE NO. 3: LEAVE COLLEGE AFTER YOUR SOPHOMORE YEAR.

Zuckerberg did just that. Imagine how the news must have been received by his parents: "Mom and Dad, I'm dropping out of Harvard to form my own company." But a precedent for such a bold move existed. In the fall of 2003, Zuckerberg had attended a computer science lecture by Bill Gates at which Gates had said that "the great thing about Harvard is that you can always come back and finish."[26] Both moved away and never went back, except to receive subsequent honorary degrees from the school. Their gutsy moves had paid off.

RISKY MOVE NO. 4: AT AGE TWENTY, MOVE TO CALIFORNIA ON YOUR OWN.

Having left college, Mark Zuckerberg now doubled down on his bet and left his family's comfortable home outside New York City to move to Palo Alto, California, the epicenter of Silicon Valley. It was another courageous move but perhaps a logical one, owing to the area's reputation as a mecca for computer engineers and venture capitalists. As Zuckerberg later reflected, "There's a feeling in Silicon Valley that you have to be there, because that's where all the engineers are."[27] The bold moves made by the titans of tech—Larry Ellison, Musk, Brin, Bezos, Gates, and Zuckerberg—all required a change of venue for their perpetrators.

SHAKESPEARE ONCE SAID, "FORTUNE BRINGS IN SOME BOATS THAT are not steer'd" (*Cymbeline*). However, it brings in no boats that are so securely anchored that they don't move. A hidden habit of geniuses? They all move to a metropolis or to a university to further their goals.

Think of the geniuses in this chapter and their opportunistic moves: Shakespeare, Franklin, and Fleming to London; Watson and Crick to Cambridge University; Pasteur to Lille and then Paris; Zuckerberg to Silicon Valley. Each as a young adult moved to a metropolitan region or to a university, or to a university within a metropolis. "I don't believe in luck," said Oprah Winfrey in 2011. "Luck is preparation meeting the moment of opportunity."[28] True, but first you have to get to the meeting. Winfrey moved to Chicago.

Think of the geniuses mentioned in this book and the cities where they did their great work. Athens: Socrates and Plato were born there, but Aristotle moved there at age seventeen. London: Faraday was born there, but Shakespeare, Dickens, and Woolf were newcomers. Vienna: Schubert and Schoenberg were natives, but Haydn, Mozart, Beethoven, Brahms, and Mahler were immigrants, as was Freud. Alexander Hamilton emigrated to New York and distantly inspired the extraordinary *Hamilton,* a work by Lin-Manuel Miranda, the son of another immigrant. And what would the world of postmodern art be without the New York arrivistes Kusama, Pollock, Robert Motherwell, Mark Rothko, and Warhol? As Kusama said about her move from rural conservative Japan to New York City in 1953, "I had to get out."[29]

As to the university: Newton had his Cambridge and Einstein his Max Planck Institute in Berlin before his last days at the Institute for Advanced Study in Princeton. Tech gurus Musk, Brin, Larry Page, and Peter Thiel spent varying amounts of time at Stanford. Geniuses don't stay home; they move to where circumstances are more favorable.

Let's call this automotive imperative the "Genius Anti-inertia Law." There are, of course, exceptions to the law, such as the Wright brothers, who stayed close to small-town Dayton, Ohio. The botanists Gregor Mendel and George Washington Carver needed access to open fields. Naturalists, such as Darwin, and *plein air* painters, such as Claude Monet and Georgia O'Keeffe, are, owing to professional necessity, also exempt from the law. But as a rule, geniuses don't stay down on the farm. Even the painter of *The Starry Night,* Vincent van Gogh, said as a young man, "I don't think that you can reasonably ask me to go back to the country for the sake of perhaps 50 francs a month less, when the whole stretch of years ahead is so closely related to the associations I have to establish in town, either here in Antwerp or later in Paris."[30] In 1886, van Gogh moved to Paris.

So, too, around that time or shortly thereafter, did Picasso, Matisse, Modigliani, Marc Chagall, Braque, Constantin Brancusi, Joan Miró, and Diego Rivera among painters; Claude Debussy, Stravinsky, and Aaron Copland among composers; Ezra

Pound, Guillaume Apollinaire, Joyce, Stein, Hemingway, and Fitzgerald among poets and writers. "If I had not gone to Paris, I would not be who I am," said Chagall. "We always returned to Paris, no matter who we were," said Hemingway.[31]

What is it that pulls a genius to a metropolis such as Belle Époque Paris, mid-twentieth-century New York, or the megalopolis of Silicon Valley? Creative cities have historically been situated at crossroads where diverse peoples—often recent immigrants—with dissimilar ideas gather.[32] The newcomers sow fresh ideas within the existing intellectual climate, and thus are born new ways of thinking. Silicon Valley draws the best tech minds from around the world by an aggressive use of the H-1B visa, known as "the genius visa" because it allows for the immigration of highly skilled foreign workers. "Nearly all the great advances in civilization . . . have been during periods of the utmost internationalism," said the historian Kenneth Clark.[33] Do we still feel the same about that southwest border wall in the United States?

Finally, to cross-pollinate, diverse ideas must flow with little governmental censure. "Genius can only breathe freely in an atmosphere of freedom," said John Stuart Mill.[34] And it must be encouraged. Silicon Valley investors provide more venture capital than any other place in the world, their largesse in 2018 ($10.5 billion) being more than three times that of their nearest competitor (Boston with $3 billion).[35] Financial support, access to new ideas, freedom of expression, competition, the chance to test oneself against the very best—these are all gravitational forces.

How big must the city be? Big enough to attain a critical mass. A composer needs theaters, performers, producers, audiences, and critics. A painter needs not only fellow artists for support but also agents, galleries, festivals, exhibition spaces, and patrons. A tech engineer needs other tech engineers, equipment, and research money. They all need competitors, and they all need jobs. Agglomeration of opportunity is what compels geniuses to move.

And like geniuses, these creative epicenters are always moving. Historically, they have progressed from east to west, from China to the Near East to Europe and the United Kingdom to the U.S. East Coast and then the West Coast. Where will the next Silicon Valley arise? Will genius go full circle back to Asia? Has it already emerged in Singapore? Where will the next center of innovation be, now that Paris is overrun with tourists and rents in New York City are astronomical? Follow the restless genius for the answer. Better still, figure out which way the favorable wind is blowing, pack a bag, and get there first.

CHAPTER 12

MOVE FAST AND BREAK THINGS

A man must be a very great genius to make up for being such a loathsome human being." With those words, the honored war correspondent Martha Gellhorn summed up her husband, Ernest Hemingway, shortly before their divorce in 1945.[1] Hemingway won the Nobel Prize in Literature in 1954. He was also a bully, a brawler, an adulterer, and an alcoholic who ultimately destroyed himself. We have a habit of wanting our geniuses to be superheroes, the highest form of the human species. "It is right," Albert Einstein said in 1934, "that those should be the best loved who have contributed most to the elevation of the human race and human life."[2] Yet geniuses habitually disappoint us, at least on a personal level.

The fault is ours. We forget that the standard for genius is based on accomplishment, not character. We fail to see that accomplishment and morality may operate independently. Judged by character, geniuses seem no better than the common herd. In fact, they often seem worse, obsessed with their personal quest to change the world. Time is on their side, however, for its passage obscures the personal destruction they have caused as it illuminates the societal good they have done. We tend to forget that the money behind Alfred Nobel's prizes was made largely from dynamite, bombs, and artillery shells; and that Cecil Rhodes, who established the Rhodes Scholarship at Oxford University, built his fortune on forced African labor in what was then Rhodesia. As our memory dims, negative associations fade and twisted personal habits get straightened out. As the writer Edmond de Goncourt said in 1864, "No one loves the genius until he is dead."[3]

Are there any geniuses who are/were exemplary human beings? Seen in the rearview mirror of history, Leonardo da Vinci, Marie Curie, and Charles Darwin appear to have been honorable people. Alexander Fleming and Jonas Salk worked for the common good. But how much can we really know about anyone's true moral compass or motivations? Some of today's geniuses, real or aspiring, profess to have altruistic aims. Oprah Winfrey has said, "I love giving people opportunities where there might not have been one. Because somebody did that for me."[4] We have no reason to doubt her sincerity. Elon Musk professes his goal to be nothing less than the salvation of the human race: "I want to contribute as much as possible to humanity becoming a multi-planet species," thereby alluding to his goal of putting people on Mars as planet earth becomes impossible for human habitation.[5] However, by all reports, closer to home Musk runs roughshod over family, friends, and employees, coming across as rude and intolerant.[6] Mark Zuckerberg has said more than once that "Facebook is about connecting and sharing—connecting with your friends, family, and communities, and sharing information with them."[7] But while we have all been connecting and sharing on Facebook, Zuckerberg has been selling our data for profit and, by many accounts, undermining democracies around the world.

Some geniuses are moral and, knowingly or unknowingly (according to the law of unintended consequences), destroy things. Some are immoral or amoral and destroy things. Some destroy institutions as part of the inevitable process of change; others destroy people as a means of generating psychic energy to feed their obsessions. Destroying things doesn't make a person a genius, but all creative geniuses make a habit of doing it.

In 1995, the Chinese artist Ai Weiwei lifted a million-dollar Han Dynasty vase over his head and smashed it to the ground. Art lovers around the world were horrified, but Ai wanted to send a message: to create new art requires that old customs, habits, and cultures be destroyed. In 1942, the Harvard economist Joseph Schumpeter formulated the concept of "creative destruction" to suggest that no new technology or industry can take hold without the destruction of a preexisting one.[8] Alan Greenspan, a former head of the U.S. Federal Reserve, expressed the symbiotic relationship this way: "Destruction is more than just an unfortunate side effect of creation. It is part and parcel of the same thing."[9] Among the "unfortunate" victims of recent creative destruction have been bank tellers, grocery clerks, travel agents, librarians, journalists, taxi drivers, and assembly-line workers, to name just a few displaced by the digital revolution. As Ai dramatically suggested, destruction is the price we pay for progress.

STEVE JOBS WAS A TECH-SAVVY VISIONARY WHO PUT SECRETARIES, telephone operators, camera manufacturers, and record companies out of business. His aim was to make our lives better, and surely he intuited that his revolutionary Apple personal computer and iPhone would create more jobs than they eliminated. In 2011, *Forbes* published an article titled "Steve Jobs: Create. Disrupt. Destroy," saying in it, "No person has done more to disrupt the existing way of doing things than Mr. Jobs."[10] But was any person more obnoxious? Only in Walter Isaacson's *Steve Jobs* do you find a biography of a genius with the following index entry: "Offensive behavior of."

That Steve Jobs was "an arrogant asshole" was known to all, even himself. "It's just the way I am," he said. In a 2008 article in the *New York Times,* business writer Joe Nocera recalled a telephone call he had received from Jobs: "This is Steve Jobs. You think I'm an arrogant [expletive] who thinks he's above the law, and I think you're a slime bucket who gets most of his facts wrong."[11] By Jobs's standards, he was being gracious. More typical was his greeting to his own Apple employees, as recounted by product manager Debi Coleman. "'You asshole, you never do anything right.' It was," she said, "like an hourly occurrence."[12] In 1981, a phone call with Xerox computer engineer Bob Belleville went this way, Jobs saying "Everything you've done in your life is shit, so why don't you come work for me?"[13] As Isaacson wrote, "Jobs's prickly behavior was partly driven by his perfectionism and his impatience with those who made compromises in order to get a product out on time and on budget."[14]

But the other driver of Jobs's destructive behavior was a habit of simply being hurtful, with no product gain in sight—to put people down and show he was smarter, simply for the sadistic pleasure it gave him. Stories abound about the way Jobs needlessly humiliated those he encountered, be they waiters or CEOs.[15] Members of his immediate family were not exempt from abusive treatment. Although a multimillionaire, he refused to acknowledge his daughter, Lisa Brennan-Jobs, denying his paternity until he was taken to court. In her book *Small Fry: A Memoir* (2018), Brennan-Jobs described how her father, Steve, would frequently use money as a way to confuse or frighten her. "Sometimes he decided not to pay for things at the very last minute," she wrote, "walking out of restaurants without paying the bill."[16] Out to dinner one night, Mr. Jobs turned to his daughter's cousin, Sarah, who had unknowingly offended the vegetarian Jobs by ordering meat. "Have you ever thought about how awful your voice is?" Jobs asked Sarah. "Please stop talking in that awful voice. You should really consider what's wrong with yourself and try to fix it." Lisa's mother, Chrisann Brennan, recalled, "He was an enlightened being who was cruel. That's a strange combination."[17] Why the cruelty?

Steve Jobs believed that the golden rule of human behavior did not apply to him. He felt he was special, a chosen one, "an enlightened being," and "above the law." He refused to put a license plate on his car and parked it in the company handicapped spot. Said software engineer Andy Hertzfeld, who worked with Jobs on the original Macintosh team, "He thinks there are a few people who are special—like Einstein and Gandhi, and the gurus he met in India, and he's one of them."[18] Sometimes Jobs knew that the moment was right to destroy his own product (the iPod, for example) by introducing a more revolutionary and potentially lucrative one (the iPhone). Sometimes his obsessive passion—having "a bug up my rear," he indecorously called it[19]—changed the world of technology, and sometimes it merely caused gratuitous personal damage. Sometimes Jobs was a genius, and sometimes he was just a jerk.

THOMAS EDISON WAS JUST CLUELESS. HE DIDN'T MEAN TO BE PERsonally destructive; he simply lacked empathy. In a poll taken in 1922, nine years before his death, 750,000 Americans identified Edison as the "greatest man in history."[20] After all, he had invented a long-burning incandescent light bulb, which had put an end to night. Granted, the light bulb had put candle makers out of business and sunk the whaling industry. But when it came to empathy for other creatures, Edison was in the dark. His approach to family and to people in general can be gleaned from his proposal of marriage to his first wife, Mary Stilwell, a sixteen-year-old employee in his Newark, New Jersey, lab, as reported in *The Christian Herald and Signs of the Times* a few years later.

"What do you think of me, little girl? Do you like me?"
"Why, Mr. Edison, you frighten me. I—that is—I—."
"Don't be in any hurry, about telling me. It doesn't matter much, unless you would like to marry me. . . . Oh, I mean it. Don't be in a rush, though. Think it over; talk to your mother about it, and let me know soon as is convenient—Tuesday say. How will Tuesday suit you, next week Tuesday, I mean?"[21]

Edison married Stilwell on Christmas Day 1871. That after-noon, he returned to his lab to work, and she became, according to biographer Neil Baldwin, "a fully fledged casualty of her hus-band's accumulated neglect."[22] In 1878, Edison's assistant Edward Johnson told a reporter from the *Chicago Tribune,* "He does not go home for days, either to eat or sleep." Later Johnson remem-bered that Edison had once warned him, "We must look out for crosses [i.e., short-circuited wires] for if we ever kill a customer it would be very bad for business."[23] To appreciate the full extent to which the obsessive Edison might go in pursuit of an idea, however, we need only revisit the history of the "War of the Cur-rents" and the execution of Topsy the elephant.

To be brief: In 1885, Thomas Edison was at war with his archrival Nikola Tesla over which current, Edison's direct (DC) or Tesla's alternating (AC), would light the United States. To dis-credit his rival's system, Edison began a public campaign to dis-parage Tesla and prove AC to be deadly. Edison began electrical experiments using AC on dogs, paying boys a 25-cent bounty for each stray they could round up; in 1890, he facilitated, at the behest of the New York State penal system, the electrocution of a human. And if AC could kill a man, why not go big and kill an el-ephant? Thus on January 3, 1903, a female circus elephant named Topsy was electrocuted on Coney Island, a public spectacle at a public amusement park. Edison stipulated how the electrodes should be placed on the feet of the unsuspecting pachyderm. To make sure the destructive force of AC was evident to all, he sent a film crew employing his new motion picture camera to record the event.[24] His short film survives today and is available on You-Tube. Often the warning "viewer discretion advised" is a tease to drum up more viewers. Here it is not.

THE DESTRUCTIVE TENDENCIES OF OTHERWISE BRILLIANT INDIVID-uals have been evident for a long time. In 1711, Sir Isaac Newton tried to destroy the reputation of Gottfried Leibniz in a squabble over who had invented calculus; Newton, as president of the Royal Academy [of Science], empaneled a court to judge the case, but then he himself rendered the verdict and wrote the opinion, one disparaging the reputation of Leibniz.[25] Newton also fudged evidence in his experiments,[26] stole data from colleagues, and failed to give credit where credit was due—all in the name of scientific advancement.[27] Perhaps the novelist Aldous Huxley exaggerated when he said ironically, "As a man [Newton] was a failure, as a monster he was superb."[28] His fellow physicist Stephen Hawking summed up Newton in just seven words: "Isaac Newton was not a pleasant man."[29]

Nor was physicist Albert Einstein, at least to his immediate kin. He fathered an illegitimate daughter but had no contact with her, and he put his second son away in a sanatorium in Switzerland, unvisited by him from 1933 until Einstein's death in 1955. As his first wife, Mileva Marić, said in December 1912, "He is tirelessly working on his problems; one can say that he lives only for them. I must confess with a bit of shame that we are unimportant to him and take second place."[30] Einstein himself acknowledged his self-centered nature when he spoke of "my pronounced lack of need for direct contact with other human beings and human communities. I am truly a 'lone traveler' and have never belonged to my country, my home, my friends, or even my immediate family, with my whole heart."[31]

WHY DO GENIUSES HAVE A HABIT OF RELEGATING OTHERS TO SECond place? Could it be simple egotism, the fact that the genius needs to be number one? "I don't care so much about making my fortune," Thomas Edison said in 1878, "as I do for getting ahead of the other fellows."[32] Or is it simply obsession? The Nobel Prize—winning writer Pearl S. Buck called creativity an "overpowering necessity." Although she used "he" and "his" in what follows, she presumably meant all geniuses: "[It is] the overpowering necessity to create, create, and create—so that without the creating of music or poetry or books or buildings or something of meaning, his very being is cut off from him. He must create, must pour out creation. By some strange, unknown, inward urgency he is not really alive unless he is creating."[33] Beethoven said, "I live entirely in my scores and hardly have I completed one composition when I have already begun another."[34] Picasso expressed the same sentiment, albeit in different words: "Worst of it is that he [the artist] is never finished. There's never a moment when you can say, 'I've worked well and tomorrow is Sunday.'" Thomas Edison said, "Restlessness is discontent, and discontent is the first necessity of progress. Show me a thoroughly satisfied man, and I will show you a failure."[35]

These are all sentiments honestly expressed. Indeed, how many of us use the excuse of "our work" as a way of avoiding familial and/or societal responsibility? A nightly dilemma of many busy professional parents: go back to work, or do homework with the child? Might obsessive geniuses teach us, in this case, by negative example?

But obsession has a positive flip side: productivity. Shakespeare wrote 37 plays, each running on average three hours, and 154 sonnets. Some critics have attributed Shakespeare's dramas to a team or a committee of writers, believing that no one person could have accomplished so much. Likely these are the same critics who have not heard about Leonardo's 100,000 drawings and 13,000 pages of notes, Bach's 300 cantatas composed at the rate of one a week, Mozart's 800 compositions (including several three-hour operas) written in thirty years, Edison's 1,093 patents, Picasso's 20,000 works of art, or Freud's 150 books and articles and 20,000 letters. Einstein is best known for his five papers of 1905, but he also published 248 others. Compulsive productivity is a habit of genius, not a reason to deny it.

Should Shakespeare have stayed home in Stratford-on-Avon to help rear his family and not have abandoned them for London, the city that made him? Perhaps, but, as William Faulkner said hurtfully to his daughter, Jill, when she pestered him to stop drinking, "Nobody remembers *Shakespeare's* children."[36] Should

Paul Gauguin have stayed with his wife and five children in Co-penhagen instead of sailing off permanently to Tahiti? Happy fam-ily but far fewer Polynesian masterpieces. In sum, does the genius deserve a free pass?

Biographers, of course, are all too willing to supply one—to excuse almost any sort of destructive behavior. A week after Mo-zart's death, on December 5, 1791, a Viennese newspaper wrote that "Mozhart [sic] unfortunately had that indifference to family circumstances which so often attaches to great minds."[37] But his sister, Nannerl, in a short biography in 1800, defended Mozart's memory, saying "It is certainly easy to understand that a great genius, who is preoccupied with the abundance of his own ideas, and who soars from earth to heaven with amazing speed, is ex-tremely reluctant to lower himself to noticing and dealing with mundane affairs."[38] And the reporter Lillian Ross, who often wrote about Robin Williams in The New Yorker, said this about the comedian in 2018: "Robin was a genius, and genius doesn't produce normal men next door who are good family men and look after their wives and children. Genius requires its own way of looking at and living in the world, and it isn't always compat-ible with conventional ways of living."[39]

Can we hate the artist but love the art? For decades the nation of Israel said "no," as it banned from its concert halls the transfor-mative music of the rabid anti-Semite Richard Wagner. In 2018, the curators of the National Gallery of Art in Washington, D.C., postponed an exhibition of the works of Chuck Close owing to allegations of sexual harassment of female models. The sales and streaming of Michael Jackson's music have declined since the damning documentary Leaving Neverland (2019) accused him of pedophilia.[40] In 2019, 20,000 students in the University of Cali-fornia system demanded that a popular course on the films of the possible child molester Woody Allen be canceled.[41] That same year, the National Gallery of London asked, "Is it time to stop looking at Gauguin altogether?," because the artist had "repeat-edly entered into sexual relations with young girls."[42]

Yet as Jock Reynolds, the director emeritus of the Yale University Art Gallery, has asked, "How much are we going to do [by way of] a litmus test on every artist in terms of how they behave?"[43] The painter Caravaggio, the genius who almost single-handedly created the dramatic chiaroscuro style of Baroque art, was accused of murder; and Egon Schiele, who was honored in 2018 with centennial exhibitions in New York, Paris, London, and Vienna, spent twenty-four days in jail on charges of statutory rape of a thirteen-year-old girl. That was more than a hundred years ago. Is there a statute of limitations regarding destructive behavior for artists? If not, what then do we do with arguably the greatest of all Western painters, the genius and monster Pablo Picasso?

IN 1965, THE CULTURAL CRITIC LIONEL TRILLING WROTE THAT great moments in art are measured by "how much damage they can do."[44] Pablo Picasso did a lot of damage to the women in his life. He was emotionally and physically abusive, terrorizing his wives, partners, and mistresses, and pitting them against one another. A list is useful for keeping them straight:

Fernande Olivier (1904–1911): A Picasso Cubist painting of her sold for $63.4 million in 2016

Olga Khokhlova (1917–1955): First wife until her death, mother of their son Paulo

Marie-Thérèse Walter (1927–1935): Mother of Maya; he painted Walter twice as often as any other woman

Dora Maar (1935–1943): Played an influential role in the creation of Picasso's painting *Guernica*

Françoise Gilot (1943–1953): Mother of Claude and Paloma, successful painter still living in New York

Geneviève Laporte (during the 1950s): First met Picasso when she was a high school student

Jacqueline Roque (1953–1973): Second wife until his death in 1973

Such a list might suggest that Picasso's women followed in sequence, but instead they came in clumps. When Picasso summered in Mougins in 1938, his new mistress, Dora, went along, but so, too, at a distance, did his wife, Olga, and Marie-Thérèse. When Picasso was resident in Paris in 1944 on Rue des Grands-Augustins, Olga, Dora, Marie-Thérèse, and Françoise came and went. In that residence, picked out by Dora, she and Marie-Thérèse once came to blows. "One of my choicest memories," recalled Picasso.[45]

If Picasso's women could not destroy one another by themselves, Picasso would assist. Among his favorite sayings: "For me, there are only two kinds of women—goddesses and doormats."[46] As to the physical abuse: Olga was struck down and dragged by her hair around the floor of the apartment on Rue La Boétie. Dora was knocked unconscious in the studio in Rue des Grands-Augustins. Françoise was attacked by three Mediterranean scorpions while Picasso laughed delightedly—the deadly Scorpio was his zodiac sign. Once in Golfe-Juan, France, he burned Gilot's face with a lighted cigarette. Burning seems to have appealed to Picasso. As he said to Gilot toward the end of their relationship in 1952, "Every time I change wives I should burn the last one. That way I'd be rid of them. They wouldn't be around now to complicate my existence. Maybe that would bring back my youth, too. You kill the woman and you wipe out the past she represents."[47]

Having terrorized the women in his life, the now-energized Picasso set about transferring the psychic electricity he had negatively generated to his art. "He first raped the woman . . . and then he worked. Whether it was me, or someone else, it was always like that," recounted Marie-Thérèse Walter.[48] Brush in hand, Picasso subjected the curvaceous body of Marie-Thérèse to his sexual

FIGURE 12.1: Pablo Picasso, *The Weeping Woman* (portrait of Dora Maar), 1937 (Tate Modern, London). "For me she is the weeping woman," Picasso said. "For years I've painted her in tortured forms."

fantasies; more than once he added to her forehead a large penis, presumably a facsimile of his own. The beautiful, talented Dora Maar began in Picasso's mind as a stylish fashion icon but became progressively *The Weeping Woman* (Figure 12.1), her features made increasingly angular and disjointed—from fashionable goddess to hysterical doormat. Marie-Thérèse, Dora, and Françoise each appears in a separate psychodrama involving the vulnerable woman and the Minotaur, she the sacrificial victim, he the frightful beast bent on rape (Figure 12.2). As Picasso surveyed one of these drawings, he mused, "He [the Minotaur] is studying her, trying to read her thoughts, trying to decide whether she loves him *because* he's a monster. Women are odd enough for that, you know. It's hard to say whether he wants to wake her or kill her."[49] At what point does the victim flee the Minotaur, flee even a genius?

More could be said about Picasso as Minotaur, but the point is made. He was a monster. And like every revolutionary, this monster could last only as long as the public allowed, as he himself realized. "They [the public] expect to be shocked and terrorized," he said. "If the monster only smiles, then they're disappointed."[50] Picasso didn't disappoint, but his artistic terror left collateral damage.

To Picasso, it didn't matter. "Nobody has any real importance for me," he told Françoise Gilot. "As far as I'm concerned, other people are like those little grains of dust floating in the sunlight. It takes only a push of the broom and out they go."[51] Out went his half-crazed first wife, Olga, who stalked Picasso wherever he went until she died in 1954; Marie-Thérèse, who hanged

FIGURE 12.2: Pablo Picasso, *Minotaur Leaning over a Sleeping Girl,* 1933 (National Gallery of Canada, Ottawa). This and similar drawings by Picasso appeared in the National Gallery's 2016 exhibition *Picasso: Man and Beast.*

herself in 1977; his second wife, Jacqueline, who shot herself in 1986; and Dora Maar, who underwent electric shock therapy and joined a semimonastic convent, dying in 1997. Wounded but surviving was Françoise Gilot, who later married a second genius, the aforementioned Dr. Jonas Salk. Arianna Huffington, the creator of Huffington Post, hit the nail on the head with the title of her 1988 comprehensive biography of the artist: *Picasso: Creator and Destroyer.*

IN 2009, MARK ZUCKERBERG SAID, "MOVE FAST AND BREAK things. . . . Unless you are breaking stuff, you are not moving fast enough."[52] Silicon Valley computer engineers quickly moved from mainframe computers to workstations to desktops to tablets and finally to smartphones, each new product destroying the exclusivity of its predecessor. What "stuff" did Zuckerberg want broken—products, institutions, or people?

Today Facebook has a market capitalization of nearly half a trillion dollars and Zuckerberg himself a net worth of more than $60 billion. Facebook is genius on a global scale. With 2.7 billion subscribers (including its subsidiaries Instagram, WhatsApp, and Messenger), Facebook reaches a third of the world's population, serving as the planet's principal source of news and connectivity to others. The advantages of Facebook are obvious: by aggregating many lines of communication and commerce on a single platform (money, messages, people searches, news feeds, photos, videos, video conferencing, focus groups, and so on) people and products can be brought together with unprecedented speed and efficiency. No longer is it necessary to paint and post signs to rally citizens to an anti-gun demonstration or to notify your neighbors about your yard sale. It can be done quickly, efficiently, and on a massive scale—and it's all "free." You only need be willing to pay at the expense of your privacy—and perhaps your freedom.

As the author of *The Handmaid's Tale,* Margaret Atwood, has observed, however, "Every aspect of human technology has a dark side, including the bow and arrow."[53] The obvious dark side of Facebook begins with the data breaches and the unauthorized use of personal information sold to advertisers. In Facebook's world of "surveillance capitalism," confidential information flows directly to Facebook itself or through partnering vendors or phone app developers. Your contacts and location, the medicines you take, your heart rate, your political affiliation, your vacation interests—it's all there for Facebook to exploit as "sponsored posts."[54]

Less well understood is the capacity of Facebook algorithms to bind people into focus groups, which are fed increasingly narrow streams of information, potentially leading to pumped-up extremist groups. On February 12, 2019, the *New York Times* ran two headlines on two successive pages of the paper: "Facebook Group of French Journalists Harassed Women for Years," and "When Facebook Spread Hate, One German Cop Tried Something Unusual." Each demonstrated the capacity of Facebook technology to harass or mislead. On March 15, 2019, a white extremist killed fifty Muslims in a mosque in New Zealand, inspired in part by his ability to stream live video on Facebook. Facebook has thus far proved incapable of regulating disinformation, harassment, bullying, and hate speech. During the 2016 U.S. presidential election, Russian agents, masquerading as Americans, acquired bogus Facebook identities, joined political advocacy groups, posted messages, and purchased Facebook ads that reached 126 million users.[55] Sometimes those "Americans" paid for the ads in rubles (*not* genius).[56] On February 14, 2019, a committee of the British House of Commons issued a report on interference in the "Brexit" vote about which a spokesperson concluded that Facebook had behaved like a "digital gangster."[57] That same month, a longtime Silicon Valley investor and observer, Roger McNamee, published a critique of Facebook titled *Zucked: Waking Up to the Facebook Catastrophe*. Manipulated by an unregulated monopoly, liberal democracies are indeed Zucked.

As to genius Zuck himself, did he foresee all the destruction caused by data theft, or is he simply a victim of unintended consequence? Recall that an article published in the *Harvard Crimson* on November 19, 2003, reported that Zuckerberg had nearly been expelled from Harvard, charged with "breaching security, violating copyrights and violating individual privacy." At the time, Zuckerberg appeared to be a socially maladroit computer geek obsessed with code.[58] Typical of his thinking then was what he said to a friend in an online exchange, as reported on Business Insider:[59]

ZUCK: yea so if you ever need info about anyone at harvard
ZUCK: just ask
ZUCK: i have over 4000 emails, pictures, addresses, sns
FRIEND: what!? how'd you manage that one?
ZUCK: people just submitted it
ZUCK: i don't know why
ZUCK: they "trust me"
ZUCK: dumb fucks

What has changed? Apparently not much, except that the number of us dumb fucks has grown to 2.7 billion.

IN HIS PLAY *JULIUS CAESAR* (1599), SHAKESPEARE SAID, "THE EVIL that men do lives after them; the good is oft interred with their bones." The power of Shakespeare's eloquence is such that we fail to see that, when it comes to genius, the Bard may be wrong. We hold on to the good but forget the destruction. This capacity for collective amnesia may be an evolutionary advantage that enables progress. We tolerate transformative jerks and the personal and institutional destruction they cause because, on the whole, it is in our long-term benefit to do so. As the novelist Arthur Koestler said in 1964, "The principal mark of genius is not perfection but originality, the opening of new frontiers."[60] If the innovations of the genius are beneficial enough, we tend to forgive and forget.

NOW RELAX

ll the really good ideas I'd ever had come to me while I was milking a cow," said the painter Grant Wood, best known for his iconic work *American Gothic* (1930).[1] Where and when do you get your best ideas? Under what circumstances? Is it while relaxing with a glass of wine at night? While taking a shower in the morning? Or while sitting at your desk after that first cup of coffee? Isaac Newton had the capacity to just stand immobile and think, think, think. Are such intense focus and relentlessly logical lucubration the key to creative insight? Not always. Remember, Archimedes had his "eureka" moment when taking a bath. Judging from the working habits of many geniuses, to be creative, one should simply unwind mindlessly—by soaking in a tub, milking a cow, listening to some music, going for a jog, or even taking a train ride. And perhaps most important for creative ideation: get a good night's sleep, one that is full of fantastic dreams.

WHAT IS A DREAM? WHY DO WE DREAM? WHAT DO OUR DREAMS mean? The genius Sigmund Freud sought to provide answers to these questions in *The Interpretation of Dreams* (1900). Freud believed that dreams are expressions of not-yet-fulfilled desires hidden in the unconscious. It was a brilliant theory, but no one could scientifically prove it or disprove it, and with the advent of brain-imaging machines, the field of dream psychotherapy shifted from Freudian analysis to neurophysiology.

The key to interpreting the "dream factory," science now suggests, rests in understanding what happens during rapid eye movement (REM) sleep. REM sleep is that deep, quasi-hallucinatory state we experience at the end of the sleep cycle, but sometimes even during naps. Magnetic resonance imaging scans reveal that during REM sleep, parts of the brain effectively shut down while others power up. The far left and right sides of the prefrontal cortex, which are responsible for decision making and logical thought, turn off, while the hippocampus, amygdala, and visual-spatial cortex, which attend to memory, emotion, and images, become hyperactive.[2] The result, perhaps counterintuitively, is that while memories, emotions, and pictures run freely, better problem solving and more creative ideas can result.[3] Modern neuroscience is proving the truth of an adage about problem solving: "Better go sleep on it."

A test by Professor Robert Stickgold at Harvard and his collaborator Professor Matthew Walker, now at Berkeley, demonstrated that subjects were 15 to 35 percent more effective at unscrambling anagram puzzles after having awakened from a REM dream state than they were at solving those same puzzles after awakening from a non-REM state or after attempting to solve the puzzles from a wakeful state.[4] In another test, Stickgold showed that if a REM dream was problem specific and the dream content was relevant to a problem to be solved after waking, the subject was ten times as likely to find a solution (in the case of this particular test, an escape from a maze).[5] In his bestselling 2017 book *Why We Sleep: Unlocking the Power of Sleep and Dreams*, Walker made the point that in the superrelaxed state of REM dreaming, the brain is occupied with trying to make sense of things by free-associating over the whole memory bank, pulling together distant and disparate strands of information. "During the dreaming sleep state," he said, "your brain will cogitate vast swaths of acquired knowledge, and then extract overarching rules and commonalities—'the gist.' . . . From this dreaming process, which I would describe as ideasthesia, have come some of the most revolutionary leaps forward in human progress."[6]

AFTER OBSESSING OVER THE RELATIONSHIP OF ALL KNOWN CHEMI-cal elements in 1869, the Russian chemist Dmitri Mendeleev fell asleep, and the solution came to him: the structure of the periodic table. The author Stephen King has said that his thriller *Salem's Lot* sprang from a recurrent childhood nightmare. Julie Taymor, the creative force behind Broadway's *The Lion King*, has noted that "a lot of my strangest ideas come from early morning sleep, and it's really an incredible moment. I get up and the thing has become clear very fast." Vincent van Gogh said, perhaps metaphorically, "I dream of painting and then I paint my dream." Much of the surrealist Salvador Dalí's art looks like the visions one might experience in a dream. Dalí was so obsessed with the creative power of dreams that he would intentionally fall asleep with a spoon in his hand. When he nodded off, the spoon would clatter to the floor, awakening him to the need to capture his sleep-induced thoughts at that somnambulant moment and put them on canvas.[7]

Just as artists see things as they dream, musicians hear things. Richard Wagner heard the beginning of *The Ring Cycle* in 1853 after taking a walk and then dozing off on a sofa. Igor Stravinsky recalled the genesis of his Octet for Wind Instruments in these terms: "The *Octet* began with a *dream,* in which I saw myself in a small room surrounded by a small group of instrumentalists playing some attractive music. I did not recognize the music, though I strained to hear it, and I could not recall any features of it the next day, but I do remember my curiosity—in the dream—to know how many the musicians were. . . . I awoke from this little concert in a state of great delight and anticipation and the next morning began to compose."[8] Billy Joel has reported dreaming of his pop tunes in orchestrally arranged versions. Keith Richards claims that the song "(I Can't Get No) Satisfaction" came to him in his sleep in a hotel room in Florida, where he had left on a slow-turning tape recorder that captured the opening motif of the tune.[9] But the fullest description of musical inspiration born of surreal slumber comes from Sir Paul McCartney.

McCartney's "Yesterday," ranked as one of the top pop songs of the twentieth century, emerged from a dream in 1963, first the music and then more gradually the lyrics. McCartney introduced the song at a concert at the Library of Congress in 2010 with the words "The song that we are going to do now ["Yesterday"] to finish the evening is a song that came to me in a dream, so I have to believe in the magic."[10] McCartney has told this story about the origins of "Yesterday" many times: how it came to him when awakening from a dream at his girlfriend's house and how he went to the piano to set some chords to it. Not believing that a melody could be the product of a dream, he went around for weeks, asking friends such as the producer George Martin, as well as fellow Beatles John Lennon and George Harrison, about its source. "'What is this song? It must have come from somewhere. I don't know where it came from.' Nobody could place it, so at the end I had to claim it as my own. Well, that's pretty magical, you wake up one morning and there's this tune in your head. And then about three thousand people go and record it. The original lyrics to it were 'Scrambled eggs, oh, baby, how I love your legs.' But I changed them."

WHAT MIGHT HAVE CAUSED McCARTNEY'S MOMENT OF NOCTUR-nal inspiration? Scientists say neurotransmitters, the electro-chemical stimulators or repressors that move impulses from cell to cell within the body. During wakeful periods, the chemical noradrenaline flows through the brain, mobilizing it for action.

It functions similarly to the way adrenaline, the "call to action" hormone, functions in the body. During REM dreaming, however, noradrenaline disappears and acetylcholine, known as the "calm and safe" neurotransmitter, comes to the fore, allowing the brain to begin its relaxed, associative free flight.[11] The German chemist Otto Loewi (1873–1961) was the first to discover the power of acetylcholine, and he did so, appropriately, in a dream.

An earlier chemist, Henry Hallett Dale, had discovered acetylcholine in 1915. But how it works as a neurotransmitter was not clear until Loewi went to bed on the evening of March 25, 1921. The specifics here are not as important as the context in which Loewi's insight occurred—in not one but two dreams on successive nights:

> The night before Easter Sunday of that year [1921] I awoke, turned on the light, and jotted down a few notes on a tiny slip of thin paper. Then I fell asleep again. It occurred to me at six o'clock in the morning that during the night I had written down something most important, but I was unable to decipher the scrawl. The next night, at three o'clock, the idea returned. It was the design of an experiment to determine whether or not the hypothesis of chemical transmission that I had uttered seventeen years ago was correct. I got up immediately, went to the laboratory, and performed a simple experiment on a frog heart according to the nocturnal design.[12]

Following his nocturnal insight, Loewi devised an experiment in which he injected acetylcholine into a frog's heart, causing it to beat, thereby showing how the heart can be stimulated not only by an external electrical charge but also by an endogenous chemical one. (Today, modern devices such as electronic loop recorders and pacemakers monitor and control electric firings within the heart.) Loewi's discovery brought him the Nobel Prize in Chemistry in 1936.

There are three important points to be drawn here, with some practical applications. First, as with many nocturnal problem solvers, Loewi had the same dream more than once. Second, he seems to have been fixated on the same problem 24/7, over a long period of time, his insight coming as the endpoint of a seventeen-year period of incubation. Finally, he slept prepared—he kept pen and paper near him. Albert Einstein, too, was determined to always be prepared when an "aha" moment arrived. Once when Einstein was staying overnight with a friend in New York, his host asked if Einstein needed pajamas. The response: "When I retire, I sleep as nature made me."[13] But Einstein did request a pen and a notepad for his bedtable.[14] Note to self: keep pen and paper by the bed.

Maybe also put them next to the shower. A 2016 survey reported by Business Insider showed that 72 percent of Americans get their best ideas in the shower. "We did a multinational study," said University of Pennsylvania psychologist Scott Kaufman, "and found that people reported more creative inspiration in their showers than they did at work."[15] Neuroscientists explain why: dream-influencing neurotransmitters, such as acetylcholine, do not turn on and off like switches in the morning but rather slosh in and out like tides.[16] Of course, the shower is relaxing owing to the warm water and the constant "white noise" background that blots out distractions. But most important, a time lag of as much as twenty minutes exists after we awaken before our mind has fully returned to its chemically wakeful state.[17] During this "twilight zone" the brain is sensorily awake but still experiences a free flow of ideas. Thus, *carpe diem,* or at least the first twenty minutes thereof—and, again, keep pen and paper handy.

TAKING A SHOWER RELAXES US, AS DO CONSONANT HARMONIES AND gently rocking rhythms in music, even in the womb. Einstein intuited as much, and thus, wherever he moved, his violin usually accompanied him. The story that Einstein's second wife, Elsa, told the actor Charlie Chaplin in 1931 suggests that music might be a not-so-silent partner during an important breakthrough moment:

> The Doctor [i.e. Einstein] came down in his dressing-gown as usual for breakfast but he hardly touched a thing. I thought something was wrong, so I asked what was troubling him. "Darling," he said, "I have a wonderful idea." And after drinking his coffee, he went to the piano and started playing. Now and again he would stop, making a few notes.[18]

Einstein continued playing in this vein for half an hour while he thought about the significance of his breakthrough. He then went up to his study and, so the story goes, when he came down two weeks later, he held in his hands several sheets on which were the equations for his General Theory of Relativity.[19]

The tale may be exaggerated, but Einstein's elder son, Hans Albert, reported similarly that when his father had reached an impasse in his study, he would reenter the family quarters and begin to play his violin to transport his mind to a different state. "Whenever he felt that he had come to the end of the road or into a difficult situation in his work he would take refuge in music and that would usually solve all his difficulties."[20]

Sometimes even experienced musicians have to relax and get out of their own way. For years, when teaching my Yale course Listening to Music, I would tell students that Mozart had been able to play the piano when upside down. Then I would say, "Actually, it's not that difficult," and prove it. I would lie on my back on the piano bench, cross my hands, reach for the keys, and then play. (A video demonstration is posted on my website.) Over time I learned that if I concentrated on where I should put my fingers, I would make mistakes, but I could play flawlessly if I said to myself, "You know this stuff, just take a deep breath, relax, go—it will come." One year a student pointed out to me something I didn't realize: "Did you notice," she said, "that when you played you closed your eyes?" No, I hadn't, but it made sense. We should all realize that we have much studied material stored in long-term memory; we just need to relax and let it come to the fore.

SUFFERING FROM WRITER'S BLOCK? IF SO, PUT ON YOUR SNEAKERS and dash outside for a two-mile run. This, at least, is the suggestion made in a 2014 article in the *Guardian* reporting the findings of recent scholarly studies on the relationship between creativity and exercise.[21] In fact, current research by several neurologists and psychologists suggests that increased exercise, even walking, enhances cognitive function as well as divergent thinking and creativity.[22] But geniuses throughout history already knew this, consciously or not.

In ancient Greece a group called the Peripatetics, followers of Aristotle, conducted their philosophical inquiries while walking around the Lyceum. Charles Dickens walked fifteen miles a day through the streets of London while he conceived *A Christmas Carol* (1843).[23] A daughter of Mark Twain recounted that his father paced while he worked: "Some of the time when dictating, Father walked the floor . . . then it always seemed as if a new spirit had flown into the room."[24] Bill Gates is a pacer, too. "It helps him organize his mind and see what others can't see," says his wife, Melinda.[25] The avid walker Henry David Thoreau said in 1851, "The moment my legs begin to move, my thoughts begin to flow."[26] Unusual for a woman in her day, the novelist Louisa May Alcott, as we have seen, was a devoted runner: "I am so full of my work I can't stop to eat or sleep, or for anything but a daily run," she wrote while working on *Little Women* in 1868.[27]

Whether you walk or run, in nature or in a gym, neurotransmitters are at work, leading to diminished inhibitions, fewer conceptual restraints, and enhanced memory resources. But a caveat for all creative movers: although the *place* of activity does not matter, the *pace* does. Increasing the speed of the walk from seventeen-minute miles to twelve-minute miles, or the run from ten- to eight-minute miles, for example, will cause the average brain to shift out of a relaxed mode and into one focused on the mechanics of walking or running.[28] Thus, if you are on an exercise treadmill, ignore all the electronic monitors; if you are outside, ditch the Fitbits; on the road, focused concentration is the enemy of creativity.

NIKOLA TESLA WAS RELAXED WHEN HE WALKED THROUGH THE City Park in Budapest one late afternoon in 1882. At age twenty-six, he was in Budapest to work for the new Budapest Telephone Company. A friend, Anital Szigety, had been impressing upon him the importance of regular exercise, so the two customarily took long walks together.[29] Tesla recounted the following in his autobiography:

> On an afternoon which is ever present in my memory, I was enjoying a walk with my friend in the City Park, and reciting poetry. At that age I knew entire books by heart, word for word. One of these was Goethe's *Faust*. The sun was just setting, and reminded me of the glorious passage:
>
> *The glow turns back and retreats, done is the day of toil;*
> *Yet it hastens forth, toward a new life;*
> *Ah, that no wing can lift me from the soil*
> *Upon its track to follow, again and again!*
> *A glorious dream!*
>
> As I uttered these inspiring words, the idea came like a flash of lightning, and in an instant the truth was revealed.[30]

What Tesla had discovered was a way of inducing magnetic fields to rotate by means of alternating current, thereby forcing a drive shaft to rotate in a constant direction. From that insight developed the polyphase electrical motor that made Europe and, more so, the United States the industrial colossuses that they would become. Washing machines, vacuums, drills, pumps, and electric fans, among other things, are still powered by Tesla's perambulatory insight.

But the important point is this: Tesla had been searching for this solution to a problem with the alternating current motor since his earliest days as an engineering student at the University of Graz back in 1875. "I may go on for months or years with the idea in the back of my head," Tesla said when asked in 1921 about his thought process.[31] The "aha" insight finally occurred when he was not consciously thinking about electric motors. He was walking in a park, reciting Goethe's *Faust* to his friend, and enjoying the setting sun as the earth rotated. The original German of the passage in question, given above, contains the word *rucken* ("to turn back")—the spinning of the earth, the spinning of a magnetic field powered by alternating current. Perhaps not coincidentally, the section of the poem he recited ended with a line beginning *Ein schöner Traum* ("a glorious dream"). Tesla was relaxed and perhaps in a semiconscious or dreamlike state. The confluence of conscious and unconscious sensations yielded a "eureka" epiphany, but that flash of insight had been seven years in the making.

Suppose you have no desire to exercise your way to an insightful state. Can a vehicle transport you there? Our geniuses suggest yes. Many did their best thinking in trains, buses, carriages, or boats. We have already seen how the journey that transformed Joanne Rowling into the bestselling author J. K. Rowling began on a train as she conceived the Harry Potter series. Walt Disney thought up Mickey Mouse on a train. Lin-Manuel Miranda says that the chorus of the song "Wait for It" in *Hamilton* came to him while riding on a subway train in New York on his way to a party. He sang the melodic refrain into his iPhone, briefly attended the party, and then completed the song on his subway ride home.[32] The common denominator in those experiences: a constant rocking motion and a gentle background rhythm. Is that why we so often fall asleep on a train?

In a letter of 1810, Ludwig van Beethoven told how he fell asleep during a carriage ride from Baden to nearby Vienna: "When I was in my carriage yesterday, on the way to Vienna, sleep overpowered me. . . . Now, as I was slumbering, I dreamed that I was travelling far away, no less far than Syria, no less far than India and back again, to Arabia, too, and at last I came even to Jerusalem. . . . Now, during my dream journey, the following canon [musical round] occurred to me. Yet I had hardly awoken when the canon was gone and I could not recall a single note or word of it to my mind."[33] The next day, by coincidence, Beethoven happened to get into the same carriage to go back to Baden and, as he described it, "Lo and behold, in accordance with the law of association of ideas, the same canon occurred to me; now, waking, I held it fast, as once Menelaus held Proteus, and only granted it one last favour, that of allowing it to transform itself into three voices." Movement, relaxation, sleep, and associative memory (the same, comfortable venue) all contributed to Beethoven's short canon created twice in a carriage.

THUS FROM THE TIME OF SOCRATES (*DEATHBED DREAM*) TO PAUL McCartney ("Yesterday"), geniuses throughout history have affirmed that creative insights arise from relaxed moments both night and day. From these accounts can be extrapolated good advice for aspiring creators today. If you need a fresh idea, go for a walk or a jog, or simply get into a relaxing conveyance so as to allow your mind to range more freely. Don't drive downtown, where you must pay attention to traffic, but head to wide-open spaces *without* focus-demanding audiobooks or radio news. Indeed, any sort of "mindless" physical activity involving repetitive motion can set your imagination free. The novelist Toni Morrison would "brood, thinking of ideas," while mowing the lawn.[34]

The choreographer George Balanchine claimed, "When I'm iron-ing, that's when I do most of my work."[35] When you wake in the morning, just lie there thinking for a few minutes—and don't reach for your smartphone! At this moment your mind may be at its best. Similarly, don't consider daydreaming or power napping to be a waste of time—think of them as opportunities to gain insight. Finally, be like Einstein: keep pen and paper by your bed or near the shower so as to be able to capture your best ideas. We all have the habit of wanting to be focused and "productive." Geniuses have the habit of knowing when *not* to be.

TIME TO CONCENTRATE!

Sometimes it takes discipline to relax. And sometimes it takes discipline so as to focus, first to analyze a problem and then to get our "product" out the door. This applies to successful people as well as geniuses. We know that we must concentrate to come up with a solution, but then do we execute or procrastinate? Leonardo da Vinci had extraordinary powers of analytical concentration, as we will see. But once he saw the solution, he often lost interest and didn't produce the product. That perhaps explains why he left us fewer than twenty-five completed paintings. The cartoonist Charles Schulz, who drew 17,897 *Peanuts* comic strips, was known for the hours that he would spend just doodling with a pencil, letting his mind wander. But then, according to his biographer David Michaelis, "Once he had an idea, he would work quickly and with intense concentration to get it onto paper before the inspiration dried up."[1] Whether arising from relaxed defocused musings or intense analytical concentration, ideas that have the capacity to change the world must be reified, verified, and publicized before they can have their transformative impact. Both analysis and execution require concentrated hard work.

ANALYTICAL CONCENTRATION PRECEDES EXECUTION. BEFORE PABLO Picasso executed with pen or brush in hand, he often analyzed using only eye and mind. Picasso's muse during the 1940s, Françoise Gilot, recounted how he would intently analyze his favorite subject, the female body:

> The next day he said, "You'd be better posing for me nude." When I had taken off my clothes, he had me stand back to the entrance, very erect, with my arms at my side. Except for the shaft of daylight coming in through the high window at my right, the whole place was bathed in a dim, uniform light that was on the edge of shadow. Pablo stood off, three or four yards from me, looking tense and remote. His eyes didn't leave me for a second. He didn't touch his drawing pad; he wasn't even holding a pencil. It seemed a very long time.
>
> Finally he said, "I see what I need to do. You can dress now. You won't have to pose again." When I went to get my clothes I saw that I had been standing there just over an hour.[2]

Leonardo da Vinci would also just stand and stare. Indeed, he seems to have spent as much time analyzing the composition of *The Last Supper* (1485–1488) in the abbey of Santa Maria delle Grazie in Milan as he did executing it. As his contemporary the writer Matteo Bandello reported, "He would sometimes remain two, three, or four days without touching his brush, although he spent several hours a day standing in front the work, arms folded, examining and criticizing the figures to himself."[3] That concentration Leonardo called his *discorso mentale* (mental discourse).

Infuriated by the slow progress of *The Last Supper*, the abbot of the monastery complained to Leonardo's patron, the duke of Milan. Called upon to explain his slow progress, Leonardo declared that "the greatest geniuses sometimes accomplish more when they work less, since they are searching for inventions in their minds, and forming those perfect ideas which their hands then express and reproduce from what they previously conceived with their intellect."[4] Atypical for Leonardo, once he had his "inventions" for *The Last Supper* securely in his mind, he continued to focus, now executing furiously. "He sometimes stayed there from dawn to sundown," said Bandello, "never putting down his brush, forgetting to eat and drink, painting without pause."

Similarly, Picasso would eventually execute his paintings, working as if possessed, according to this report from his longtime secretary, Jaime Sabartés:

> Even while he is attending to his palette, he goes on contemplating the picture from a corner of his eye. The canvas and the palette compete for his attention, which does not abandon either; both remain within the focus of his vision, which embraces the totality of each, and both together. He surrenders body and soul to the activity which is his *raison d'etre*, dabbing the bristles of the brush in the oily paste of colour with a loving gesture, with all his senses focused upon a single aim, as if he were bewitched.[5]

No matter where he happened to be, Albert Einstein could concentrate in his own mental silo. A friend described the apartment in which Einstein, as a new father, worked in Basel around 1903:

> The room smelled of diapers and stale smoke, and puffs of smoke arose every so often from the stove, but these things didn't seem to bother Einstein. He had the baby on one knee and a pad on the other, and every so often he would write an equation on the pad, then quickly rock the baby a little faster as he began to fuss.[6]

Later that grown son said, "Even the loudest baby-crying didn't seem to disturb Father. He could go on with his work completely impervious to noise."[7] According to Einstein's sister Maja, the same might happen in the midst of a crowd: "In a large, quite noisy group, he could withdraw to the sofa, take pen and paper in hand, . . . and lose himself so completely in a problem that the conversation of many voices stimulated rather than disturbed him."[8]

Sometimes Einstein's powers of concentration led to comical results. Once during a speech at a reception in his honor, Einstein took out his pen and started to scribble equations on the back of his program, apparently oblivious to all the things being said about him. "The speech ended with a great flourish. Everybody stood up, clapping hands and turning to Einstein. Helen [his secretary] whispered to him that he had to get up, which he did. Unaware of the fact that the ovation was for him, he clapped his hands too."[9]

Mozart had the same power to "get into the zone." His wife, Constanze, recounted that during an outdoor lawn bowling party in 1787 he continued to work on the opera *Don Giovanni*, oblivious to all around him; when called upon to take his turn, he stood up, bowled, and "then went back to work without the speech and laughter of the others disturbing him in the least."[10] But how amused was Constanze in 1783 when her husband wrote his String Quartet no. 15, K. 421 at her bedside while she gave birth to their first child, Raimund? He would briefly comfort her but then return to writing his music.[11]

TODAY, CONCENTRATING IN THE MIDST OF CHAOS MAY REQUIRE mentally constructing a "fourth wall." The expression derives from the theater, where actors are asked to build an imaginary barrier so as to separate themselves from the audience out front, and thereby stay within their own psychological space. Next time you are waiting at LaGuardia Airport or Heathrow or are packed in a middle coach seat on a noisy flight, try erecting your own fourth wall and finding therein your own Zen realm in which you are the only citizen. Within your own mentally imposed domain, you, like Einstein and Mozart, can work oblivious to all outside interference.

Isaac Newton's powers of concentration seem to have bordered on mental disorder. His manservant Humphrey Newton (no relation) wrote, "So intent, so serious upon his Studies that he eat very sparingly, nay, oftimes he has forgot to eat at all, so that going into his Chamber, I have found his Mess untouch'd, of which when I have reminded him, would reply, Have I; & then making to the Table, would eat a bit or two standing, for I cannot say, I ever saw Him sit at Table by himself."[12] To appreciate Newton's ability to focus, consider Figure 14.1. Here we see him working out the beginning of an infinite sequence: fifty-five columns of figures marching along in neat, tidy rows, and all done, as far as can be determined, entirely in his head. Another genius, the economist John Maynard Keynes, summed up Newton's ability to concentrate: "I fancy his pre-eminence is due to his muscles of intuition being the strongest and most enduring with which a man has ever been gifted. Anyone who has ever attempted pure scientific or philosophical thought knows how one can hold a problem momentarily in one's mind and apply all one's powers of concentration to piercing through it, and how it will dissolve and escape and you find that what you are surveying is a blank. I believe that Newton could hold a problem in his mind for hours and days and weeks until it surrendered to him its secret."[13] As Keynes observed, when trying to concentrate, we all experience the way the object of thought can "dissolve and escape." Concentration requires a good memory.

ROBERT HESS ARRIVED AS A FRESHMAN AT YALE IN 2011 AS THE highest-ranking U.S. chess player of native birth. He had achieved the title "international grandmaster" two years before at age seventeen. In 2008, the chess journalist Jerry Hanken called a recent

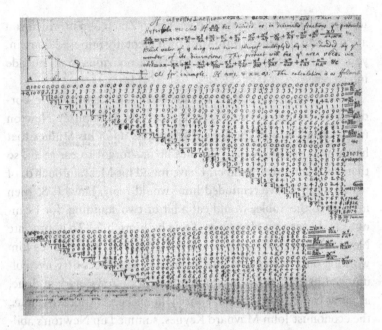

FIGURE **14.1**: Newton calculating the area under a hyperbola to fifty-five decimal places by adding values from each term of an infinite series, ca. 1665. Newton apparently wrote his page, part of his development of calculus, while at home in Lincolnshire "quarantining" from the plague that then ravaged the university town of Cambridge (Additional Manuscript 3958, fol. 78v, Cambridge University Library, Cambridge, UK).

Hess match "one of the greatest performances by an American teenager since the heyday of Bobby Fischer."[14] Being curious about freshman Robert, I tracked him down and invited him to join the Yale "genius class" on "chess day." To make things interesting, I auditioned three other experienced players to do battle with Robert simultaneously—while he was blindfolded. Spotters knowing chess notation moved the pieces for him as he called out the moves (P to K4, for example). Students and visitors crowded around looking anxiously at the boards. Within ten to fifteen minutes each adversary was defeated. The crowd went crazy.

That was impressive. But more astonishing was what was to

come. "Robert," I said, "how good is your memory?[15] How well do you remember those games?" "I remember all of them," he said with polite nonchalance, and he wrote on the blackboard the succession of ten to twenty moves in sequence for each of the three games. "I could have done this against ten players blindfolded," he said, not bragging but as a simple statement of fact. "Of course," a student piped up, "he has a photographic memory." "Think about it," responded another dismissively, "he was blindfolded and couldn't see a thing. What's to photograph?" Maybe Robert can "photograph" what he sees in his mind.

Many great minds throughout history seem to have possessed a photographic or eidetic memory—the ability to recall an image after only seeing it once—and used it as a tool of concentration. Once, when in a tavern, Michelangelo argued with fellow artists over who could create the ugliest image. Michelangelo drew his way to victory and said he owed it to the fact that he had seen and could remember all the graffiti in Rome.[16] Those around Picasso believed that he, too, had a photographic memory for visual images, for he once described an assumed-to-be-lost photograph in every detail, later to have his mnemonic powers validated when the image resurfaced.[17] James Joyce was known to his Jesuit teachers at Clongowes Wood College as "the boy with the ink-blotter mind."[18] Elon Musk was called "genius boy" by his mother because, she said, he possessed a photographic memory.[19] In 1951, the conductor Arturo Toscanini wanted the N.B.C. Symphony to perform the slow movement of Quartet no. 5 by Joachim Raff, but no score of the obscure ten-minute piece could be located in New York. So Toscanini, who had not seen the piece for years, laboriously wrote it out, note for note. Later, a collector of musical autographs found the original score and checked it against Toscanini's manuscript, finding only one error.[20]

Few of us possess a photographic memory like the geniuses named above. Even the gifted have had to work to attain mnemonic prowess. Robert Hess had been playing chess since the age of five under the watchful eye of paid tutors; day after day he had practiced by memorizing standard openings, positions, and end-games, as well as famous matches throughout history. Leonardo da Vinci willfully worked to improve his memory. According to his contemporary biographer Giorgio Vasari, "He so loved bizarre physiognomies, with beards and hair like savages, that he would follow someone who had caught his attention for a whole day. He would memorize his appearance so well that on his return home he would be able to draw him as if he had him before his very eyes."[21] At night Leonardo would rest in bed, trying to re-create in his mind the images he had seen during the day.[22] We can follow the spirit of Leonardo by engaging in mind-challenging activities such as playing chess or Sudoku, sight-reading a score for a musical instrument, or assembling something that requires following instructions sequentially and to the letter. According to Harvard Health Publishing, we'd all improve our memory by avoiding alcohol and exercising regularly, so as to increase blood flow to the brain.[23] As Leonardo's biographer Fritjof Capra reported, Leonardo himself regularly lifted weights.[24]

Averse to pumping iron? There is an alternate practical technique that we can all employ: set a deadline. Geniuses are intrinsically motivated, passionate about what they are doing. But sometimes even they benefit from last-minute external motivation to assure that the job gets done. Charles Schulz had to finish his cartoon before the next edition of the 2,600 newspapers in which his work was syndicated; Mozart had a theater rented and an audience arriving to hear *Don Giovanni*. Elon Musk has production quotas he has to meet for his Tesla automobiles; Jeff Bezos guarantees that your Amazon Prime package will be delivered in one to two days. Even imposing an arbitrary deadline on ourselves can enhance our concentration and help us remove the inconsequential.

STEPHEN HAWKING WAS SOMEONE WHO HAD THINGS BOTH CONSE-quential and inconsequential removed from him. Hawking has been called "the greatest genius since Einstein,"[25] as well as "the genius in the wheelchair." Hawking himself maintained that the latter designation was media hype, driven by the public's thirst for heroes.[26] To be sure, the public has always had a soft spot for the genius trapped in a wrecked body. Think of the Hunchback of Notre Dame, the Phantom of the Opera, and Alastor "Mad-Eye" Moody in *Harry Potter*—each a genius hidden behind a deformed exterior.

Hawking only seriously began to concentrate at age twenty-one—and only because he had to, due to the onset of amyotrophic lateral sclerosis (ALS), also known as Lou Gehrig's disease. Before that year, he seems to have been an underachieving bon vivant. By his own admission, he did not read until the age of eight; in school he was only in the middle of the class academically; and in college he spent his time socializing, working only an hour a day.[27] But in 1963, at the age of twenty-one, Hawking suddenly faced a literal deadline: he was given a diagnosis of ALS that came with a life expectancy of two to three years. Confined to a wheelchair, he had few distractions. By 1985, he had lost the ability to speak and was unable to communicate except through his computer. Of necessity, he focused on his chosen field, astrophysics. When I asked Kitty Ferguson, Hawking's friend and principal biographer, whether Hawking's isolation had enhanced his ability to concentrate, she offered this important insight: "I would say that his disability probably didn't increase his capacity to concentrate, but it did increase his *inclination* to concentrate, finally to grow up, focus, and quit wasting time. As he once said to me, 'What choice did I have?'"[28]

By the early 1970s, Hawking had lost the use of his hands. That posed a problem because all physicists do their thinking as they work through equations, writing endlessly on paper, blackboards, walls, doors, or almost any other flat surface—analytical concentration toggling with execution. To continue in that vein, Hawking developed a workaround: he would see the problem in his mind and hold it there, concentrating in a way similar to the way Newton had. A Nobel Prize winner and friend of Hawking, Kip Thorne, said, "He learned to do [math and physics] entirely in his head without writing things down. He did it by manipulating images of the shapes of objects, the shapes of curves, the shapes of surface, not merely in three-dimensional space but four-dimensional space plus time. What makes him unique among all physicists is his ability to do wide ranging calculations far better than if he had not had ALS."[29] Hawking confessed that in the midst of distractions, he, like Einstein, would focus by entering his own zone of focused thought: "Turning problems over in my mind has been my method of discovery for nearly half my life now. While all around me people have buzzed away deep in conversation, I have often been transported afar, lost in my own thoughts, trying to fathom how the universe works."[30] Kitty Ferguson summed up Hawking's capacity to focus: "Few have Hawking's powers of concentration and self-control. Few have his genius."[31] The master of black holes had managed to thrive in his own.

ON JULY 1, 2014, I HAD AN ISCHEMIC STROKE, AND MY WIFE rushed me to the hospital in Sarasota, Florida, where we currently live. Scans showed that I had (and still have) a completely blocked left interior carotid artery; attempts to clear it through an endarterectomy were pointless. For three days I was hooked up to wires in a hospital bed in my own black hole. I could think, but I could not speak. A virtual prisoner inside my body, I said silently, "Craig, this is serious. You are going to have to dig your way out of this. Think, concentrate, and pull your life together." I started doing some mental exercises that I invented in an effort to reunite my short-term memory and speech, proceeding in order of increasing difficulty: (1) Say "blue bull dog" and remember the first word after you have finished the third; (2) Identify two composers who lived between Bach and Brahms; (3) Name three restaurants on Longboat Key from south to north; (4) Say all four syllables in the name of the road that runs from Tampa to Miami (Tamiami). Hour after hour I concentrated—what else was there to do? Whether or not this self-willed exercise contributed to a sudden turn of mind, I cannot say, but on the third day my blocked blood flow reversed itself, and thereafter, over a period of months, I gradually regained normal cognitive function. I was lucky. Of course my experience, although serious at the time, was trivial compared to Hawking's ALS. Yet it did give me a glimpse of what it might have been like there inside his mental silo. "Keeping the mind active was the key to my survival,"[32] he once said, and he lived more than fifty years longer than doctors had initially expected. Sometimes in life it is imperative to relax, defocus, and let your mind carry you away to original insights. But at other times, whether you are a genius like Hawking or a plodder like me, there are practical problems to be solved in space or elsewhere. At such moments, you must find the discipline to concentrate.

EVERY GENIUS HAS A TIME, PLACE, AND ENVIRONMENT FOR WORKing and getting the job done.[33] You may call this "habit" (as I do in this book and as did Vladimir Nabokov and Shel Silverstein), "routine" (Leo Tolstoy and John Updike), "schedule" (Isaac Asimov, Yayoi Kusama, and Stephen King), "rut" (Andy Warhol), or "ritual" (Confucius and Twyla Tharp). The habits of these great minds are neither glamorous nor exalted. "Inspiration is for amateurs," says the painter Chuck Close. "The rest of us just show up and get to work."[34]

Just as every genius is different, so each has his or her own unique way of concentrating. The author Thomas Wolfe, standing six feet, six inches tall, wrote on top of a kitchen refrigerator beginning around midnight. Ernest Hemingway started in the morning, typing on his Underwood portable set on top of a bookcase in the annex to his Key West home. John Cheever would put on his only suit in the morning, as if preparing to join other professional men going to work. Descending in the elevator to the basement of his New York City apartment building, he would then take off his suit coat and write while leaning on storage boxes until noon. Then he would put his coat on again and ascend home for lunch.[35]

Intense concentration, in some cases, requires a break involving physical exercise. Victor Hugo would take a two-hour break and head toward the ocean, working out vigorously on the beach. Igor Stravinsky, if energy and concentration were flagging, would stand on his head for a short period of time. Nobel Prize winner Saul Bellow did the same—perhaps to increase blood flow to the brain. The choreographer Twyla Tharp, for whom physical conditioning was part of her creative process, went daily to the Pumping Iron Gym at 5:30 A.M. But as she said in her book *The Creative Habit: Learn It and Use It for Life,* "The ritual is not the stretching and weight training I put my body through each morning at the gym; the ritual is the cab. The moment I tell the driver where to go I have completed the ritual." Having a disciplined ritual makes life simpler and increases productivity. "It's actively antisocial," Tharp said. "On the other hand, it is pro-creative."[36]

Most geniuses create in offices, labs, or studios walled off from the outside world. Once inside his studio, painter N. C. Wyeth taped cardboard "blinders" to the sides of his glasses so as not to see beyond his canvas. Tolstoy locked his door. Dickens had an extra door built to his study to block noise. Nabokov, when writing *Lolita,* worked every night in the back seat of his parked car, "the only place in the country," he said, "with no noise and no drafts." Marcel Proust had his apartment walls lined with cork. The point of all this: geniuses need to concentrate. Einstein more than once encouraged fledgling scientists to get a job as a lighthouse keeper so as to "devote themselves undisturbed" to thinking.[37]

Call it a lighthouse or a safe house, all great minds have a space in which they get into the zone. The mystery writer Agatha Christie was often beset by social and professional interruptions, yet, as she recalled, "Once I could get away, however, shut the door and get people not to interrupt me, then I was able to go full speed ahead, completely lost in what I was doing."[38]

Follow her lead but go one step further: *Don't* interrupt yourself with diverting web searches or email. But *do* give yourself confidence and encouragement by placing marks of your previous accomplishments (diplomas, certificates, awards) in view, as well as portraits of your heroes or heroines. Brahms kept a lithograph of Beethoven above his piano. Einstein kept inspirational likenesses of Newton, Faraday, and Maxwell in his study; and Darwin had portraits of his idols—Hooker, Lyell, and Wedgewood—in his. The creative process itself is frightening—often "the great work" seems suddenly to be nothing of value—and simple tricks like these can help. With a ritual to fall back upon, you can get up and try again tomorrow. "A solid routine," said John Updike, "saves you from giving up."[39]

Thus, a final lesson for the rest of us from the geniuses of this book: to be more efficient and productive, create a daily routine for yourself that comes with a four-wall safe zone for constructive concentration. Get to the office, or to your study or studio, and secure some space and time for interior thinking. Of course, give yourself access to a wide array of opinions and information, but remember that at the end of the day, you alone are responsible for synthesizing that information and producing something. We need successful people to make the world function well today. We need geniuses to ensure that it will function better tomorrow.

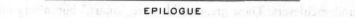

UNEXPECTED OUTCOMES

We teach our children to "behave" and to follow the rules. Many of our kids will continue on to college, where they will take courses from professors, such as myself, centering on those great minds who, it turns out, *didn't* "behave" and who *broke* the rules—the transformative geniuses of Western culture. This is just one of the many unexpected outcomes that have emerged during the dozen years that I have spent teaching my "genius course" at Yale and through the process of writing this book. Here are a few others in no particular order.

At the beginning of this project, I had in my mind a picture of the genius: someone with a superhigh IQ who, even as a youth, has sudden "aha" insights, yet is eccentric and unpredictable. Every feature of this stereotypical image, I have now learned, is wrong or inaccurate in most cases. Take, for example, the notion that the genius is a brainiac who aces all the standardized tests of life. In truth, my study of geniuses reveals just as many examples of poor-to-middling students as Phi Beta Kappa candidates. Hawking didn't read until he was eight, and recall that Picasso and Beethoven couldn't do basic math. Jack Ma, John Lennon, Thomas Edison, Winston Churchill, Walt Disney, Charles Darwin, William Faulkner, and Steve Jobs likewise were all academic underachievers. These great minds were "smart," but in very unstandardized, unpredictable ways. Thus, my cohort of geniuses has taught me that it is impossible to predict who will become a genius; no longer will I make the mistake of judging a young person's potential based on standardized tests and grades, or even prodigious acts. Indeed, I would caution all parents against pushing their children along the prodigy track. Let's all check back in twenty years to see if that prodigy has begun to change the world—few do.

Other unexpected revelations: Successful people may produce successful offspring, but geniuses, it turns out, don't produce dynasties of little geniuses—genius is not a heritable trait but a "one-off" phenomenon. Successful people need mentors—we all know that—but apparently geniuses can do without. Geniuses generally absorb material quickly, intuit more, and move rapidly past any mentor. True, genius by definition presupposes an inequality of outcome (the exceptional thoughts of Einstein or extraordinary music of Bach) and it generates a concomitant inequality of reward (eternal fame for Bach, fabulous wealth of Bezos); that's just the way the world works. Similarly, acts of genius are usually attended by acts of destruction; that's generally called progress.

Genius also proves not to be sudden. That "aha" moment is really the culmination of a lengthy period of cerebral gestation. Remember, Albert Einstein wrestled with general relativity for two years before having his "happiest thought"; Nikola Tesla took seven years before envisioning the induction motor; and Otto Loewi needed nearly twenty before having his nocturnal epiphany about acetylcholine. Why, then, does every genius have a *sudden* "eureka" moment in Hollywood films? Because the audience can't sit and watch for twenty years, or even two.

"All geniuses die young," said the comedian Groucho Marx. But statistically that proves not to be true; obstinate obsession drives them on. Geniuses change the world, yes, but they often do so, it turns out, accidentally; sometimes society is made better as an unintended consequence of the creator's need for self-salvation. How many masterpieces are created for the benefit of the psyche of the painter? How many great books are written more for the author than the reader?

Finally, my Yale students and I have experienced one enduring insight that we perhaps should have seen coming: Many great minds turn out to be not-so-great human beings. At the beginning of the course, I invariably ask the students, just to get a laugh and provoke discussion, "Who here is a genius? All geniuses, please raise your hands." A few souls do so timidly; the class clowns elevate emphatically for all to see. Next I ask, "But if you are not already a genius, how many of you would *like* to be one?" To this about three-quarters of the class responds affirmatively. In the final session of the course, I ask, "Having studied all these geniuses, how many of you *still* want to be one?" Now, only about a quarter of the group says, "I do." As one student volunteered on the point: "At the beginning of the course I thought I did, but now I'm not so sure. So many of them seem like obsessive, self-centered jerks—not the kind of person I'd want as a friend or a suitemate." Point taken: obsessive and self-centered. As much as we stand to benefit from the habits of genius, be on guard if there is one in your midst. If you work for a genius, you may be berated or abused, or you may lose your job. If someone close to you is a genius, you may find that his or her work or passion always comes first. Yet to those so abused, made redundant, exploited, or ignored, we offer sincere thanks for "taking one for the team," the team being all of us who subsequently benefit from the greater cultural good that "your" genius has done. To paraphrase the writer Edmond de Goncourt, "Almost no one loves the genius until he or she is dead." But then we do, because now life is better.

ACKNOWLEDGMENTS

I t takes a village to write my books. Helpful inhabitants thereof include our four children, to whom the book is dedicated, as well as fellow dedicatees Dr. Fred and M.A. Sue Finkelstein, our best friends and spirited co-debaters for forty-five years, and finally my sharpest critic, my beloved wife, Sherry, who read every word of everything more than once. Likewise, I am indebted to my agent, Peter Bernstein, who kept faith in the project, and my editor at Dey Street/HarperCollins, Jessica Sindler, who possesses an uncanny capacity for shaping material to make it speak to the modern world. During my heyday at Yale, I benefited greatly from the insights and kindness of several valued colleagues who annually visited the "genius course" to serve as "guest presenters." Among them were physics professor Doug Stone, from whom I learned enormously; mathematician Jim Rolf; microbiologist and now Yale provost Scott Strobel; and, finally, Chief Investment Officer David Swensen, whom I always saved for the last class because, as a generous philanthropist, he understood that, although the genius needs money, money isn't genius. In addition, over the years I benefited from half a dozen class presentations by the gifted neuroscientist Caroline Robertson, now at Dartmouth, as well as visits by the late novelist

Anita Shreve, the late art historian David Rosand, entrepreneurs Roger McNamee and Kevin Ryan, director of the Metropolitan Opera Peter Gelb, and cultural provocateur extraordinaire Adam Glick. With a topic as broad as genius, I was continually casting about for help on specific topics, and I received it generously from longtime friend Leon Plantinga (Beethoven), Kitty Ferguson (Hawking), Nobel Prize winner Kip Thorne (ideation among physicists), Lucas Swineford (online education), and Jack Meyers, president of the Rockefeller Archives. Several people kindly critiqued chapters, among them my son Christopher, my daughter-in-law Melanie, my colleague Keith Polk, my neighbors Pam Reiter, Ken Marsh, and Bashar Nejidwi, and literary gadfly Clark Baxter, who has a special talent for sending out "zingers" to hit a target that no one else can see. Thanks to you all!

NOTES

Introduction: Hitting the Hidden Target

1. George Eliot, *Middlemarch* (Ware, Hertfordshire, UK: Wordsworth Editions, 1994), 620.
2. Darrin M. McMahon, *Divine Fury: A History of Genius* (New York: Basic Books, 2013), 229.
3. The bizarre posthumous history of Einstein's brain is recounted in Michael Paterniti, *Driving Mr. Albert: A Trip Across America with Einstein's Brain* (New York: Random House, 2001).
4. Paul G. Bahn, "The Mystery of Mozart's Skull: The Face of Mozart," *Archeology* (March–April 1991): 38–41; Luke Harding, "DNA Detectives Discover More Skeletons in Mozart Family Closet," *Guardian,* January 8, 2006, https://www.theguardian .com/world/2006/jan/09/arts.music.
5. "Leonardo da Vinci's DNA: Experts Unite to Shine Modern Light on a Renaissance Genius," EurekAlert!, May 5, 2016, https:// www.eurekalert.org/pub_releases/2016-05/tca-ldv050316.php.
6. Paul Israel, *Edison: A Life of Invention* (New York: John Wiley & Sons, 1998), 119–20.
7. As translated from the original German in Arthur Schopenhauer, *Die Welt als Wille und Vorstellung,* 3rd ed., vol. 2, book 3, chap. 31

(Leipzig: Brockhaus, 1859), https://www.amazon.com/Die-Welt
-Wille-Vorstellung-German/dp/3843040400, 627.

8. Dylan Love, "The 13 Most Memorable Quotes from Steve Jobs,"
Business Insider, October 5, 2011, https://www.businessinsider
.com/the-13-most-memorable-quotes-from-steve-jobs-2011-10.

9. Nikola Tesla, *My Inventions: The Autobiography of Nikola Tesla,*
edited by David Major (Middletown, DE: Philovox, 2016), 55.

10. Immanuel Kant, *Critique of Pure Reason,* quoted in McMahon,
Divine Fury, 90.

11. See Mihaly Csikszentmihalyi, "Implications of a Systems
Perspective for the Study of Creativity," in *Handbook of
Creativity,* edited by Robert J. Sternberg (Cambridge, UK:
Cambridge University Press, 1999), 311–34.

Chapter 1: Gift or Hard Work?

1. Plato, *Apology,* translated by Benjamin Jowett, para. 8, http://
classics.mit.edu/Plato/apology.html.

2. Charles Darwin, *The Autobiography of Charles Darwin,* edited by
Nora Barlow (New York: W. W. Norton, 1958), 38.

3. Simone de Beauvoir, *The Second Sex,* edited and translated by
H. M. Parshley (New York: Random House, 1989), 133.

4. Giorgio Vasari, *The Lives of the Artists,* translated by Julia
Conaway Bondanella and Peter Bondanella (Oxford, UK: Oxford
University Press, 1991), 284.

5. Leonardo da Vinci, *Codex Atlanticus,* quoted in Walter Isaacson,
Leonardo da Vinci (New York: Simon & Schuster, 2017), 179.

6. Carmen C. Bambach, *Michelangelo: Divine Draftsman and
Designer* (New Haven, CT: Yale University Press, 2017), 35, 39.

7. Quoted in Helia Phoenix, *Lady Gaga: Just Dance: The Biography*
(London: Orion Books, 2010), 84.

8. Lewis Lockwood, *Beethoven: The Music and the Life* (New York:
W. W. Norton, 2003), 12.

9. Tom Lutz, "Viewers Angry After Michael Phelps Loses Race to
Computer-Generated Shark," *Guardian,* July 24, 2017, https://
www.theguardian.com/sport/2017/jul/24/michael-phelps
-swimming-race-shark-discovery-channel.

10. Danielle Allentuck, "Simone Biles Takes Gymnastics to a New Level. Again," *New York Times,* August 9, 2019, https://www .nytimes.com/2019/08/09/sports/gymnastics-simone-biles.html.

11. Sade Strehlke, "How August Cover Star Simone Biles Blazes Through Expectations," *Teen Vogue* (June 30, 2016), https:// www.teenvogue.com/story/simone-biles-summer-olympics-cover -august-2016.

12. "Simone Biles Teaches Gymnastic Fundamentals," MasterClass, 2019, lesson 3, at 0:50.

13. Francis Galton, *Hereditary Genius: An Inquiry into Its Laws and Consequences* (London: MacMillan, 1869), http://galton.org/books /hereditary-genius/1869-FirstEdition/hereditarygenius1869galt.pdf, 1.

14. On horse breeding and inbreeding, see Allison Schrager, "Secretariat's Kentucky Derby Record Is Safe, Thanks to the Taxman," *Wall Street Journal,* May 3, 2019, https://www.wsj.com /articles/secretariats-kentucky-derby-record-is-safe-thanks-to-the -taxman-11556920680. On the subject of biological determinism generally, see Stephen Jay Gould, *The Mismeasure of Man* (New York: W. W. Norton, 1981), chap. 5.

15. See Robert Plomin, *Nature and Nurture: An Introduction to Human Behavioral Genetics* (Belmont, CA: Wadsworth, 2004).

16. Andrew Robinson, *Sudden Genius? The Gradual Path to Creative Breakthroughs* (Oxford, UK: Oxford University Press, 2010), 9.

17. Quoted in ibid., 256.

18. Dean Keith Simonton, "Talent and Its Development: An Emergenic and Epigenetic Model," *Psychological Review* 106, no. 3 (July 1999): 440.

19. David T. Lykken, "The Genetics of Genius," in *Genius and the Mind: Studies of Creativity and Temperament,* edited by Andrew Steptoe (Oxford, UK: Oxford University Press, 1998), 28; Robinson, *Sudden Genius?,* 256.

20. Havelock Ellis, *A Study of British Genius* (London: Hurst and Blackett, 2017 [1904]), 94 ff.

21. Gilbert Gottlieb, "Normally Occurring Environmental and Behavioral Influences on Gene Activity: From Central Dogma to Probabilistic Epigenesis," *Psychological Review* 105, no. 3 (1995): 792–802.

22. K. Anders Ericsson, Ralf Th. Krampe, and Clemens Tesch-Römer, "The Role of Deliberate Practice in the Acquisition of Expert Performance," *Psychological Review* 100, vol. 3 (July 1993): 363–406. See also John A. Sloboda, Jane W. Davidson, Michael J. A. Howe, and Derek G. Moore, "The Role of Practice in the Development of Performing Musicians," *British Journal of Psychology* 87 (May 1996): 287–309.

23. Ericsson et al., "The Role of Deliberate Practice," 397.

24. Ellen Winner, *Gifted Children: Myths and Realities* (New York: Basic Books, 1997), 3.

25. On the career of Cézanne, see Alex Danchev, *Cézanne: A Life* (New York: Random House, 2012), 106, 110, 116; Lawrence Gowing, *Cézanne: The Early Years* (New York: Harry N. Abrams, 1988), 110.

26. *La Voz de Galicia,* February 21, 1895, quoted in John Richardson, *A Life of Picasso: The Prodigy, 1881–1906* (New York: Alfred A. Knopf, 1991), 55.

27. Richardson, *A Life of Picasso,* 67.

28. David W. Galenson, *Old Masters and Young Geniuses* (Princeton, NJ: Princeton University Press, 2006), 24.

29. Ibid., 23.

30. Danchev, *Cézanne,* 12.

31. "'The Father of Us All,'" Artsy, February 6, 2014, https://www.artsy.net/article/matthew-the-father-of-us-all.

32. Brooke N. MacNamara, David Z. Hambrick, and Frederick L. Oswald, "Deliberate Practice and Performance in Music, Games, Sports, Education, and Professions: A Meta-analysis," *Psychological Science* 8 (July 2014): 1608–18.

33. Condensation of email of August 4, 2019, to which Mr. Chen appended the following: "P.S. I read this to my (Chinese) mother, and she doesn't agree with the 20% to 80% argument. She thinks that work is above everything, 80% work 20% luck/ opportunity. Tiger mom mentality, right? It's interesting how different cultures/upbringing can influence one's opinion over these issues."

34. On the development of a standardized IQ test, see Simonton, "Talent and Its Development," 440–48; Darrin McMahon, *Divine Fury: A History of Genius* (New York: Basic Books, 2013), 178–85.

35. Deborah Solomon, "The Science of Second-Guessing," *New York*

Times, December 12, 2004, https://www.nytimes.com/2004 /12/12/magazine/the-science-of-secondguessing.html.

36. Martin André Rosanoff, "Edison in His Laboratory," *Harper's Magazine* (September 1932), https://harpers.org/archive/1932/09 /edison-in-his-laboratory/.

37. Gould, *The Mismeasure of Man,* 56–57.

38. *Griggs v. Duke Power Company,* 1971. IQ and similar tests can continue to be used, however, if they are a predictor of job performance and do not discriminate on the basis of race, religion, nationality, or gender.

39. William E. Sedlacek, *Beyond the Big Test: Noncognitive Assessment in Higher Education* (San Francisco: Jossey-Bass, 2004), 61–63.

40. Catherine Rampell, "SAT Scores and Family Income," *New York Times,* August 27, 2009, https://economix.blogs.nytimes.com /2009/08/27/sat-scores-and-family-income/; Zachary Goldfarb, "These Four Charts Show How the SAT Favors Rich, Educated Families," *Washington Post,* March 5, 2014, https://www .washingtonpost.com/news/wonk/wp/2014/03/05/these-four -charts-show-how-the-sat-favors-the-rich-educated-families/; Sedlacek, *Beyond the Big Test,* 68.

41. Aamer Madhani, "University of Chicago Becomes the First Elite College to Make SAT, ACT Optional for Applicants," *USA Today,* June 14, 2018, https://www.usatoday.com/story/news/2018/06/14 /university-chicago-sat-act-optional/701153002/.

42. Anemona Hartocollis, "University of California Is Sued over Use of SAT and ACT," *New York Times,* December 10, 2019, https:// www.nytimes.com/2019/12/10/us/sat-act-uc-lawsuit.html.

43. See, e.g., Lenora Chu, *Little Soldiers: An American Boy, a Chinese School, and the Global Race to Achieve* (New York: HarperCollins, 2017), 252; Sedlacek, *Beyond the Big Test,* 60.

44. Caitlin Macy, "AP Tests Are Still a Great American Equalizer," *Wall Street Journal,* February 22, 2019, https://www.wsj.com /articles/ap-tests-are-still-a-great-american-equalizer-11550854920.

45. See, e.g., Caroline Goldenberg, "School Removes AP Courses for Incoming Freshmen," *Horace Mann Record,* June 5, 2018, https:// record.horacemann.org/2078/uncategorized/school-removes-ap -courses-for-incoming-freshman-class/.

46. Adam Grant, "What Straight-A Students Get Wrong," *New York Times,* December 8, 2018, https://www.nytimes.com/2018/12/08/opinion/college-gpa-career-success.html.

47. Tom Clynes, "How to Raise a Genius," *Nature* (September 7, 2016), https://www.nature.com/news/how-to-raise-a-genius-lessons-from-a-45-year-study-of-super-smart-children-1.20537.

48. As summarized in Nancy Andreasen, *The Creating Brain: The Neuroscience of Genius* (New York: Dana Foundation, 2005), 10–13. See also Barbara Burks, Dortha Jensen, and Lewis Terman, *Genetic Studies of Genius,* vol. 3: *The Promise of Youth: Follow-Up Studies of a Thousand Gifted Students* (Stanford, CA: Stanford University Press, 1930).

49. Marjorie Garber, "Our Genius Problem," *The Atlantic* (December 2002), https://www.theatlantic.com/magazine/archive/2002/12/our-genius-problem/308435/.

50. Malcolm Jones, "How Darwin and Lincoln Shaped Us," *Newsweek* (June 28, 2008), https://www.newsweek.com/how-darwin-and-lincoln-shaped-us-91091.

51. Thomas Montalbo, "Churchill: A Study in Oratory: Seven Lessons in Speechmaking from One of the Greatest Orators of All Time," International Churchill Society, https://winstonchurchill.org/publications/finest-hour/finest-hour-069/churchill-a-study-in-oratory/.

52. Ann Hulbert, *Off the Charts* (New York: Alfred A. Knopf, 2018), 56. Andrew Robinson, "Is High Intelligence Necessary to be a Genius?," *Psychology Today* (January 2, 2011), https://www.psychologytoday.com/us/blog/sudden-genius/201101/is-high-intelligence-necessary-be-genius.

53. J. K. Rowling, *Very Good Lives: The Fringe Benefits of Failure and the Importance of Imagination* (New York: Little, Brown, 2008), 23.

54. Walter Isaacson, *Albert Einstein: His Life and Universe* (New York: Simon & Schuster, 2007), 48.

55. Duncan Clark, *Alibaba: The House That Jack Ma Built* (New York: HarperCollins, 2016), 44.

56. Michael Barrier, *The Animated Man: A Life of Walt Disney* (Berkeley: University of California Press, 2007), 18–19.

57. Jaime Sabartés, *Picasso: An Intimate Portrait* (London: W. H.

Allen, 1948), 36–39. See also Roland Penrose, *Picasso: His Life and Work,* 3rd ed. (Berkeley: University of California Press, 1981), 18–19; Richardson, *A Life of Picasso,* 33.

58. Howard Gardner, *Frames of Mind: The Theory of Multiple Intelligences* (New York: Basic Books, 1983), esp. chap. 4.

59. Rowling, *Very Good Lives,* 11–23.

60. Alison Flood, "JK Rowling's Writing Advice: Be a Gryffindor," *Guardian,* January 8, 2019, https://www.theguardian.com/books /booksblog/2019/jan/08/jk-rowlings-writing-advice-be-a-gryffindor.

61. Some psychologists have done just that. See Robert Sternberg, Juan-Luis Castejon, M. Prieto, et al., "Confirmatory Factor Analysis of the Sternberg Triarchic Abilities Test in Three International Samples: An Empirical Test of the Triarchic Theory of Intelligence," *European Journal of Psychological Assessment* 17, no. 1 (2001): 1–16.

62. Abraham J. Tannenbaum, "The IQ Controversy and the Gifted," in *Intellectual Talent,* edited by Camilla Benbow and David Lubinsky (Baltimore: Johns Hopkins University Press, 1996), 70–74; Anders Ericsson and Robert Pool, *Peak: Secrets from the New Science of Expertise* (Boston: Houghton Mifflin Harcourt, 2016), 235. See also Robert Sternberg, *Wisdom, Intelligence, and Creativity Synthesized* (Cambridge, UK: Cambridge University Press, 2003).

63. Quoted in Casey Miller and Keivan Stassun, "A Test That Fails," *Nature* 510 (2014): 303–4, https://www.nature.com/naturejobs /science/articles/10.1038/nj7504-303a. See also Robert J. Sternberg and Wendy M. Williams, "Does the Graduate Record Exam Predict Meaningful Success and Graduate Training of Psychologists? A Case Study," *American Psychologist* 52, no. 6 (June 1997): 630–41.

64. William Sedlacek, email to the author, October 2, 2019.

65. See George Anders, "You Can Start Anywhere," in Anders, *You Can Do Anything: The Surprising Power of a "Useless" Liberal Arts Education* (New York: Little, Brown, 2017), esp. 58.

66. Malcolm Gladwell, *Outliers: The Story of Success* (New York: Little, Brown, 2008), 80–84.

67. Billy Witz, Jennifer Medina, and Tim Arango, "Bribes and Big-Time Sports: U.S.C. Finds Itself, Once Again, Facing

Scandal," *New York Times,* March 14, 2019, https://www.nytimes
.com/2019/03/14/us/usc-college-cheating-scandal-bribes.html.

68. Melissa Korn and Jennifer Levitz, "In College Admissions
Scandal, Families from China Paid the Most," *Wall Street Journal,*
April 26, 2019, https://www.wsj.com/articles/the-biggest-clients
-in-the-college-admissions-scandal-were-from-china-11556301872.

69. John Bacon and Joey Garrison, "Ex–Yale Coach Pleads Guilty
for Soliciting Almost $1 Million in Bribes in College Admissions
Scandal," *USA Today,* March 28, 2019, https://www.usatoday
.com/story/news/nation/2019/03/28/rudy-meredith-ex-yale-coach
-expected-plead-guilty-college-admissions-scam/3296720002/;
Melissa Korn, "How to Fix College Admissions," *Wall Street
Journal,* November 29, 2019, https://www.wsj.com/articles/how
-to-fix-college-admissions-11575042980.

70. Long attributed to Einstein, but see "Everybody Is a Genius. But
If You Judge a Fish by Its Ability to Climb a Tree, It Will Live Its
Whole Life Believing That It Is Stupid," Quote Investigator, April 6,
2013, https://quoteinvestigator.com/2013/04/06/fish-climb/.

Chapter 2: Genius and Gender

1. Catherine Nichols, "Homme de Plume: What I Learned Sending
My Novel Out Under a Male Name," Jezebel, August 4, 2015,
https://jezebel.com/homme-de-plume-what-i-learned-sending-my
-novel-out-und-1720637627.

2. See, e.g., "Employers' Replies to Racial Names," National Bureau
of Economic Research, https://www.nber.org/digest/sep03/w9873
.html.

3. See, e.g., "Publishing Industry is Overwhelmingly White and
Female, US Study Finds," *Guardian,* January 27, 2016, https://
www.theguardian.com/books/2016/jan/27/us-study-finds
-publishing-is-overwhelmingly-white-and-female.

4. Sheryl Sandberg, "Women at Work: Speaking While Female,"
New York Times, January 12, 2015, https://www.nytimes.com
/2015/01/11/opinion/sunday/speaking-while-female.html.

5. Christopher F. Karpowitz, Tali Mendelberg, and Lee Shaker,
"Gender Inequality in Deliberative Participation," *American*

Political Science Review 106, no. 3 (August 2012): 533–47, https://pdfs.semanticscholar.org/c0ef/981e1191a7ff3ca6a63f205aef12f64d2f4e.pdf?_ga=2.81127703.1000116753.15841352521227194247.1574373344.

6. Catherine Hill, Christianne Corbett, and Andresse St. Rose, *Why So Few? Women in Science, Technology, Engineering, and Mathematics,* AAUW, February 2010, https://www.aauw.org/aauw_check/pdf_download/show_pdf.php?file=why-so-few-research.

7. Suzanne Choney, "Why Do Girls Lose Interest in STEM? New Research Has Some Answers—and What We Can Do About It," Microsoft Stories, March 13, 2018, https://news.microsoft.com/features/why-do-girls-lose-interest-in-stem-new-research-has-some-answers-and-what-we-can-do-about-it/.

8. Dean Keith Simonton, *Greatness: Who Makes History and Why* (New York: Guilford Press, 1994), 33–34.

9. Ibid., 37.

10. Virginia Woolf, *A Room of One's Own* (New York: Fountain Press, 2012 [1929]), 24.

11. Ibid., 48.

12. Ibid., 56.

13. Quoted in George Gordon, Lord Byron, *The Works of Lord Byron, with His Letters and Journals, and His Life,* vol. 2, edited by Thomas Moore (New York: J. & J. Harper, 1830–31), 275.

14. Sean Smith, *J. K. Rowling: A Biography: The Genius Behind Harry Potter* (London: Michael O'Mara Books, 2001), 132.

15. Woolf, *A Room of One's Own,* 53–54.

16. Ibid., 56.

17. Ibid., 35.

18. Byron, *The Works of Lord Byron,* vol. 2, 399.

19. Quoted in Cecil Gray, *A Survey of Contemporary Music* (London: Oxford University Press, 1924), 246.

20. Charles Darwin, "This Is the Question," in *The Autobiography of Charles Darwin, 1809–1882,* edited by Nora Barlow (New York: W. W. Norton, 1958), 195–96.

21. Françoise Gilot and Carlton Lake, *Life with Picasso* (London: McGraw-Hill, 2012 [1964]), 77.

22. Arthur Schopenhauer, *The World as Will and Idea,* 6th ed., vol. 3,

translated by R. B. Haldane and J. Kemp (London: Kegan Paul, 1909), Project Gutenberg, http://www.gutenberg.org/files /40868/40868-h/40868-h.html, 158.

23. Arthur Schopenhauer, *The Essays of Schopenhauer,* edited by Juliet Sutherland, Project Gutenberg, https://www.gutenberg.org /files/11945/11945-h/11945-h.htm#link2H_4_0009.

24. Quoted in Darrin McMahon, *Divine Fury: A History of Genius* (New York: Basic Books, 2013), 161.

25. Emma Brockes, "Return of the Time Lord," *Guardian,* September 27, 2005, https://www.theguardian.com/science/2005 /sep/27/scienceandnature.highereducationprofile.

26. Suzanne Goldenberg, "Why Women Are Poor at Science, by Harvard President," *Guardian,* January 18, 2005, https://www .theguardian.com/science/2005/jan/18/educationsgendergap .genderissues.

27. Alexander Moszkowski, *Conversations with Einstein,* translated by Henry L. Brose (New York: Horizon Press, 1970), 79.

28. Nikolaus Pevsner, *Academies of Art, Past and Present* (Cambridge, UK: Cambridge University Press, 1940), 231; Linda Nochlin, "Why Have There Been No Great Women Artists?," 1971, http://davidrifkind.org/fiu/library_files/Linda%20Nochlin%20 %20Why%20have%20there%20been%20no%20Great%20 Women%20Artists.pdf.

29. Peter Saenger, "The Triumph of Women Artists," *Wall Street Journal,* November 23, 2018, https://www.wsj.com/articles/the -triumph-of-women-artists-1542816015.

30. Anna Klumpke, *Rosa Bonheur: Sa vie, son oeuvre* (Paris: Flammarion, 1908), 308–9.

31. Alan Greenspan and Adrian Wooldridge, *Capitalism in America: A History* (New York: Random House, 2018), 363.

32. Quoted in Jerome Karabel, *The Chosen: The Hidden History of Admission and Exclusion at Harvard, Yale and Princeton* (New York: Mariner Books, 2014), 444.

33. Celestine Bohlen, "Breaking the Cycles That Keep Women Out of Tech-Related Professions," *New York Times,* November 26, 2018, https://www.nytimes.com/2018/11/20/world/europe/women-in -stem.html?searchResultPosition=9.

34. This and the Mendelssohn quote are drawn from Craig Wright, *Listening to Music*, 7th ed. (Boston: Cengage Learning, 2017), 252–53.

35. Mason Currey, *Daily Rituals: How Artists Work* (New York: Alfred A. Knopf, 2018), 44.

36. Alexandra Popoff, *The Wives: The Women Behind Russia's Literary Giants* (New York: Pegasus, 2012), 68.

37. "Hatshepsut," Western Civilization, ER Services, https://courses .lumenlearning.com/suny-hccc-worldhistory/chapter/hatshepsut/.

38. On the sculptures of Hatshepsut and their histories in the Metropolitan Museum of Art, New York, see "Large Kneeling Statue of Hatshepsut, ca. 1479–1458 B.C.," https://www.met museum.org/art/collection/search/544449 and especially "Sphinx of Hatshepsut," https://www.metmuseum.org/toah/works-of-art /31.3.166/.

39. For an overview of Hildegard of Bingen, see Barbara Newman's introduction to her *Saint Hildegard of Bingen: Symphonia* (Ithaca, NY: Cornell University Press, 1988) and Mathew Fox, *Hildegard of Bingen: A Saint for Our Times* (Vancouver: Namaste, 2012). For sample writings, see Sabina Flanagan, *Secrets of God: Writings of Hildegard of Bingen* (Boston: Shambhala, 1996). For samples of her letters, see Matthew Fox, ed., *Hildegard of Bingen's Book of Divine Works with Letters and Songs* (Santa Fe, NM: Bear & Co, 1987).

40. One example is the painting *Lot and his Daughters,* formerly attributed to Bernardo Cavallino, in the Toledo Museum of Art. See Josef Grabski, "On Seicento Painting in Naples: Some Observations on Bernardo Cavallino, Artemisia Gentileschi and Others," *Artibus et Historiae* 6, no. 11 (1985): 23–63. See also Sarah Cascone, "Sotheby's Offers Lost Artemisia Gentileschi Masterpiece," Artnet News, June 10, 2014, https://news.artnet.com/market/sothebys -offers-lost-artemisia-gentileschi-masterpiece-37273.

41. On the trial, see Tracy Marks, "Artemisia: The Rape and the Trial," http://www.webwinds.com/artemisia/trial.htm.

42. On Ada Lovelace, see, e.g., Betty A. Toole, *Ada, the Enchantress of Numbers: Prophet of the Computer Age* (Moreton-in-Marsh, Gloucestershire, UK: Strawberry Press, 1998) and William Gibson and Bruce Sterling, *The Difference Engine: A Novel* (New

York: Bantam Books, 1991). A good synopsis of Lovelace as computer visionary is given in Walter Isaacson, *The Innovators: How A Group of Hackers, Geniuses, and Geeks Created the Digital Revolution* (New York: Simon & Schuster, 2014), 7–33.

43. See Ruth Levin Sime, *Lise Meitner: A Life in Physics* (Berkeley: University of California Press, 1996), https://www.washington post.com/wp-srv/style/longterm/books/chap1/lisemeitner.htm ?noredirect=on.

44. Adam Parfrey and Cletus Nelson, *Citizen Keane: The Big Lies Behind the Big Eyes* (Port Townsend, WA: Feral House, 2014).

45. Ariane Hegewisch and Emma Williams-Baron, "The Gender Wage Gap: 2017 Earnings Differences by Race and Ethnicity," Institute for Women's Policy Research, March 7, 2018, https:// iwpr.org/publications/gender-wage-gap-2017-race-ethnicity/.

46. Rachel Bachman, "Women's Team Sues U.S. Soccer," *Wall Street Journal,* March 9, 2019, https://www.wsj.com/articles/u-s -womens-soccer-team-alleges-gender-discrimination-11552059299.

47. Gené Teare, "In 2017, Only 17% of Startups Have a Female Founder," TC, April 19, 2017, https://techcrunch.com/2017/04/19 /in-2017-only-17-of-startups-have-a-female-founder/; Valentina Zarya, "Female Founders Got only 2% of Venture Capital in 2017," *Fortune* (January 31, 2018), https://fortune.com/2018/01 /31/female-founders-venture-capital-2017/.

48. Adnisha Padnani, "How an Obits Project on Overlooked Women Was Born," *New York Times,* March 8, 2018, https://www.ny times.com/2018/03/08/insider/overlooked-obituary.html.

49. Mary Ann Sieghart, "Why Are Even Women Biased Against Women?," BBC Radio 4, February 4, 2018, https://www.bbc.co .uk/programmes/b09pl66d. See also Caroline Heldman, Meredith Conroy, and Alissa R. Ackerman, *Sex and Gender in the 2016 Presidential Election* (Santa Barbara, CA: Praeger, 2018).

50. Adrian Hoffmann and Jochen Musch, "Prejudice Against Women Leaders: Insights from an Indirect Questioning Approach," *Sex Roles* 80, nos. 11–12 (June 2019): 681–92, https://link.springer .com/article/10.1007/s11199-018-0969-6.

51. Mahzarin R. Banaji and Anthony G. Greenwald, *Blind Spot: Hidden Biases of Good People* (New York: Bantam Books, 2013).

52. Hill et al., *Why So Few?*, 74.
53. Corinne A. Moss-Racusin, John F. Dovidio, Victoria L. Brescoll, et al., "Science Faculty's Subtle Gender Biases Favor Male Students," *Proceedings of the National Academy of Sciences of the United States of America*, October 9, 2012, https://www.pnas.org/content/109/41/16474.
54. Banaji and Greenwald, *Blind Spot*, 115.
55. Brigid Schulte, "A Woman's Greatest Enemy? A Lack of Time to Herself," *Guardian*, July 21, 2019, https://www.theguardian.com/commentisfree/2019/jul/21/woman-greatest-enemy-lack-of-time-themselves.
56. Seth Stephens-Davidowitz, "Google, Tell Me. Is My Son a Genius?," *New York Times*, January 18, 2014, https://www.nytimes.com/2014/01/19/opinion/sunday/google-tell-me-is-my-son-a-genius.html.
57. Simonton, *Greatness*, 37.

Chapter 3: Avoid the Prodigy Bubble

1. See also Melissa Eddy, "A Musical Prodigy? Sure, but Don't Call Her 'a New Mozart,'" *New York Times*, June 14, 2019, https://www.nytimes.com/2019/06/14/world/europe/alma-deutscher-prodigy-mozart.html.
2. "British Child Prodigy's Cinderella Opera Thrills Vienna," BBC News, December 30, 2016, https://www.bbc.com/news/world-europe-38467218.
3. Otto Erich Deutsch, *Mozart: A Documentary Biography*, translated by Eric Blom, Peter Branscombe, and Jeremy Noble (Stanford, CA: Stanford University Press, 1965), 9.
4. Mozart had two sons who more than dabbled in music: Carl Thomas (1784–1858), who trained to be a musician but ended up a civil servant in Milan, and Franz Xaver (1791–1844), who earned his living as a composer, piano instructor, and occasional public performer. Neither left progeny.
5. Erich Schenk, "Mozarts Salzburger Vorfahren," *Mozart-Jahrbuch* 3 (1929): 81–93; Erich Schenk, *Mozart and His Times*, edited and translated by Richard and Clara Winston (New York: Knopf,

1959), 7–8; Erich Valentin, "Die Familie der Frau Mozart geb. Pertl," in Valentin, *"Madame Mutter": Anna Maria Walburga Mozart (1720–1778)* (Augsburg, Germany: Die Gesellschaft, 1991).

6. Deutsch, *Mozart*, 445.

7. Ibid., 27.

8. "Prodigy," *The Compact Oxford English Dictionary* (Oxford, UK: Oxford University Press, 1991).

9. *Inside Bill's Brain: Decoding Bill Gates,* Netflix, September 2019, episode 1.

10. Yo-Yo Ma, conversation with the author, Tanglewood, MA, August 14, 2011.

11. Dean Keith Simonton, Kathleen A. Taylor, and Vincent Cassandro, "The Creative Genius of William Shakespeare: Histiometric Analyses of His Plays and Sonnets," in *Genius and the Mind: Studies of Creativity and Temperament,* edited by Andrew Steptoe (Oxford, UK: Oxford University Press, 1998), 180.

12. Deutsch, *Mozart*, 360.

13. Cliff Eisen, *New Mozart Documents: A Supplement to O. E. Deutsch's Documentary Biography* (Stanford, CA: Stanford University Press, 1991), 14.

14. Alissa Quart, *Hothouse Kids: The Dilemma of the Gifted Child* (New York: Penguin, 2006), 77; *My Kid Could Paint That,* Sony Pictures Classic, 2007.

15. Deutsch, *Mozart*, 494.

16. Marin Alsop, conversation with the author, New Haven, CT, May 22, 2017.

17. Scott Barry Kaufman and Carolyn Gregoire, *Wired to Create: Unraveling the Mysteries of the Creative Mind* (New York: Random House, 2016), 151.

18. Quoted in Helia Phoenix, *Lady Gaga: Just Dance: The Biography* (London: Orion House, 2010), 44–45.

19. Quoted in Dean Keith Simonton, *Greatness: Who Makes History and Why* (New York: Guilford Press, 1994), 243.

20. Ellen Winner, *Gifted Children: Myths and Realities* (New York: Basic Books, 1996), 10; Alissa Quart, *Hothouse Kids: The Dilemma of the Gifted Child* (New York: Alfred A. Knopf, 2006), 204–5; Ann Hulbert, *Off the Charts: The Hidden Lives and*

Lessons of American Child Prodigies (New York: Alfred A. Knopf, 2018), 283, 291.

21. Maynard Solomon, *Mozart: A Life* (New York: Simon & Schuster, 1995), 177–209.

22. Leopold, letter to Wolfgang, February 12, 1778, in *The Letters of Mozart and His Family,* edited by Emily Anderson (London: Macmillan, 1985), 478.

23. Leopold, letter to Wolfgang, December 18, 1777, in ibid., 423.

24. Wolfgang Mozart, letter to Leopold, July 21, 1778, in ibid., 587.

25. Liz Schumer, "Why Mentoring Matters and How to Get Started," *New York Times,* September 30, 2018, https://www.nytimes.com /2018/09/26/smarter-living/why-mentoring-matters-how-to-get -started.html.

26. Quoted in John Richardson, *A Life of Picasso: The Prodigy, 1881–1906* (New York: Alfred A. Knopf, 2007), 45.

27. Douglas Stone, class presentation, Exploring the Nature of Genius course, Yale University, February 2, 2014.

28. The results of the initial study, which could not be duplicated, were published in Frances H. Rauscher, Gordon L. Shaw, and Catherine N. Ky, "Music and Spatial Task Performance," *Nature* 365, no. 611 (October 14, 1993). The expansion "Makes you smarter" was introduced by music critic Alex Ross in "Listening to Prozac . . . Er, Mozart," *New York Times,* August 28, 1994, https://www.nytimes.com/1994/08/28/arts/classical-view-listening -to-prozac-er-mozart.html.

29. Tamar Levin, "No Einstein in Your Crib? Get a Refund," *New York Times,* October 23, 2009, https://www.nytimes.com/2009 /10/24/education/24baby.html.

30. Winner, *Gifted Children,* 280–81.

31. Hulbert, *Off the Charts,* 291. On the "regrets of the prodigy," see Quart, *Hothouse Kids,* 210.

Chapter 4: Imagine the World as Does a Child

1. The description of the night comes from Mary Shelley, *History of a Six Weeks' Tour Through a Part of France, Switzerland, Germany and Holland, with Letters . . .* (London: T. Hookham and C. and

J. Ollier, 1817), https://archive.org/details/sixweekhistoryof00 shelrich/page/98/mode/2up, 99–100. The identification of the day is given in Fiona Sampson, *In Search of Mary Shelley* (New York: Pegasus, 2018), 124.

2. On *Frankenstein* and popular culture, see *Frankenstein: How a Monster Became an Icon*, edited by Signey Perkowitz and Eddy von Mueller (New York: Pegasus, 2018).

3. See, e.g., Kathryn Harkup, *Making the Monster: The Science Behind Mary Shelley's Frankenstein* (London: Bloomsbury, 2018).

4. Mary Shelley, *Frankenstein: Annotated for Scientists, Engineers, and Creators of All Kinds*, edited by David H. Guston, Ed Finn, and Jason Scott Robert (Cambridge, MA: MIT Press, 2017), 84.

5. The introduction is reproduced at *Frankenstein*, Romantic Circles, https://www.rc.umd.edu/editions/frankenstein/1831v1/intro.html.

6. For the publication history and reception of *Frankenstein*, see Harkup, *Making the Monster*, 253–55.

7. "Harry Potter and Me," BBC Christmas Special, British Version, December 28, 2001, transcribed by "Marvelous Marvolo" and Jimmi Thøgersen, http://www.accio-quote.org/articles/2001 /1201-bbc-hpandme.htm.

8. Ibid.

9. See, e.g., Arianna Stassinopoulos Huffington, *Picasso: Maker and Destroyer* (New York: Simon & Schuster, 1988), 379.

10. Quoted in Ann Hulburt, *Off the Charts: The Hidden Lives and Lessons of American Child Prodigies* (New York: Alfred A. Knopf, 2018), 260.

11. Quoted in Howard Gardner, *Creating Minds: An Anatomy of Creativity* (New York: Basic Books, 1993), 145.

12. Natasha Staller, "Early Picasso and the Origins of Cubism," *Arts Magazine* 61 (1986): 80–90; Gertrude Stein, *Gertrude Stein on Picasso*, edited by Edward Burns (New York: Liveright, 1970).

13. As told to Françoise Gilot, in Françoise Gilot and Carlton Lake, *Life with Picasso* (New York: McGraw-Hill, 1990 [1964]), 113.

14. Quoted in Max Wertheimer, *Productive Thinking* (New York: Harper & Row, 1959), 213.

15. Albert Einstein, *Autobiographical Notes*, translated and edited by Paul Schlipp (La Salle, IL: Open Court, 1979), 6–7.

16. Ibid., 49; Walter Isaacson, *Einstein: His Life and Universe* (New York: Simon & Schuster, 2007), 26; Peter A. Bucky, *The Private Albert Einstein* (Kansas City, MO: Universal Press, 1992), 26.

17. Quoted in Isaacson, *Einstein,* 196.

18. J. Robert Oppenheimer, *Robert Oppenheimer: Letters and Recollections,* edited by Alice Kimball Smith and Charles Weiner (Cambridge, MA: Harvard University Press, 1980), 190.

19. Justin Gammill, "10 ACTUAL Quotes from Albert Einstein," October 22, 2015, I Heart Intelligence, https://iheartintelligence .com/2015/10/22/quotes-from-albert-einstein/.

20. Albert Einstein, letter to Otto Juliusburger, September 29, 1942, Albert Einstein Archives, Hebrew University, Jerusalem, folder 38, document 238.

21. J. Randy Taraborelli, *Michael Jackson: The Magic, the Madness, the Whole Story, 1958–2009* (New York: Grand Central Publishing, 2009), 201.

22. Goodreads, https://www.goodreads.com/quotes/130291-the -secret-of-genius-is-to-carry-the-spirit-of.

23. Dann Hazel and Josh Fippen, *A Walt Disney World Resort Outing: The Only Vacation Planning Guide Exclusively for Gay and Lesbian Travelers* (San Jose: Writers Club Press, 2002), 211.

24. "The Birth of a Mouse," referencing Walt Disney's essay "What Mickey Means to Me," Walt Disney Family Museum, November 18, 2012, https://www.waltdisney.org/blog/birth -mouse.

25. Otto Erich Deutsch, *Mozart: A Documentary Biography,* translated by Eric Blom, Peter Branscombe, and Jeremy Noble (Stanford, CA: Stanford University Press, 1965), 462.

26. Mozart, letter to Maria Anna Thekla Mozart, November 5, 1777, in Wolfgang Amadeus Mozart, *The Letters of Mozart and His Family,* edited by Emily Anderson (London: Macmillan, 1985), 358.

27. M. J. Coren, "John Cleese—How to Be Creative," Vimeo, https:// vimeo.com/176474304.

28. Frida Kahlo, *The Diary of Frida Kahlo: An Intimate Self-Portrait* (New York: Abrams, 2005), 245–47.

29. Deutsch, *Mozart,* 493.

30. Letter of January 15, 1787, in Mozart, *The Letters of Mozart and His Family*, 904.

31. Jeff Bezos, *First Mover: Jeff Bezos in His Own Words*, edited by Helena Hunt (Chicago: Agate Publishing, 2018), 93.

32. Amihud Gilead, "Neoteny and the Playground of Pure Possibilities," *International Journal of Humanities and Social Sciences* 5, no. 2 (February 2015): 30–39, http://www.ijhssnet .com/journals/Vol_5_No_2_February_2015/4.pdf.

33. Stephen Jay Gould, "A Biological Homage to Mickey Mouse," https://faculty.uca.edu/benw/biol4415/papers/Mickey.pdf.

34. George Sylvester Viereck, "What Life Means to Einstein," *Saturday Evening Post* (October 26, 1929), http://www.saturdayevening post.com/wp-content/uploads/satevepost/einstein.pdf, 117.

35. Author's translation from Charles Baudelaire, *Le Peintre de la vie moderne* (Paris: FB Editions, 2014 [1863]), 13.

Chapter 5: Develop a Lust for Learning

1. Frank A. Mumby and R. S. Rait, *The Girlhood of Queen Elizabeth* (Whitefish, MT: Kessinger, 2006), 69–72.

2. "Queen Elizabeth I of England," Luminarium: Anthology of English Literature, http://www.luminarium.org/renlit/elizlet1544 .htm.

3. Elizabeth I, *Elizabeth I: Collected Works*, edited by Leah S. Marcus, Janel Mueller, and Mary Beth Rose (Chicago: University of Chicago Press, 2002), 182.

4. William Camden, *The Historie of the Most Renowned and Victorious Princess Elizabeth, Late Queen of England* (London: Benjamin Fisher, 1630), 6.

5. Elizabeth I, *Elizabeth I: Collected Works*, 332–35. See Folger Library, Washington, D.C., V.a.321, fol. 36, as well as *Modern History Sourcebook: Queen Elizabeth I of England (b. 1533, r. 1558–1603); Selected Writing and Speeches*, https://sourcebooks .fordham.edu/mod/elizabeth1.asp.

6. Susan Engel, *The Hungry Mind: The Origins of Curiosity in Childhood* (Cambridge, MA: Harvard University Press, 2015), 17 and chap. 4.

7. Kenneth Clark, "The Renaissance," in *Civilisation: A Personal View*, 1969, http://www.historyaccess.com/therenaissanceby.html.

8. Drawn from Leonardo's *Codex Atlanticus*, fol. 611, quoted in Ian Leslie, *Curious: The Desire to Know and Why Your Future Depends on It* (New York: Basic Books, 2014), 16.

9. Fritjof Capra, *The Science of Leonardo: Inside the Mind of the Great Genius of the Renaissance* (New York: Random House, 2007), 2.

10. Sigmund Freud, *Leonardo da Vinci and a Memory of His Childhood*, edited and translated by Alan Tyson (New York: W. W. Norton, 1964), 85.

11. A list of confirmed left-handed luminaries, and some supposed, is given in Dean Keith Simonton, *Greatness: Who Makes History and Why* (New York: Guilford Press, 1994), 22–24.

12. Sherwin B. Nuland, *Leonardo da Vinci: A Life* (New York: Penguin, 2000), 17.

13. Quoted in ibid., 18.

14. Amelia Noor, Chew Chee, and Asina Ahmed, "Is There a Gay Advantage in Creativity?" *The International Journal of Psychological Studies* 5, no. 2 (2013), ccsenet.org/journal/index.php/ijps/article/view/24643.

15. Giorgio Vasari, "Life of Leonardo da Vinci," in Vasari, *Lives of the Most Eminent Painters, Sculptors, and Architects*, translated by Lulia Conaway Bondanella and Peter Bondanella (Oxford, UK: Oxford University Press, 1991), 284, 294, 298.

16. Walter Isaacson, *Leonardo da Vinci* (New York: Simon & Schuster, 2017), 397.

17. Leonardo da Vinci, *The Notebooks of Leonardo da Vinci*, edited by Edward MacCurdy (New York: George Braziller, 1939), 166.

18. J. B. Bellhouse and F. H. Bellhouse, "Mechanism of Closure of the Aortic Valve," *Nature* 217 (1968), https://www.nature.com/articles/217086b0, 86–87.

19. Alastair Sooke, "Leonardo da Vinci—The Anatomist," *The Culture Show at Edinburgh*, BBC, December 31, 2013, https://www.youtube.com/watch?v=-J6MdN_fucUu&t=9s.

20. Isaacson, *Leonardo da Vinci*, 412.

21. "Blurring the Lines," *National Geographic* (May 2019): 68–69.

22. Quoted in Marilyn Johnson, "A Life in Books," *Life* (September 1997): 47.

23. Ibid., 53.

24. Ibid., 60.

25. Oprah Winfrey, *Own It: Oprah Winfrey in Her Own Words,* edited by Anjali Becker and Jeanne Engelmann (Chicago: Agate, 2017), 77.

26. Benjamin Franklin, *Benjamin Franklin: The Autobiography and Other Writings,* edited by L. Jesse Lemisch (New York: Penguin, 2014), 15.

27. Richard Bell, "The Genius of Benjamin Franklin," lecture, Northwestern University Law School, Chicago, September 28, 2019.

28. Franklin, *Autobiography,* 18.

29. Quoted in Bill Gates, *Impatient Optimist: Bill Gates in His Own Words,* edited by Lisa Rogak (Chicago: Agate, 2012), 107.

30. Franklin, *Autobiography,* 112.

31. Most of the primary source documents are given in J. Bernard Cohen, *Benjamin Franklin's Experiments* (Cambridge, MA: Harvard University Press, 1941), 49 ff.

32. *The Papers of Benjamin Franklin,* March 28, 1747, https://franklinpapers.org/framedVolumes.jsp, 3, 115.

33. Ibid., December 25, 1750, https://franklinpapers.org/framedVolumes.jsp, 4, 82–83.

34. Peter Dray, *Stealing God's Thunder* (New York: Random House, 2005), 97.

35. Franklin, letter to Jonathan Shipley, February 24, 1786, in Franklin, *Autobiography,* 290.

36. Nikola Tesla, *My Inventions: An Autobiography,* edited by David Major (San Bernardino, CA: Philovox, 2013), 15.

37. Extrapolating from what Tesla is reading in a similarly staged photo of him taken earlier in 1899 in his lab at 46–48 Houston Street in lower Manhattan.

38. W. Bernard Carlson, *Tesla: Inventor of the Electrical Age* (Princeton, NJ: Princeton University Press, 2013), 191.

39. Ibid., 282.

40. Both quotes are from Ashlee Vance, *Elon Musk: Tesla, SpaceX,*

and the Quest for a Fantastic Future (New York: HarperCollins, 2015), 33.

41. shazmosushi, "Elon Musk Profiled: Bloomberg Risk Takers," January 3, 2013, YouTube, https://www.youtube.com/watch ?v=CTJt547--AM, at 4:02.

42. Ibid., at 17:00.

43. Engel, *The Hungry Mind*, 33, 38.

44. Mary-Catherine McClain and Steven Pfeiffer, "Identification of Gifted Students in the United States Today: A Look at State Definitions, Policies, and Practices," *Journal of Applied School Psychology* 28, no. 1 (2012): 59–88, https://eric.ed.gov /?id=EJ956579.

45. "Eleanor Roosevelt: Curiosity Is the Greatest Gift," Big Think, December 23, 2014, quoting *Today's Health* (October 1966), https://bigthink.com/words-of-wisdom/eleanor-roosevelt -curiosity-is-the-greatest-gift.

46. Scott Kaufman, "Schools Are Missing What Matters About Learning," *The Atlantic* (July 24, 2017), https://www.theatlantic .com/education/archive/2017/07/the-underrated-gift-of-curiosity /534573/.

47. Henry Blodget, "I Asked Jeff Bezos the Tough Questions— No Profits, the Book Controversies, the Phone Flop—and He Showed Why Amazon Is Such a Huge Success," Business Insider, December 13, 2014, https://www.businessinsider.com/amazons -jeff-bezos-on-profits-failure-succession-big-bets-2014-12.

48. See, e.g., Engel, *The Hungry Mind*, 17–18; Amihud Gilead, "Neoteny and the Playground of Pure Possibilities," *International Journal of Humanities and Social Sciences* 5, no. 2 (February 2015): 30–33, http://www.ijhssnet.com/journals/Vol_5_No_2 _February_2015/4.pdf; and Cameron J. Camp, James R. Rodrigue, and Kenneth R. Olson, "Curiosity in Young, Middle-Aged, and Older Adults," *Educational Gerontology* 10, no. 5 (1984): 387–400, https://www.tandfonline.com/doi/abs/10.1080 /0380127840100504?journalCode=uedg20.

49. Albert Einstein, letter to Cal Seelig, March 11, 1952, quoted in Einstein, *The New Quotable Einstein*, edited by Alice Calaprice (Princeton, NJ: Princeton University Press, 2005), 14.

50. Albert Einstein, *Autobiographical Notes,* edited and translated by Paul Schlipp (La Salle, IL: Open Court, 1979), 9.

51. Quoted in Walter Isaacson, *Einstein: His Life and Universe* (New York: Simon & Schuster, 2007), 18.

52. Max Talmey, *The Relativity Theory Simplified and the Formative Period of Its Inventor* (New York: Falcon Press, 1932), 164.

53. Einstein, *Autobiographical Notes,* 17.

54. Albert Einstein, *Ideas and Opinions,* edited by Cal Seelig (New York: Random House, 1982), 63.

55. I am indebted to Latinist Tim Robinson for helping me correctly craft this Latin phrase.

56. "Self-education Is the Only Kind of Education There Is," Quote Investigator, https://quoteinvestigator.com/2016/07/07/self -education/.

Chapter 6: Find Your Missing Piece

1. Vincent van Gogh, letter to Theo, Cuesmes, July 1880, http:// www.webexhibits.org/vangogh/letter/8/133.htm.

2. Alan C. Elms, "Apocryphal Freud: Sigmund Freud's Most Famous Quotations and Their Actual Sources," in *Annual of Psychoanalysis* 29 (2001): 83–104, https://elms.faculty.ucdavis .edu/wp-content/uploads/sites/98/2014/07/20011Apocryphal -Freud-July-17-2000.pdf.

3. Jon Interviews, "Gabe Polsky Talks About 'In Search of Greatness,'" October 26, 2018, https://www.youtube.com /watch?v=fP8baSEK7HY, at 14:16.

4. Jean F. Mercier, "Shel Silverstein," *Publishers Weekly* (February 24, 1975), http://shelsilverstein.tripod.com/ShelPW.html.

5. Andrew Robinson, *Sudden Genius?: The Gradual Path to Creative Breakthroughs* (Oxford, UK: Oxford University Press, 2010), 164.

6. Marie Curie, "Autobiographical Notes," in Curie, *Pierre Curie,* translated by Charlotte and Vernon Kellogg (New York: Dover, 2012 [1923]), 84.

7. Ibid., 92.

8. Eve Curie, *Madame Curie: A Biography by Eve Curie,* translated by Vincent Sheean (New York: Dover, 2001 [1937]), 157.

9. This and the following quote are drawn from Marie Curie, "Autobiographical Notes," 92.

10. Eve Curie, *Madame Curie,* 174.

11. Curie, "Autobiographical Notes," 92.

12. https://www.quotetab.com/quote/by-frida-kahlo/passion-is-the -bridge-that-takes-you-from-pain-to-change#GOQJ7pxSyy EPUTYw.97. I have been unable to identify the original source.

13. John Stuart Mill, *Autobiography* (New York: H. Holt, 1873), chap. 5, paraphrased in Eric Weiner, *The Geography of Bliss* (New York: Hachette, 2008), 74.

14. Arthur Schopenhauer, *The World as Will and Idea,* translated by R. B. Haldane and J. Kemp (London: Kegan Paul, 1909), vol. 1, http://www.gutenberg.org/files/38427/38427-h/38427-h.html #pglicense, 240.

15. Harriet Reisen, *Louisa May Alcott: The Woman Behind Little Women* (New York: Henry Holt, 2009), 216.

16. Louisa May Alcott, *Little Women,* pt. 2, chap. 27, http://www .literaturepage.com/read/littlewomen-296.html.

17. Mason Currey, *Daily Rituals: Women at Work* (New York: Knopf, 2019), 52.

18. John Maynard Keynes, "Newton, the Man," July 1946, http:// www-groups.dcs.st-and.ac.uk/history/Extras/Keynes_Newton .html.

19. Anecdotes of this sort, coming from Newton's manservant Humphrey Newton, are preserved in Cambridge, King's College Library, Keynes MS 135, and redacted at "The Newton Project," http://www.newtonproject.ox.ac.uk/view/texts/normalized /THEM00033.

20. See "Newton Beats Einstein in Polls of Scientists and Public," The Royal Society, November 23, 2005, https://royalsociety.org/news /2012/newton-einstein/.

21. "Newton's Dark Secrets," *Nova,* PBS, https://www.youtube.com /watch?v=sdmhPfGo3fE&t=105s.

22. John Henry, "Newton, Matter, and Magic," in *Let Newton Be!: A New Perspective on his Life and Works,* edited by John Fauvel, Raymond Flood, Michael Shortland, and Robin Wilson (Oxford, UK: Oxford University Press, 1988), 142.

23. Jan Golinski, "The Secret Life of an Alchemist," in *Let Newton Be*, 147–67.

24. Isaac Newton, letter to John Locke, July 7, 1692, in *The Correspondence of Isaac Newton,* vol. 3, edited by H. W. Turnbull (Cambridge, UK: Cambridge University Press, 1961), 215.

25. See Thomas Levenson, *Newton and the Counterfeiter: The Unknown Detective Career of the World's Greatest Scientist* (Boston: Houghton Mifflin Harcourt, 2009), 223–32.

26. As paraphrased in James Gleick, *Isaac Newton* (New York: Random House, 2003), 190.

27. Charles Darwin, *The Autobiography of Charles Darwin,* edited by Nora Barlow (New York: W. W. Norton, 2005), 53.

28. Janet Browne, *Charles Darwin: Voyaging* (Princeton, NJ: Princeton University Press, 1995), 102.

29. Darwin, *Autobiography,* 53.

30. Browne, *Charles Darwin,* 88–116.

31. American Museum of Natural History, Twitter, February 12, 2018, https://twitter.com/AMNH/status/963159916792963073.

32. Darwin, *Autobiography,* 115.

33. Abigail Elise, "Orson Welles Quotes: 10 of the Filmmaker's Funniest and Best Sayings," International Business Times, May 6, 2015, https://www.ibtimes.com/orson-welles-quotes-10-film makers-funniest-best-sayings-1910921.

34. *Harper's Magazine* (September 1932), cited in Thomas Alva Edison, *The Quotable Edison,* edited by Michele Albion (Gainesville: University Press of Florida, 2011), 82.

35. Randall Stross, *The Wizard of Menlo Park: How Thomas Alva Edison Invented the Modern World* (New York: Random House, 2007), 66.

36. Ibid., 229. See also "Edison at 75 Still a Two-Shift Man," *New York Times,* February 12, 1922, https://www.nytimes.com/1922 /02/12/archives/edison-at-75-still-a-twoshift-man-submits-to -birthday-questionnaire.html.

37. "Mr. Edison's Use of Electricity," *New York Tribune,* September 28, 1878, Thomas A. Edison Papers, Rutgers University, http://edison.rutgers.edu/digital.htm, SB032142a.

38. *Ladies' Home Journal* (April 1898), quoted in Edison, *The Quotable Edison,* 101.
39. "I Have Gotten a Lot of Results. I Know of Several Thousand Things that Won't Work," Quote Investigator, July 31, 2012, https://quoteinvestigator.com/2012/07/31/edison-lot-results/.
40. Jim Clash, "Elon Musk Interview," AskMen, 2014, https://www.askmen.com/entertainment/right-stuff/elon-musk-interview-4.html.
41. Dana Gioia, "Work, for the Night Is Coming," *Los Angeles Times,* January 23, 1994, https://www.latimes.com/archives/la-xpm-1994-01-23-bk-14382-story.html.

Chapter 7: Leverage Your Difference

1. A recently discovered letter from a provincial French doctor, Félix Rey, reveals how much of his ear van Gogh cut off. The discovery is discussed in Bernadette Murphy, *Van Gogh's Ear* (New York: Farrar, Straus and Giroux, 2016), chap. 14.
2. Plato discussed four different types of madness in *Phaedrus* (c. 360 B.C.), translated by Benjamin Jowett, The Internet Classics Archive, http://classics.mit.edu/Plato/phaedrus.html.
3. Aristotle, *Problems: Books 32–38,* translated by W. S. Hett and H. Rackham (Cambridge, MA: Harvard University Press, 1936), problem 30.1.
4. John Dryden, "Absalom and Achitophel," Poetry Foundation, https://www.poetryfoundation.org/poems/44172/absalom-and-achitophel.
5. Edgar Allan Poe, "Eleonora," quoted in Scott Barry Kaufman and Carolyn Gregoire, *Wired to Create: Unraveling the Mysteries of the Creative Mind* (New York: Random House, 2016), 36.
6. "Quotes from Alice in Wonderland—by Lewis Caroll," Book Edition, January 31, 2013, https://booksedition.wordpress.com/2013/01/31/quotes-from-alice-in-wonderland-by-lewis-caroll/.
7. "Live at the Roxy," HBO (1978), https://www.youtube.com/watch?v=aTRtH1uJh0g.
8. Cesare Lombroso, *The Man of Genius,* 3rd ed. (London: Walter Scott, 1895), 66–99.

9. Kay R. Jamison, *Touched with Fire: Manic-Depressive Illness and the Artistic Temperament* (New York: Simon & Schuster, 1993), esp. chap. 3, "Could It Be Madness—This?" See also Nancy C. Andreasen, "Creativity and Mental Illness: Prevalence Rates in Writers and Their First-Degree Relatives," *American Journal of Psychiatry* 144 (1987): 1288–92, as well as Andreasen's *The Creating Brain: The Neuroscience of Genius* (New York: Dana Press, 2005), esp. chap. 4, "Genius and Insanity."

10. Kay Redfield Jamison, "Mood Disorders and Patterns of Creativity in British Writers and Artists," *Psychiatry* 52, no. 2 (1989): 125–34; Jamison, *Touched with Fire*, 72–73.

11. François Martin Mai, "Illness and Creativity," in Mai, *Diagnosing Genius: The Life and Death of Beethoven* (Montreal: McGill-Queens University Press, 2007), 187; Andrew Robinson, *Sudden Genius?: The Gradual Path to Creative Breakthroughs* (Oxford, UK: Oxford University Press, 2010), 58–61; Jamison, *Touched with Fire*, 58–75.

12. Quoted on the back cover of Christopher Zara, *Tortured Artists: From Picasso and Monroe to Warhol and Winehouse, the Twisted Secrets of the World's Most Creative Minds* (Avon, MA: Adams Media, 2012).

13. Roger Dobson, "Creative Minds: The Links Between Mental Illness and Creativity," LewRockwell.com, May 22, 2009, https://www.lewrockwell.com/2009/05/roger-dobson/creative-minds-the-links-between-mentalillness-andcreativity/.

14. M. Schneider, "Great Minds in Economics: An Interview with John Nash," *Yale Economic Review* 4, no. 2 (Summer 2008): 26–31, http://www.markschneideresi.com/articles/Nash_Interview.pdf.

15. Sylvia Nasar, *A Beautiful Mind* (New York: Simon & Schuster, 2011), back cover.

16. See, e.g., Anna Greuner, "Vincent van Gogh's Yellow Vision," *British Journal of General Practice* 63, no. 612 (July 2013): 370–71, https://bjgp.org/content/63/612/370.

17. Derek Fell, *Van Gogh's Women: Vincent's Love Affairs and Journey into Madness* (New York: Da Capo Press, 2004), 242–43, 248.

18. Vincent van Gogh, letter to Theo, January 28, 1889, Vincent van

Gogh: The Letters, http://vangoghletters.org/vg/letters/let743 /letter.html.

19. See Alastair Sooke, "The Mystery of Van Gogh's Madness," BBC, July 25, 2016, YouTube, https://www.youtube.com/watch?v=Ag MBRQLhgFE.

20. See, e.g., the middle of the letter to Theo of January 28, 1886, Vincent van Gogh: The Letters, http://vangoghletters.org/vg /letters/let555/letter.html.

21. See, e.g., Marije Vellekoop, Van Gogh at Work (New Haven, CT: Yale University Press, 2013); Nina Siegal, "Van Gogh's True Palette Revealed," New York Times, April 30, 2013, https://www .nytimes.com/2013/04/30/arts/30iht-vangogh30.html.

22. Vincent van Gogh, letter to Theo, July 1, 1882, Vincent van Gogh: The Letters, http://vangoghletters.org/vg/letters/let241 /letter.html.

23. Vincent van Gogh, letter to Theo, July 6, 1882, Vincent van Gogh: The Letters, http://vangoghletters.org/vg/letters/let244 /letter.html.

24. Vincent van Gogh, letter to Theo, July 22, 1883, Vincent van Gogh: The Letters, http://vangoghletters.org/vg/letters/let364 /letter.html.

25. Gordon Claridge, "Creativity and Madness: Clues from Modern Psychiatric Diagnosis," in Genius and the Mind, edited by Andrew Steptoe (Oxford, UK: Oxford University Press, 1998), 238–40.

26. Quoted in Thomas C. Caramagno, The Flight of the Mind: Virginia Woolf's Art and Manic-Depressive Illness (Berkeley: University of California Press, 1991), 48.

27. Leonard Woolf, Beginning Again: An Autobiography of the Years 1911 to 1918 (Orlando, FL: Harcourt Brace Jovanovich, 1963), 79.

28. Caramagno, The Flight of the Mind, 75.

29. Virginia Woolf, Virginia Woolf: Women and Writing, edited by Michèle Barrett (Orlando, FL: Harcourt Brace Jovanovich, 1979), 58–60.

30. The Diary of Virginia Woolf, vol. 3: 1925–30, edited by Anne Olivier Bell (Orlando, FL: Harcourt Brace & Company, 1981), 111.

31. The Diary of Virginia Woolf, vol. 4: 1931–35, edited by Anne Olivier Bell (San Diego: Harcourt Brace & Company, 1982), 161.

32. Yayoi Kusama, *Infinity Net: The Autobiography of Yayoi Kusama* (London: Tate Publishing, 2011), 205.

33. Ibid., 57, 191.

34. Ibid., 20.

35. Natalie Frank, "Does Yayoi Kusama Have a Mental Disorder?," Quora, January 29, 2016, https://www.quora.com/Does-Yayoi -Kusama-have-a-mental-disorder.

36. Kusama, *Infinity Net,* 66.

37. Vincent van Gogh, letter to Theo, July 8 or 9, 1888, Vincent van Gogh: The Letters, http://vangoghletters.org/vg/letters /let637. Woolf: Woolf, *The Diary of Virginia Woolf,* vol. 3, 287. Kusama: Natalie Frank, "Does Yayoi Kusama Have a Mental Disorder?" Picasso: quoted in Jack Flam, *Matisse and Picasso* (Cambridge, MA: Westview Press, 2003), 34; Sexton: Kaufman and Gregoire, *Wired to Create,* 150. Churchill: quoted in his 1921 essay "Painting as a Pastime." Graham: quoted in her *Blood Memory: An Autobiography* (New York: Doubleday, 1991). Lowell: Patricia Bosworth, "A Poet's Pathologies: Inside Robert Lowell's Restless Mind," *New York Times,* March 1, 2017. Close: Society for Neuroscience, "My Life as a Rolling Neurological Clinic," Dialogues between Neuroscience and Society, New Orleans, October 17, 2012, YouTube, https://www.youtube.com /watch?v=qWadil0W5GU, at 11:35. Winehouse: interview with *Spin* (2007), quoted in Zara, *Tortured Artists,* 200.

38. Ludwig van Beethoven, "Heiligenstadt Testament," October 6, 1802, in Maynard Solomon, *Beethoven,* 2nd rev. ed. (New York: Schirmer Books, 1998), 152; see also 144 for a facsimile of the document.

39. Author's translation from Paul Scudo, "Une Sonate de Beethoven," *Revue des Deux Mondes,* new series 15, no. 8 (1850): 94.

40. Mai, *Diagnosing Genius;* D. Jablow Hershman and Julian Lieb, "Beethoven," in *The Key to Genius: Manic-Depression and the Creative Life* (Buffalo, NY: Prometheus Books, 1988), 59–92; Solomon, *Beethoven,* see index under "mood swings" and "alcohol excesses"; Leon Plantinga, author of *Beethoven's Concertos: History, Style, Performance* (1999), conversations with the author, March 7, 2017.

41. Beethoven, letter to Franz Wegeler, June 29, 1801, reproduced in Ludwig van Beethoven, *Beethoven: Letters, Journals and Conversations,* edited and translated by Michael Hamburger (Garden City, NY: Doubleday, 1960), 24.

42. Solomon, *Beethoven,* 158.

43. A point emphasized to me by the Beethoven scholar Leon Plantinga in a personal conversation, December 11, 2019.

44. Solomon, *Beethoven,* 161.

45. I owe my awareness of this issue to the kindness of Professor Caroline Robertson of Dartmouth College.

46. Caroline Robertson, "Creativity in the Brain: The Neurobiology of Autism and Prosopagnosia," lecture, Yale University, March 4, 2015.

47. Close, "My Life as a Rolling Neurological Clinic," at 46:00. See also Eric Kandel, *The Disordered Mind: What Unusual Brains Tell Us About Ourselves* (New York: Farrar, Straus and Giroux, 2018), 131.

48. Close, "My Life as a Rolling Neurological Clinic," at 28:20.

49. For an overview of the question of autistic savants, see Joseph Straus, "Idiots Savants, Retarded Savants, Talented Aments, Mono-Savants, Autistic Savants, Just Plain Savants, People with Savant Syndrome, and Autistic People Who Are Good at Things: A View from Disability Studies," in *Disability Studies Quarterly* 34, no. 3 (2014), http://dsq-sds.org/article/view/3407/3640.

50. Oliver Sacks, *The River of Consciousness* (New York: Alfred A. Knopf, 2019), 142. See also Oliver Sacks, *An Anthropologist on Mars: Seven Paradoxical Tales* (New York: Vintage, 1995), 197–206; Kandel, *The Disordered Mind,* 152; Eric Kandel, *The Age of Insight: The Quest to Understand the Unconscious in Art, Mind, and Brain, from Vienna 1900 to the Present* (New York: Random House, 2012), 492–94.

51. Hans Asperger, "'Autistic Psychopathy' in Childhood," in *Autism and Asperger Syndrome,* edited by Ute Firth (Cambridge, UK: Cambridge University Press, 1991), 37–92. On this topic generally, see Ioan James, *Asperger's Syndrome and High Achievement: Some Very Remarkable People* (London: Jessica Kingsley, 2006), and Michael Fitzgerald, *Autism and Creativity:*

Is There a Link Between Autism in Men and Exceptional Ability? (London: Routledge, 2004).

52. Many Things, *Robin Williams: Live on Broadway*, HBO, 2002, YouTube, www.youtube.com/watch?v=FS376sohiXc.

53. James Lipton, interview with Robin Williams, *Inside the Actors Studio: 2001*, www.dailymotion.com/video/x64ojf8.

54. Zoë Kessler, "Robin Williams' Death Shocking? Yes and No," PsychCentral, August 28, 2014, https://blogs.psychcentral.com /adhd-zoe/2014/08/robin-williams-death-shocking-yes-and-no/.

55. Dave Itzkoff, *Robin* (New York: Henry Holt, 2018), 41.

56. See, e.g., johanna-khristina, "Celebrities with a History of ADHD or ADD," IMDb, March 27, 2012, https://www.imdb.com/list /ls004079795/; Kessler, "Robin Williams' Death Shocking?"

57. Leonard Mlodinow, "In Praise of A.D.H.D," *New York Times*, March 17, 2018, https://www.nytimes.com/2018/03/17/opinion /sunday/praise-adhd-attention-hyperactivity.html; Scott Kaufman, "The Creative Gifts of ADHD," *Scientific American* (October 21, 2014), blogs.scientificamerican.com/beautiful-minds/2014/10/21 /the-creative-gifts-of-adhd.

58. A. Golimstok, J. I. Rojas, M. Romano, et al., "Previous Adult Attention-Deficit and Hyperactivity Disorder Symptoms and Risk of Dementia with Lewy Bodies: A Case-Control Study," *European Journal of Neurology* 18, no. 1 (January 2011): 78–84, https://www.ncbi.nlm.nih.gov/pubmed/20491888. See also Susan Schneider Williams, "The Terrorist Inside My Husband's Brain," *Neurology* 87 (2016): 1308–11, https://demystifyingmedicine.od .nih.gov/DM19/m04d30/reading02.pdf.

59. Jamison, *Touched with Fire*, 43.

60. Lisa Powell, "10 Things You Should Know About Jonathan Winters, the Area's Beloved Comic Genius," *Springfield News-Sun*, November 10, 2018, https://www.springfieldnewssun.com /news/local/things-you-should-know-about-jonathan-winters-the -area-beloved-comedic-genius/Dp5hazcCY9z2sBpVDfaQGI/.

61. Quoted in Dick Cavett, "Falling Stars," in *Time: Robin Williams* (November 2014): 28–30.

62. *Robin Williams: Live on Broadway*, 2002, YouTube, www.you tube.com/watch?v=FS376sohiXc.

63. YouTube Movies, *Robin Williams: Come Inside My Mind,* HBO, January 20, 2019, YouTube, https://www.youtube.com/watch ?v=6xrZBgP6NZo, at 1:08 and 1:53.

64. "The Hawking Paradox," *Horizon,* BBC, 2005, https://www .dailymotion.com/video/x226awj, at 10:35.

65. Simon Baron-Cohen, quoted in Lizzie Buchen, "Scientists and Autism: When Geeks Meet," *Nature* (November 2, 2011), https:// www.nature.com/news/2011/111102/full/479025a.html; Judith Gould, quoted in Vanessa Thorpe, "Was Autism the Secret of Warhol's Art?," *Guardian,* March 13, 1999, https://www.the guardian.com/uk/1999/mar/14/vanessathorpe.theobserver.

66. This was the question asked by the Scottish psychiatrist J. D. Laing. See Bob Mullan, *Mad to Be Normal: Conversations with J. D. Laing* (London: Free Association Books, 1995).

67. Martin Luther King, Jr., "1966 Ware Lecture: Don't Sleep Through the Revolution," speech delivered at the Unitarian Universalist Association General Assembly, Hollywood, Florida, May 18, 1966, https://www.uua.org/ga/past/1966/ware.

68. Motoko Rich, "Yayoi Kusama, Queen of Polka Dots, Opens Museum in Tokyo," *New York Times,* September 26, 2017, https:// www.nytimes.com/2017/09/26/arts/design/yayoi-kusama-queen -of-polka-dots-museum-tokyo.html?mcubz=3&_r=0.

69. Itzkoff, *Robin,* 221–22.

70. Lewina O. Lee, Peter James, Emily S. Zevon, et al., "Optimism Is Associated with Exceptional Longevity in 2 Epidemiologic Cohorts of Men and Women," *Proceedings of the National Academy of Sciences of the United States of America* 116, no. 37 (August 26, 2019): 18357–62, https://www.pnas.org/content /116/37/18357.

71. "New Evidence That Optimists Live Longer," Harvard T. H. Chan School of Public Health, August 27, 2019, https://www .hsph.harvard.edu/news/features/new-evidence-that-optimists -live-longer/?utm_source=SilverpopMailing&utm_medium =email&utm_campaign=Daily%20Gazette%2020190830 (2)%20(1).

72. Catherine Clifford, "This Favorite Saying of Mark Zuckerberg Reveals the Way the Facebook Billionaire Thinks About Life,"

CNBC Make It, November 30, 2017, https://cnbc/207/11/30/why
-facebook-ceo-mark-zuckerberg-thinks-the-optimists-are
-successful.html.

Chapter 8: Rebels, Misfits, and Troublemakers

1. John Waller, *Einstein's Luck: The Truth Behind Some of the Greatest Scientific Discoveries* (Oxford, UK: Oxford University Press, 2002), 161.

2. David Wootton, *Galileo: Watcher of the Skies* (New Haven, CT: Yale University Press, 2010), 259.

3. Dennis Overbye, "Peering into Light's Graveyard: The First Image of a Black Hole," *New York Times,* April 11, 2019, https://www.nytimes.com/2019/04/10/science/black-hole-picture.html.

4. Jonathan Swift, *Essay on the Fates of Clergymen,* Forbes Quotes, https://www.forbes.com/quotes/5566/.

5. Recent research on this point is summarized in Jennifer S. Mueller, Shimul Melwani, and Jack A. Goncalo, "The Bias Against Creativity: Why People Desire but Reject Creative Ideas," *Psychological Science* 23, no. 1 (November 2011): 13–17, https://digitalcommons.ilr.cornell.edu/cgi/viewcontent.cgi?article=1457&context=articles.

6. Erik L. Wesby and V. L. Dawson, "Creativity: Asset or Burden in the Classroom?," *Creativity Research Journal* 8, no. 1 (1995): 1–10, https://www.tandfonline.com/doi/abs/10.1207/s15326934crj0801_1.

7. Amanda Ripley, "Gifted and Talented and Complicated," *New York Times,* January 17, 2018, https://www.nytimes.com/2018/01/17/books/review/off-the-charts-ann-hulbert.html.

8. Wootton, *Galileo,* 218.

9. Ibid., 145–47.

10. Ibid., 222–23.

11. Printed with English translations in Eric Metaxas, *Martin Luther: The Man Who Rediscovered God and Changed the World* (New York: Viking, 2017), 115–22.

12. Ibid., 104.

13. On Luther's escape from Augsburg and Worms, see ibid., 231–36.

14. Ibid., 113.

15. Martin Luther, *Luther's Works,* vol. 32, edited by George W. Forell (Philadelphia and St. Louis: Concordia Publishing House, 1957), 113.

16. On Darwin and the subversion of God, see Janet Browne, *Charles Darwin: Voyaging* (Princeton, NJ: Princeton University Press, 1995), 324–27.

17. Quoted in Walter Isaacson, *Albert Einstein: His Life and Universe* (New York: Simon & Schuster, 2007), 527.

18. Steve Jobs, *I, Steve: Steve Jobs in His Own Words,* edited by George Beahm (Chicago: Agate, 2012), 75.

19. The Art Channel, *Andy Warhol: A Documentary Film,* pt. 2, directed by Ric Burns, PBS, 2006, YouTube, https://www.youtube.com/watch?v=r47Nk4o08pI&t=5904s.

20. Bob Colacello, *Holy Terror: Andy Warhol Close Up,* 2nd ed. (New York: Random House, 2014), xxiv.

21. Ibid., xiii.

22. Quoted in Cameron M. Ford and Dennis A. Gioia, eds., *Creative Action in Organizations: Ivory Tower Visions and Real World Voices* (Thousand Oaks, CA: Sage Publications, 1995), 162.

23. Ryan Riddle, "Steve Jobs and NeXT: You've Got to Be Willing to Crash and Burn," Zurb, February 10, 2012, https://zurb.com/blog/steve-jobs-and-next-you-ve-got-to-be-will.

24. A biography of Harriet Tubman, *Scenes in the Life of Harriet Tubman,* was published by Sarah Hopkins Bradford as early as 1869. A recent scholarly biography is Kate Clifford Larson, *Bound for the Promised Land: Harriet Tubman: Portrait of an American Hero* (New York: Random House, 2004).

25. The obituary is printed in Becket Adams, "103 Years Later, Harriet Tubman Gets Her Due from the New York Times," *Washington Examiner* (April 20, 2016), https://www.washingtonexaminer.com/103-years-later-harriet-tubman-gets-her-due-from-the-new-york-times.

26. See Jennifer Schuessler, Binyamin Appelbaum, and Wesley Morris, "Tubman's In. Jackson's Out. What's It Mean?," *New York Times,* April 20, 2016, https://www.nytimes.com/2016/04/21

/arts/design/tubmans-in-jacksons-out-whats-it-mean.html?mtrref
=query.nytimes.com.

27. Will Ellsworth-Jones, *Banksy: The Man Behind the Wall* (New
York: St. Martin's Press, 2012), 14–16; Banksy, *Wall and Piece*
(London: Random House, 2005), 178–79.

28. Hermione Sylvester and Ashleigh Kane, "Five of Banksy's Most
Infamous Pranks," Dazed, October 9, 2018, https://www.dazed
digital.com/art-photography/article/41743/1/banksy-girl-with
-balloon-painting-pranks-sotherbys-london.

29. Christina Burrus, "The Life of Frida Kahlo," in *Frida Kahlo*,
edited by Emma Dexter and Tanya Barson (London: Tate, 2005),
200–201.

30. Andrea Kettenmann, *Kahlo* (Cologne: Taschen, 2016), 85.

31. Christina Burrus, *Frida Kahlo: I Paint My Reality* (London:
Thames and Hudson, 2008), 206.

32. Frida Kahlo, *Pocket Frida Kahlo Wisdom* (London: Hardie Grant,
2018), 78.

33. Nikki Martinez, "90 Frida Kahlo Quotes for Strength and
Inspiration," Everyday Power, https://everydaypower.com/frida
-kahlo-quotes/.

34. Oprah Winfrey, *Own It: Oprah Winfrey in Her Own Words*,
edited by Anjali Becker and Jeanne Engelmann (Chicago: Agate,
2017), 35.

35. Randall Stross, *The Wizard of Menlo Park: How Thomas Alva
Edison Invented the Modern World* (New York: Random House,
2007), 28.

36. "Edison's New Phonograph," *Scientific American* (October 29,
1887), 273; reproduced in Thomas Edison, *The Quotable Edison*,
edited by Michele Wehrwein Albion (Gainesville: University of
Florida Press, 2011), 7.

37. Rich Winley, "Entrepreneurs: 5 Things We Can Learn from Elon
Musk," *Forbes* (October 8, 2015), https://www.forbes.com/sites
/richwinley/2015/10/08/entrepreneurs-5-things-we-can-learn-from
-elon-musk/#24b3688c4098.

38. Jeff Bezos, "Read Jeff Bezos's 2018 Letter to Amazon
Shareholders," *Entrepreneur* (April 11, 2019), https://www
.entrepreneur.com/article/332101.

39. Jobs, *I, Steve,* 63.
40. J. K. Rowling, *Very Good Lives: The Fringe Benefits of Failure and the Importance of Imagination* (New York: Little, Brown, 2015), 9.
41. Ibid., 32, 37.
42. Sean Smith, *J. K. Rowling: A Biography: The Genius Behind Harry Potter* (London: Michael O'Mara Books, 2001), 122.
43. Alex Carter, "17 Famous Authors and Their Rejections," Mental Floss, May 16, 2017, http://mentalfloss.com/article/91169/16 -famous-authors-and-their-rejections.
44. Testimony of fellow student Victor Hageman as recorded in Louis Pierard, *La Vie tragique de Vincent van Gogh* (Paris: Correa & Cie, 1939), 155–59, http://www.webexhibits.org/vangogh/data /letters/16/etc-458a.htm.
45. See, e.g., Andrea Petersen, "The Overprotected American Child," *Wall Street Journal,* June 2–3, 2018, https://www.wsj.com/articles /the-overprotected-american-child-1527865038.
46. Among college students surveyed by the American College Health Association, 21.6% reported that they had been diagnosed with or treated for anxiety problems during the previous year (2017), up from 10.4% in a 2008 survey. Ibid.
47. Christopher Ingraham, "There Has Never Been a Safer Time to Be a Kid in America," *Washington Post,* April 14, 2015, https:// www.washingtonpost.com/news/wonk/wp/2015/04/14/theres -never-been-a-safer-time-to-be-a-kid-in-america/; "Homicide Trends in the United States, 1980–2008," U.S. Department of Justice, November 2011, https://www.bjs.gov/content/pub/pdf /htus8008.pdf; Swapna Venugopal Ramaswamy, "Schools Take on Helicopter Parenting with Free-Range Program Taken from 'World's Worst Mom,'" *Rockland/Westchester Journal News,* September 4, 2018, https://www.usatoday.com/story/life/allthe moms/2018/09/04/schools-adopt-let-grow-free-range-program -combat-helicopter-parenting/1191482002/.
48. Libby Copeland, "The Criminalization of Parenthood," *New York Times,* August 26, 2018, https://www.nytimes.com/2018/08/22 /books/review/small-animals-kim-brooks.html.
49. Nim Tottenham, Mor Shapiro, Jessica Flannery, et al., "Parental

Presence Switches Avoidance to Attraction Learning in Children," *Nature Human Behaviour* 3, no. 7 (2019): 1070–77.

50. See Hanna Rosin, "The Overprotected Kid," *The Atlantic* (April 2014), https://www.theatlantic.com/magazine/archive/2014/04/hey-parents-leave-those-kids-alone/358631/.

Chapter 9: Be the Fox

1. Samuel Johnson, *The Works of Samuel Johnson,* vol. 2, edited by Arthur Murray (New York: Oxford University Press, 1842), 3.

2. Leonardo da Vinci, *A Treatise on Painting,* translated by John Francis Rigaud (London: George Bell, 2005 [1887]), 10.

3. Albert Einstein, letter to David Hilbert, November 12, 1915, as quoted in Walter Isaacson, *Einstein: His Life and Universe* (New York: Simon & Schuster, 2007), 217.

4. Carl Swanson and Katie Van Syckle, "Lady Gaga: The Young Artist Award Is the Most Meaningful of Her Life," *New York* (October 20, 2015), http://www.vulture.com/2015/10/read-lady-gagas-speech-about-art.html.

5. From an interview in *Entertainment Weekly* quoted in Helia Phoenix, *Lady Gaga: Just Dance: The Biography* (London: Orion, 2010), 19.

6. Kevin Zimmerman, "Lady Gaga Delivers Dynamic Dance-Pop," BMI, December 10, 2008, https://www.bmi.com/news/entry/lady_gaga_delivers_dynamic_dance_pop.

7. Jessica Iredale, "Lady Gaga: 'I'm Every Icon,'" *WWD,* July 28, 2013, https://wwd.com/eye/other/lady-gaga-im-every-icon-7068388/.

8. Benjamin Franklin, "Proposals Relating to the Education of Youth in Pennsylvania," September 13, 1749, reprinted in Franklin, *The Papers of Benjamin Franklin,* vol. 3, 404, https://franklinpapers.org/framedVolumes.jsp. What follows is drawn from this source, 401–17. See also Franklin's earlier broadside "A Proposal for Promoting Useful Knowledge," May 14, 1743.

9. C. Custer, "Jack Ma: 'What I Told My Son About Education,'" Tech in Asia, May 13, 2015, https://www.techinasia.com/jack-ma-what-told-son-education.

10. Abby Jackson, "Cuban: Don't Go to School for Finance—Liberal

Arts Is the Future," Business Insider, February 17, 2017, https://
www.businessinsider.com/mark-cuban-liberal-arts-is-the-future
-2017-2.

11. Rebecca Mead, "All About the Hamiltons," *The New Yorker*
(February 9, 2015), https://www.newyorker.com/magazine
/2015/02/09/hamiltons.

12. Todd Haselton, "Here's Jeff Bezos's Annual Shareholder Letter,"
CNBC, April 11, 2019, https://www.cnbc.com/2019/04/11/jeff
-bezos-annual-shareholder-letter.html.

13. Interview with Tim Berners-Lee, Academy of Achievement,
June 22, 2007, quoted in Walter Isaacson, *The Innovators: How
a Group of Hackers, Geniuses, and Geeks Created the Digital
Revolution* (New York: Simon & Schuster, 2014), 408.

14. Isaacson, *Einstein*, 67.

15. From Nabokov's 1974 novel *Look at the Harlequins!*, in "Genius:
Seeing Things That Others Don't See. Or Rather the Invisible
Links Between Things," Quote Investigator, May 11, 2018,
https://quoteinvestigator.com/2018/05/11/on-genius/.

16. Gary Wolf, "Steve Jobs: The Next Insanely Great Thing," *Wired*
(February 1, 1996), https://www.wired.com/1996/02/jobs-2/.

17. Matt Rosoff, "The Only Reason the Mac Looks like It Does,"
Business Insider, March 8, 2016, https://www.businessinsider.sg
/robert-palladino-calligraphy-class-inspired-steve-jobs-2016-3/.

18. Walter Isaacson, *Steve Jobs* (New York: Simon & Schuster, 2011),
64–65.

19. Aristotle, *The Poetics of Aristotle*, XXII, translated by S. H.
Butcher, Project Gutenberg, https://www.gutenberg.org/files
/1974/1974-h/1974-h.htm.

20. Quoted in David Epstein, *Range: Why Generalists Triumph in a
Specialized World* (New York: Random House, 2019), 103.

21. See, e.g., Leah Barbour, "MSU Research: Effective Arts
Integration Improves Test Scores," Mississippi State Newsroom,
2013, https://www.newsarchive.msstate.edu/newsroom/article
/2013/10/msu-research-effective-arts-integration-improves
-test-scores; Brian Kisida and Daniel H. Bowen, "New Evidence
of the Benefits of Arts Education," Brookings, February 12, 2019,
https://www.brookings.edu/blog/brown-center-chalkboard

/2019/02/12/new-evidence-of-the-benefits-of-arts-education/; and Tom Jacobs, "New Evidence of Mental Benefits from Music Training," *Pacific Standard,* June 14, 2017, https://psmag.com /social-justice/new-evidence-brain-benefits-music-training-83761.

22. Samuel G. B. Johnson and Stefan Steinerberger, "Intuitions About Mathematical Beauty: A Case Study in the Aesthetic Experience of Ideas," *Cognition* 189 (August 2019): 242–59, https://www.ncbi .nlm.nih.gov/pubmed/31015078.

23. Barry Parker, *Einstein: The Passions of a Scientist* (Amherst, NY: Prometheus Books, 2003), 13.

24. For a complete treatment of the subject, see Wright, "Mozart and Math," available at the author's website.

25. Friedrich Schlichtegroll, *Necrolog auf das Jahr 1791,* in Franz Xaver Niemetschek, *Vie de W. A. Mozart,* edited and translated by Georges Favier (Paris: CIERCE, 1976), 126, surely reporting information acquired from Nannerl.

26. Peter Bucky, *The Private Albert Einstein* (Kansas City, MO: Andrews McMeel, 1992), 156.

27. Donald W. MacKinnon, "Creativity: A Multi-faceted Phenomenon," paper presented at Gustavus Adolphus College, 1970, https://webspace.ringling.edu/~ccjones/curricula/01-02 /sophcd/readings/creativity.html.

28. Jack Flam, *Matisse and Picasso: The Story of Their Rivalry and Friendship* (Cambridge, MA: Westview Press, 2018), 33–39.

29. Ibid., 34.

30. "Copyright, Permissions, and Fair Use in the Visual Arts Communities: An Issues Report," Center for Media and Social Impact, February 2015, https://cmsimpact.org/resource/copyright -permissions-fair-use-visual-arts-communities-issues-report/; "Fair Use," in *Copyright & Fair Use,* Stanford University Libraries, 2019, https://fairuse.stanford.edu/overview/fair-use/.

31. On the state of thinking regarding human evolution prior to Darwin, see in particular Janet Browne, *Darwin: Voyaging* (Princeton, NJ: Princeton University Press, 1995), chap. 16.

32. On this point, see Steven Johnson, *Where Good Ideas Come From* (New York: Riverhead, 2010), 80–82.

33. Charles Darwin, *The Autobiography of Charles Darwin,* edited by Nora Barlow (New York: W. W. Norton, 2005), 98.

34. As posited in Charles Darwin, *On the Origin of Species by Means of Natural Selection* (London: Taylor and Francis, 1859), introduction.

35. Browne, *Darwin,* 227.

36. Among many treatments of this topic, see "Thomas Edison: 'The Wizard of Menlo Park,'" chap. 3 in Jill Jonnes, *Empires of Light: Edison, Tesla, Westinghouse, and The Race to Electrify the World* (New York: Random House, 2003).

37. Paul Israel, *Edison: A Life of Invention* (New York: John Wiley & Sons, 1999), 208–11.

38. David Robson, *The Intelligence Trap: Why Smart People Make Dumb Mistakes* (New York: W. W. Norton, 2019), 75.

39. Donald W. MacKinnon, "Creativity: A Multi-faceted Phenomenon," paper presented at Gustavus Augustus College, 1970, https://webspace.ringling.edu/~ccjones/curricula/01-02/sophcd/readings/creativity.html.

40. Quoted in Margaret Cheney, *Tesla: Man Out of Time* (Mattituck, NY: Amereon House, 1981), 268.

41. Daniel Kahneman, *Thinking, Fast and Slow* (New York: Farrar, Straus and Giroux, 2011), 216–20.

42. Research summarized in Epstein, *Range,* 107–9.

43. For this and the following statement, see Robert Root-Bernstein, Lindsay Allen, Leighanna Beach, et al., "Arts Foster Scientific Success: Avocations of Nobel, National Academy, Royal Society, and Sigma Xi Members," *Journal of Psychology of Science and Technology* 1, no. 2 (2008): 51–63, https://www.researchgate.net/publication/247857346_Arts_Foster_Scientific_Success_Avocations_of_Nobel_National_Academy_Royal_Society_and_Sigma_Xi_Members; and Robert S. Root-Bernstein, Maurine Bernstein, and Helen Garnier, "Correlations Between Avocations, Scientific Style, Work Habits, and Professional Impact of Scientists," *Creativity Research Journal* 8, no. 2 (1995): 115–37, https://www.tandfonline.com/doi/abs/10.1207/s15326934crj0802_2.

44. Patricia Cohen, "A Rising Call to Promote STEM Education and

Cut Liberal Arts Funding," *New York Times*, February 21, 2016, https://www.nytimes.com/2016/02/22/business/a-rising-call-to -promote-stem-education-and-cut-liberal-arts-funding.html. See also Adam Harris, "The Liberal Arts May Not Survive the 21st Century," *The Atlantic* (December 13, 2018), https://www.the atlantic.com/education/archive/2018/12/the-liberal-arts-may-not -survive-the-21st-century/577876/; and "New Rules for Student Loans: Matching a Career to Debt Repayment," LendKey, September 1, 2015, https://www.lendkey.com/blog/paying-for -school/new-rules-for-student-loans-matching-a-career-to-debt -repayment/.

45. Frank Bruni, "Aristotle's Wrongful Death," *New York Times*, May 26, 2018, https://www.nytimes.com/2018/05/26/opinion /sunday/college-majors-liberal-arts.html.

46. Scott Jaschik, "Obama vs. Art History," Inside Higher Ed, January 31, 2014, https://www.insidehighered.com/news/2014 /01/31/obama-becomes-latest-politician-criticize-liberal-arts -discipline.

47. Tad Friend, "Why Ageism Never Gets Old," *The New Yorker* (November 20, 2017), https://www.newyorker.com/magazine /2017/11/20/why-ageism-never-gets-old.

48. Alina Tugent, "Endless School," *New York Times*, October 13, 2019, https://www.nytimes.com/2019/10/10/education /learning/60-year-curriculum-higher-education.html; author's conversation with Christopher Wright, director of strategic partnerships, 2U, December 17, 2019.

49. Steve Jobs, *I, Steve: Steve Jobs in His Own Words*, edited by George Beahm (Agate: Chicago, 2011), 73.

50. Albert Einstein, *Ideas and Opinions* (New York: Crown, 1982), 69.

Chapter 10: Think Opposite

1. "NASA Announces Launch Date and Milestones for SpaceX Flight," December 9, 2011, https://www.nasa.gov/home/hqnews /2011/dec/HQ_11-413_SpaceX_ISS_Flight.html.

2. Mariella Moon, "SpaceX Is Saving a Ton of Money by Re-using Falcon 9 Rockets," Engadget, April 6, 2017, https://www.engadget

.com/2017/04/06/spacex-is-saving-a-ton-of-money-by-re-using
-falcon-9-rockets/.

3. Quoted in Elon Musk, *Rocket Man: Elon Musk in His Own
    Words,* edited by Jessica Easto (Chicago: Agate, 2017), 16.

4. For a discussion of left-handed persons and creativity, see Dean
    Keith Simonton, *Greatness: Who Makes History and Why* (New
    York: Guilford Press, 1994), 20–24.

5. I am indebted to the late David Rosand for introducing me to the
    mirror images present in many of Leonardo's drawings. See his
    Drawing Acts: Studies in Graphic Representation and Expression
    (Cambridge, UK: Cambridge University Press, 2002).

6. Bronwyn Hemus, "Understanding the Essentials of Writing a
    Murder Mystery," Standout Books, May 5, 2014, https://www
    .standoutbooks.com/essentials-writing-murder-mystery/.

7. Bruce Hale, "Writing Tip: Plotting Backwards," Booker's Blog,
    March 24, 2012, https://talltalestogo.wordpress.com/2012/03/24
    /writing_tip_plotting_backwards/.

8. Kip Thorne, *Black Holes and Time Warps: Einstein's Outrageous
    Legacy* (New York: W. W. Norton, 1994), 147.

9. Quoted in David M. Harrison, "Complementarity and the
    Copenhagen Interpretation of Quantum Mechanics," *UPSCALE,*
    October 7, 2002, https://www.scribd.com/document/166550158
    /Physics-Complementarity-and-Copenhagen-Interpretation-of
    -Quantum-Mechanics.

10. Albert Rothenberg, *Creativity and Madness: New Findings and
    Old Stereotypes* (Baltimore: Johns Hopkins University Press,
    1990), 14.

11. Author's translation from Albert Einstein, *The Collected Papers
    of Albert Einstein,* vol. 7: *The Berlin Years: Writings, 1918–1921,*
    edited by Michael Janssen, Robert Schulmann, József Illy, et al.,
    document 31: "Fundamental Ideas and Methods of the Theory of
    Relativity, Presented in Their Development," II: "The Theory of
    General Relativity," https://einsteinpapers.press.princeton.edu
    /vol7-doc/293, 245.

12. Albert Rothenberg, *Flight from Wonder: An Investigation of
    Scientific Creativity* (Oxford, UK: Oxford University Press, 2015),
    28–29.

13. Cade Metz, "Google Claims a Quantum Breakthrough That Could Change Computing," *New York Times,* October 23, 2019, https://www.nytimes.com/2019/10/23/technology/quantum-computing-google.html.

14. Elon Musk, "The Secret Tesla Motors Master Plan (Just Between You and Me)," Tesla, August 2, 2006, https:/www.tesla.com/blog/secret-tesla-motors-master-plan-just-between-you-and-me.

15. Franklin Foer, "Jeff Bezos's Master Plan," *The Atlantic* (November 2019), https://www.theatlantic.com/magazine/archive/2019/11/what-jeff-bezos-wants/598363/.

16. Jeff Bezos, *First Mover: Jeff Bezos in His Own Words,* edited by Helena Hunt (Chicago: Agate, 2018), 95.

17. Quoted in Foer, "Jeff Bezos's Master Plan."

18. Rothenberg, *Creativity and Madness,* 25.

19. Martin Luther King, Jr., "I Have a Dream," "Great Speeches of the Twentieth Century," *Guardian,* April 27, 2007, https://www.theguardian.com/theguardian/2007/apr/28/greatspeeches.

20. Bradley J. Adame, "Training in the Mitigation of Anchoring Bias: A Test of the Consider-the-Opposite Strategy," *Learning and Motivation* 53 (February 2016): 36–48, https://www.sciencedirect.com/science/article/abs/pii/S0023969015000739?via%3Dihub.

Chapter 11: Get Lucky

1. First published in *Harper's Magazine* (December 1904): 10; reprinted in John Cooley, ed., *How Nancy Jackson Married Kate Wilson and Other Tales of Rebellious Girls and Daring Young Women* (Lincoln, NE: University of Nebraska Press, 2001), 209.

2. "The Harder I Practice, the Luckier I Get," Quote Investigator, https://quoteinvestigator.com/2010/07/14/luck/. I owe my knowledge of this quote to the kindness of Clark Baxter.

3. Frances Wood, "Why Does China Love Shakespeare?," *Guardian,* June 28, 2011, https://www.theguardian.com/commentisfree/2011/jun/28/china-shakespeare-wen-jiabao-visit.

4. Quoted in Noah Charney, *The Thefts of the Mona Lisa: On Stealing the World's Most Famous Painting* (Columbia, SC: ARCA Publications, 2011).

5. Evan Andrews, "The Heist That Made the Mona Lisa Famous," History, November 30, 2018, https://www.history.com/news/the -heist-that-made-the-mona-lisa-famous.

6. Charney, The Thefts of the Mona Lisa, 74.

7. Quoted in the introduction to James D. Watson and Francis Crick, "Molecular Structure of Nucleic Acids: A Structure for Deoxyribose Nucleic Acid," Nature 171, no. 4356 (April 25, 1953): 737–38, in The Francis Crick Papers, U.S. National Library of Medicine, https://profiles.nlm.nih.gov/spotlight/sc /catalog/nlm:nlmuid-101584582X381-doc.

8. Reprinted with facsimile in James D. Watson, The Double Helix: A Personal Account of the Discovery of the Structure of DNA, edited by Gunther S. Stent (New York: W. W. Norton, 1980), 237–41.

9. On Pauling's error, see Linus Pauling, "The Molecular Basis of Biological Specificity," reproduced in ibid., 152.

10. Ibid., 105; Robert Olby, The Path to the Double Helix: The Discovery of DNA (New York: Dover, 1994), 402–3.

11. Watson, The Double Helix, 14.

12. "Statutes of the Nobel Foundation," The Nobel Prize, https:// www.nobelprize.org/about/statutes-of-the-nobel-foundation/.

13. For an update on the odds of winning the Nobel for CRISPR, see Amy Dockser Marcus, "Science Prizes Add Intrigue to the Race for the Nobel," Wall Street Journal, June 1, 2018, https://www .wsj.com/articles/science-prizes-add-intrigue-to-the-race-for-the -nobel-1527870861.

14. Author's translation from Louis Pasteur, inaugural address, Faculty of Sciences, University of Lille, December 7, 1854, Gallica Bibliothèque Numérique, https://upload.wikimedia.org/wikipedia /commons/6/62/Louis_Pasteur_Universit%C3%A9_de_Lille _1854-1857_dans_les_champs_de_l%27observation_le_hasard _ne_favorise_que_les_esprits_pr%C3%A9par%C3%A9s.pdf.

15. John Waller, Einstein's Luck: The Truth Behind the Greatest Scientific Discoveries (Oxford, UK: Oxford University Press, 2002), 247.

16. Upon his appointment as prime minister, May 10, 1940, in Winston Churchill, The Second World War, vol. 1: The Gathering Storm (1948), quoted in "Summer 1940: Churchill's Finest Hour,"

International Churchill Society, https://winstonchurchill.org/the-life-of-churchill/war-leader/summer-1940/.

17. Waller, *Einstein's Luck*, 249.

18. Kevin Brown, *Penicillin Man: Alexander Fleming and the Antibiotic Revolution* (London: Sutton, 2005), 102.

19. Ibid., 120.

20. Mark Zuckerberg, *Mark Zuckerberg: In His Own Words*, edited by George Beahm (Chicago: Agate, 2018), 1.

21. Ben Mezrich, *The Accidental Billionaires: The Founding of Facebook: A Tale of Sex, Money, Genius, and Betrayal* (New York: Random House, 2010), 45.

22. Katharine A. Kaplan, "Facemash Creator Survives Ad Board," *Harvard Crimson*, November 19, 2003, https://www.thecrimson.com/article/2003/11/19/facemash-creator-survives-ad-board-the/.

23. Mezrich, *The Accidental Billionaires*, 105.

24. Roger McNamee, *Zucked: Waking Up to the Facebook Catastrophe* (New York: Random House, 2019), 54; David Enrich, "Spend Some Time with the Winklevii," *New York Times*, May 21, 2019, https://www.nytimes.com/2019/05/21/books/review/ben-mezrich-bitcoin-billionaires.html?searchResultPosition=5.

25. Farhad Manjoo, "How Mark Zuckerberg Became Too Big to Fail," *New York Times*, November 1, 2018, https://www.nytimes.com/2018/11/01/technology/mark-zuckerberg-facebook.html.

26. Mezrich, *The Accidental Billionaires*, 108.

27. Zuckerberg, *Mark Zuckerberg*, 46.

28. Oprah Winfrey, *Own It: Oprah Winfrey in Her Own Words*, edited by Anjali Becker and Jeanne Engelmann (Chicago: Agate, 2017), 7.

29. Yayoi Kusama, *Infinity Net: The Autobiography of Yayoi Kusama* (London: Tate Publishing, 2011), 77.

30. Vincent van Gogh, letter to Theo, January 12–16, 1886, Vincent van Gogh: The Letters, http://vangoghletters.org/vg/letters/let552/letter.html.

31. Both quotes in *Paris: The Luminous Years: Towards the Making of the Modern*, written, produced, and directed by Perry Miller Adato, PBS, 2010, at 0:40 and 1:10.

32. Eric Weiner, *The Genius of Geography* (New York: Simon & Schuster, 2016), 167.

33. Quoted in Dan Hofstadter, "'The Europeans' Review: Engines of Progress," *Wall Street Journal*, October 18, 2019, https://www.wsj.com/articles/the-europeans-review-engines-of-progress-11571409900.

34. James Wood, *Dictionary of Quotations from Ancient and Modern, English and Foreign Sources* (London: Wame, 1893), 120.

35. Richard Florida and Karen M. King, "Rise of the Global Startup City: The Geography of Venture Capital Investment in Cities and Metros Across the Globe," Martin Prosperity Institute, January 26, 2016, http://martinprosperity.org/content/rise-of-the-global-start up-city/.

Chapter 12: Move Fast and Break Things

1. Quoted in Mary Dearborn, *Ernest Hemingway: A Biography* (New York: Vintage, 2018), 475.

2. Albert Einstein, *Ideas and Opinions* (New York: Random House, 1982), 12.

3. Author's translation and paraphrase of the original French. See also Edmond and Jules de Goncourt, *Pages from the Goncourt Journals,* edited and translated by Robert Baldick (Oxford, UK: Oxford University Press, 1962), 100.

4. Oprah Winfrey, *Own It: Oprah Winfrey in Her Own Words,* edited by Anjali Becker and Jeanne Engelmann (Chicago: Agate, 2017), 65.

5. Quoted in Andrew Ross Sorkin, "Tesla's Elon Musk May Have Boldest Pay Plan in Corporate History," *New York Times,* January 23, 2018, https://www.nytimes.com/2018/01/23/business/dealbook/tesla-elon-musk-pay.html/.

6. David Kiley, "Former Employees Talk About What Makes Elon Musk Tick," *Forbes* (July 14, 2016), https://www.forbes.com/sites/davidkiley5/2016/07/14/former-employees-talk-about-what-makes-elon-musk-tick/#a48d8e94514e; "What Is It Like to Work with/ for Elon Musk?," Quora, https://www.quora.com/What-is-it-like-to-work-with-for-Elon-Musk.

7. Mark Zuckerberg, *Mark Zuckerberg: In His Own Words,* edited by George Beahm (Chicago: Agate, 2018), 189.

8. Joseph Schumpeter, *Capitalism, Socialism and Democracy,* 3rd ed. (New York: Harper, 1962), chap. 11.

9. Alan Greenspan and Adrian Wooldridge, *Capitalism in America: A History* (New York: Random House, 2018), 420–21.

10. Zaphrin Lasker, "Steve Jobs: Create. Disrupt. Destroy," *Forbes* (June 14, 2011), https://www.forbes.com/sites/marketshare /2011/06/14/steve-jobs-create-disrupt-destroy/#6276e77f531c.

11. Joe Nocera, "Apple's Culture of Secrecy," *New York Times,* July 26, 2008, https://www.nytimes.com/2008/07/26/business /26nocera.html.

12. Quoted in Walter Isaacson, *Steve Jobs* (New York: Simon & Schuster, 2011), 124.

13. Dylan Love, "16 Examples of Steve Jobs Being a Huge Jerk," Business Insider, October 25, 2011, https://www.businessinsider .com/steve-jobs-jerk-2011-10#everything-youve-ever-done-in -your-life-is-shit-5.

14. Isaacson, *Steve Jobs,* 122–23.

15. See, e.g., the story of Steve Jobs and freshly squeezed orange juice in Nick Bilton, "What Steve Jobs Taught Me About Being a Son and a Father," *New York Times,* August 7, 2015, https://www.ny times.com/2015/08/07/fashion/mens-style/what-steve-jobs-taught -me-about-being-a-son-and-a-father.html.

16. This and the following quote are from Nellie Bowles, "In 'Small Fry,' Steve Jobs Comes Across as a Jerk. His Daughter Forgives Him. Should We?," *New York Times,* August 23, 2018, https:// www.nytimes.com/2018/08/23/books/steve-jobs-lisa-brennan -jobs-small-fry.html.

17. Quoted in Isaacson, *Steve Jobs,* 32.

18. Quoted in ibid., 119.

19. Kevin Lynch, *Steve Jobs: A Biographical Portrait* (London: White Lion, 2018), 73.

20. "On Thomas Edison and Beatrix Potter," *Washington Times,* April 7, 2007, https://www.washingtontimes.com/news/2007 /apr/7/20070407-095754-2338r/.

21. "Thomas A. Edison," *The Christian Herald and Signs of Our*

Times, July 25, 1888, http://edison.rutgers.edu/digital/files/full size/fp/fp0285.jpg. See also Randall Stross, *The Wizard of Menlo Park: How Thomas Alva Edison Invented the Modern World* (New York: Random House, 2007), 15–16.

22. Neil Baldwin, *Edison: Inventing the Century* (Chicago: University of Chicago Press, 2001), 60.

23. Stross, *The Wizard of Menlo Park,* 174.

24. Much of the information is drawn from Michael Daly, *Topsy: The Startling Story of the Crooked-Tailed Elephant, P. T. Barnum, and the American Wizard, Thomas Edison* (New York: Grove Press, 2013), chap. 26.

25. James Gleick, *Isaac Newton* (New York: Random House, 2003), 169–70.

26. The relationship between the color spectrum and the harmonic series in music is a good example. See Penelope Gouk, "The Harmonic Roots of Newtonian Science," in *Let Newton Be!: A New Perspective on his Life and Works,* edited by John Fauvel, Raymond Flood, Michael Shortland, and Robin Wilson (Oxford, UK: Oxford University Press, 1988), 101–26.

27. Sheldon Lee Glashow, "The Errors and Animadversions of Honest Isaac Newton," *Contributions to Science* 4, no. 1 (2008): 105–10.

28. Quoted in ibid., 105.

29. Stephen Hawking, *A Brief History of Time* (New York: Bantam Books, 1998), 196.

30. Walter Isaacson, *Einstein: His Life and Universe* (New York: Simon & Schuster, 2007), 174–75.

31. Albert Einstein, *Ideas and Opinions* (New York: Crown, 1982), 9.

32. Stross, *The Wizard of Menlo Park,* 81.

33. Quoted in Scott Barry Kaufman and Carolyn Gregoire, *Wired to Create: Unraveling the Mysteries of the Creative Mind* (New York: Random House, 2016), 122.

34. Ludwig van Beethoven, letter to Franz Wegeler, June 29, 1801, in *Beethoven: Letters, Journals and Conversations,* edited and translated by Michael Hamburger (Garden City: Doubleday, 1960), 25.

35. Thomas Alva Edison, *The Diary and Sundry Observations of Thomas Alva Edison,* edited by Dagobert D. Runes (New York: Greenwood, 1968), 110.

36. Sam Bush, "Faulkner as a Father: Do Great Novelists Make Bad Parents?," Mockingbird, July 31, 2013, https://www.mbird.com /2013/07/faulkner-as-a-father-do-great-novelists-make-bad -parents/.

37. Otto Erich Deutsch, *Mozart: A Documentary Biography*, translated by Eric Blom, Peter Branscombe, and Jeremy Noble (Stanford, CA: Stanford University Press, 1965), 423.

38. Maria Anna Mozart, letter to Friedrich Schlichtegroll, 1800, translated from *Mozart-Jahrbuch* (Salzburg: Internationale Stiftung Mozarteum, 1995), 164.

39. Quoted in Dave Itzkoff, *Robin* (New York: Henry Holt, 2018), 354.

40. Keith Caulfield, "Michael Jackson Sales, Streaming Decline After 'Leaving Neverland' Broadcast," *The Hollywood Reporter*, March 8, 2019, https://www.hollywoodreporter.com/news /michael-jacksons-sales-streaming-decline-leaving-neverland -1193509.

41. Emma Goldberg, "Do Works by Men Implicated by #MeToo Belong in the Classroom?," *New York Times*, October 7, 2019, https://www.nytimes.com/2019/10/07/us/metoo-schools.html.

42. Farah Nayeri, "Is It Time Gauguin Got Canceled?," *New York Times*, November 18, 2019, https://www.nytimes.com/2019/11/18 /arts/design/gauguin-national-gallery-london.html.

43. Robin Pogrebin and Jennifer Schuessler, "Chuck Close Is Accused of Harassment. Should His Artwork Carry an Asterisk?," *New York Times*, January 28, 2018, https://www.nytimes.com/2018 /01/28/arts/design/chuck-close-exhibit-harassment-accusations .html.

44. Lionel Trilling, *Beyond Culture: Essays on Literature and Learning* (New York: Viking, 1965), 11.

45. Arianna Stassinopoulos Huffington, *Picasso: Creator and Destroyer* (New York: Simon & Schuster, 1988), 234.

46. Françoise Gilot and Carlton Lake, *Life with Picasso* (New York: McGraw-Hill, 1964), 77.

47. Ibid., 326.

48. Author's translation from Pierre Cabanne, quoting Marie-Thérèse Walter, in "Picasso et les joies de la paternité," *L'Oeil: Revue d'Art* 226 (May 1974): 7.

49. Gilot and Lake, *Life with Picasso,* 42.

50. Huffington, *Picasso,* 345.

51. Gilot and Lake, *Life with Picasso,* 77.

52. Henry Blodget, "Mark Zuckerberg on Innovation," Business Insider, October 1, 2009, https://www.businessinsider.com/mark -zuckerberg-innovation-2009-10.

53. Brainyquote, https://www.brainyquote.com/authors/margaret _atwood. The quote appears to be a compilation of phrases taken from Maddie Crum, "A Conversation with Margaret Atwood About Climate Change, Social Media and World of Warcraft," Huffpost, November 12, 2014, https://www.huffpost.com/entry /margaret-atwood-interview_n_6141840.

54. See Sam Schechner and Mark Secada, "You Give Apps Sensitive Personal Information. Then They Tell Facebook," *Wall Street Journal,* February 22, 2019, https://www.wsj.com/articles/you -give-apps-sensitive-personal-information-then-they-tell-face book-11550851636.

55. Sandy Parakilas, "We Can't Trust Facebook to Regulate Itself," *New York Times,* November 19, 2017, https://www.nytimes.com /2017/11/19/opinion/facebook-regulation-incentive.html?ref =todayspaper.

56. Ibid.

57. Digital, Culture, Media and Sport Committee, "Disinformation and 'Fake News': Final Report," House of Commons, https:// publications.parliament.uk/pa/cm201719/cmselect/cmcumeds /1791/1791.pdf; and Graham Kates, "Facebook 'Misled' Parliament on Data Misuse, U.K. Committee Says," CBS News, February 17, 2019, https://www.cbsnews.com/news/facebook -misled-parliament-on-data-misuse-u-k-committee-says/.

58. Discussions of Zuckerberg's obsession with computer code as the solution to all of Facebook's problems can be found in Roger McNamee, *Zucked: Waking Up to the Facebook Catastrophe* (New York: Random House, 2019), 64–65, 159, 193. See also Shoshona Zuboff, *The Age of Surveillance Capitalism: The Fight for a Human Future at the New Frontier of Power* (New York: Public Affairs, 2019), 480–88.

59. Nicholas Carlson, "'Embarrassing and Damaging' Zuckerberg

IMs Confirmed by Zuckerberg, The New Yorker," Business Insider, September 13, 2010, https://www.businessinsider.com /embarrassing-and-damaging-zuckerberg-ims-confirmed-by -zuckerberg-the-new-yorker-2010-9.

60. Arthur Koestler, *The Act of Creation* (London: Hutchinson, 1964), 402.

Chapter 13: Now Relax

1. Jean Kinney, "Grant Wood: He Got His Best Ideas While Milking a Cow," *New York Times,* June 2, 1974, https://www.nytimes.com /1974/06/02/archives/grantwood-he-got-his-best-ideas-while-milking -a-cow-grant-wood-he.html.

2. Amir Muzur, Edward F. Pace-Schott, and J. Allan Hobson, "The Prefrontal Cortex in Sleep," *Trends in Cognitive Sciences* 6, no. 11 (November 2002): 475–81, https://www.researchgate.net/publication /11012150_The_prefrontal_cortex_in_sleep; Matthew Walker, *Why We Sleep: Unlocking the Power of Sleep and Dreams* (New York: Scribner, 2017), 195.

3. Walker, *Why We Sleep,* chap. 11.

4. Matthew P. Walker, Conor Liston, J. Allan Hobson, and Robert Stickgold, "Cognitive Flexibility Across the Sleep-Wake Cycle: REM-Sleep Enhancement of Anagram Problem Solving," *Brain Research* 14, no. 3 (November 2002): 317–24, https://www.ncbi .nlm.nih.gov/pubmed/12421655.

5. Robert Stickgold and Erin Wamsley, "Memory, Sleep, and Dreaming: Experiencing Consolidation," *Journal of Sleep Research* 6, no. 1 (March 1, 2011): 97–108, https://www.ncbi.nlm .nih.gov/pmc/articles/PMC3079906/.

6. Walker, *Why We Sleep,* 219.

7. Tori DeAngelis, "The Dream Canvas: Are Dreams a Muse to the Creative?," *Monitor on Psychology* 34, no. 10 (November 2003): 44, https://www.apa.org/monitor/nov03/canvas.

8. Igor Stravinsky, *Dialogues and a Diary,* edited by Robert Craft (Garden City, NY: Doubleday, 1963), 70.

9. Jay Cridlin, "Fifty Years Ago, the Rolling Stones' Song 'Satisfaction' Was Born in Clearwater," *Tampa Bay Times,* May 3,

2015, https://www.tampabay.com/things-to-do/music/50-years
-ago-the-rolling-stones-song-satisfaction-was-born-in-clearwater
/2227921/.

10. The concert/interview is available at "Paul McCartney Singing
    Yesterday at the Library of Congress," YouTube, https://www
    .youtube.com/watch?v=ieu_5o1LiQQ.

11. Walker, *Why We Sleep*, 202.

12. Quoted in Elliot S. Valenstein, *The War of the Soups and the
    Sparks: The Discovery of Neurotransmitters and the Dispute over
    How Nerves Communicate* (New York: Columbia University
    Press, 2005), 58.

13. Leon Watters, quoted in Walter Isaacson, *Albert Einstein: His Life
    and Universe* (New York: Simon & Schuster, 2007), 436.

14. In 2017, Kip Thorne won the Nobel Prize in Physics, in part for
    having proved, as part of the LIGO project, Einstein's theory
    about collapsing black holes to be correct. I don't know how
    Professor Thorne sleeps, but in an email to me he reminded me
    of a passage in his 2014 book *The Science of Interstellar* (p. 9), in
    which he says "my best thinking was in the dead of night. The
    next morning I would write up my thoughts in a several-paged
    memo with diagrams and pictures."

15. Jacquelyn Smith, "72% of People Get Their Best Ideas in the
    Shower—Here's Why," Business Insider, January 14, 2016,
    https://www.businessinsider.com/why-people-get-their-best-ideas
    -in-the-shower-2016-1.

16. Walker, *Why We Sleep*, 208, 223.

17. A. R. Braun, T. J. Balkin, N. J. Wesenten, et al., "Regional
    Cerebral Blood Flow Throughout the Sleep-Wake Cycle. An
    H2(15)O PET Study," *Brain* 120, no. 7 (July 1997): 1173–97,
    https://www.ncbi.nlm.nih.gov/pubmed/9236630.

18. Quoted in Jagdish Mehra, *Einstein, Hilbert, and the Theory of
    Gravitation* (Boston: Reidel, 1974), 76.

19. Barry Parker, *Einstein: The Passions of a Scientist* (Amherst, NY:
    Prometheus Books, 2003), 30.

20. Quoted in Gerald Whitrow, *Einstein: The Man and His
    Achievement* (New York: Dover Publications, 1967), 21.

21. David Hindley, "Running: An Aid to the Creative Process,"

Guardian, October 30, 2014, https://www.theguardian.com
/lifeandstyle/the-running-blog/2014/oct/30/running-writers-block
-creative-process.

22. Among these are Marily Oppezzo and Daniel L. Schwarz, "Give
    Your Ideas Some Legs: The Positive Effect of Walking on Creative
    Thinking," *Journal of Experimental Psychology: Learning,
    Memory, and Cognition* 40, no. 4 (2014): 1142–52, https://www
    .apa.org/pubs/journals/releases/xlm-a0036577.pdf; Lorenza S.
    Colzato, Ayca Szapora, Justine N. Pannekoek, and Bernhard
    Hommel, "The Impact of Physical Exercise on Convergent
    and Divergent Thinking," *Frontiers in Human Neuroscience* 2
    (December 2013), https://doi.org/10.3389/fnhum.2013.00824;
    and Prabha Siddarth, Alison C. Burggren, Harris A. Eyre, et al.,
    "Sedentary Behavior Associated with Reduced Medial Temporal
    Lobe Thickness in Middle-Aged and Older Adults," *PLOS ONE*
    (April 12, 2018), http://journals.plos.org/plosone/article?id
    =10.1371/journal.pone.0195549.

23. Eric Weiner, *The Geography of Genius: A Search for the World's
    Most Creative Places from Ancient Athens to Silicon Valley* (New
    York: Simon & Schuster, 2016), 21.

24. Ibid., 21.

25. *Inside Bill's Brain: Decoding Bill Gates,* Netflix, 2019, https://
    www.netflix.com/watch/80184771?source=35.

26. Henry David Thoreau, journal, August 19, 1851, in *The Portable
    Thoreau,* edited by Jeffrey S. Cramer, https://www.penguin.com
    /ajax/books/excerpt/9780143106500.

27. Mason Currey, *Daily Rituals: Women at Work* (New York:
    Random House, 2019), 52.

28. Daniel Kahneman, *Thinking, Fast and Slow* (New York: Farrar,
    Straus and Giroux, 2011), 40.

29. W. Bernard Carlson, *Tesla: Inventor of the Electrical Age*
    (Princeton, NJ: Princeton University Press, 2013), 50–51.

30. Nikola Tesla, *My Inventions,* edited by David Major (Middletown,
    DE: Philovox, 2016), 35. The original German of the poem has
    been translated by the author.

31. Carlson, *Tesla,* 404.

32. Rebecca Mead, "All About the Hamiltons," *The New Yorker* (February 9, 2015), https://www.newyorker.com/magazine/2015/02/09/hamiltons.

33. Ludwig van Beethoven, letter to Tobias Haslinger, September 10, 1821, in *Beethoven: Letters, Journals and Conversations,* edited and translated by Michael Hamburger (Garden City, NY: Doubleday, 1960), 174–75. The autograph letter is preserved in the Beethoven-Haus, Bonn, and the canon carries the Kinsky number WoO 182.

34. Danille Taylor-Guthrie, ed., *Conversations with Toni Morrison* (Jackson: University Press of Mississippi, 2004), 43.

35. Francis Mason, ed., *I Remember Balanchine: Recollections of the Ballet Master by Those Who Knew Him* (New York: Doubleday, 1991), 418.

Chapter 14: Time to Concentrate!

1. David Michaelis, *Schulz and Peanuts: A Biography* (New York: Harper Perennial, 2007), 370, quoted and condensed in Mason Currey, *Daily Rituals: How Artists Work* (New York: Alfred A. Knopf, 2018), 217–18.

2. Françoise Gilot and Carlton Lake, *Life with Picasso* (New York: McGraw-Hill, 1964), 109–10.

3. Fritjof Capra, *The Science of Leonardo* (New York: Random House, 2007), 30.

4. Giorgio Vasari, *The Lives of the Artists,* translated by Julia Conaway Bondanella and Peter Bondanella (Oxford, UK: Oxford University Press, 1991), 290.

5. Jaime Sabartés, *Picasso: An Intimate Portrait* (London: W. H. Allen, 1948), 79.

6. Quoted in Barry Parker, *Einstein: The Passions of a Scientist* (Amherst, NY: Prometheus Books, 2003), 137.

7. Walter Isaacson, *Einstein: His Life and Universe* (New York: Simon & Schuster, 2007), 161.

8. Albert Einstein, *The Complete Papers of Albert Einstein,* vol. 1, xxii, quoted in ibid., 24.

9. Abraham Pais, *Subtle Is the Lord: The Science and the Life of Albert Einstein* (New York: Oxford University Press, 1982), 454.

10. Author's translation from Joseph Heinze Eibl, "Ein Brief Mozarts über seine Schaffensweise?," *Österreichische Musikzeitschrift* 35 (1980): 586.

11. *Allgemeine musikalische Zeitung* 1 (September 1799): 854–56. This account of Constanze Mozart was repeated by her in Salzburg in 1829; see Vincent and Mary Novello, *A Mozart Pilgrimage: Being the Travel Diaries of Vincent & Mary Novello in the Year 1829*, edited by Nerina Medici di Marignano and Rosemary Hughes (London: Novello, 1955), 112.

12. Humphrey Newton, letter to John Conduitt, January 17, 1728, The Newton Project, http://www.newtonproject.ox.ac.uk/view/texts/normalized/THEM00033.

13. *Let Newton Be!: A New Perspective on his Life and Works*, edited by John Fauvel, Raymond Flood, Michael Shortland, and Robin Wilson (Oxford, UK: Oxford University Press, 1988), 15.

14. Jerry Hanken, "Shulman Wins, but Hess Wows," *Chess Life* (June 2008): 16, 20.

15. For a discussion of memory for chess and memory in general, see William G. Chase and Herbert A. Simon, "The Mind's Eye in Chess," in *Visual Information Processing: Proceedings of the Eighth Annual Carnegie Psychology Symposium on Cognition*, edited by William G. Chase (New York: Academic Press, 1972). For related studies by Simon, Chase, and others, see David Shenk, *The Immortal Game: A History of Chess* (New York: Random House, 2006), 303–4.

16. David Rosand, Meyer Shapiro Professor of Art History, Columbia University, presentation in the Yale "genius course," January 29, 2009.

17. Howard Gardiner, *Creating Minds: An Anatomy of Creativity* (New York: Basic Books, 1993), 148, 157.

18. Elyse Graham, Joyce scholar and professor of modern literature at Stony Brook University, conversation with the author, August 1, 2010.

19. Bloomberg, "Elon Musk: How I Became the Real 'Iron Man,'" https://www.youtube.com/watch?v=mh45igK4Esw, at 3:50.

20. Alan D. Baddeley, *Human Memory*, 2nd ed. (East Essex, UK: Psychology Press, 1997), 24.

21. Giorgio Vasari, *Lives of the Artists*, 1550 edition, quoted in Capra, *The Science of Leonardo*, 25.

22. Rosand, presentation in the Yale "genius course," January 29, 2009.

23. Heidi Godman, "Regular Exercise Changes the Brain to Improve Memory, Thinking Skills," Harvard Health Publishing, April 9, 2018, https://www.health.harvard.edu/blog/regular-exercise-changes-brain-improve-memory-thinking-skills-201404097110.

24. Capra, *The Science of Leonardo*, 20.

25. "The Hawking Paradox," *Horizon*, BBC, 2005, https://www.dailymotion.com/video/x226awj, at 3:00.

26. Dennis Overbye, "Stephen Hawking Taught Us a Lot About How to Live," *New York Times*, March 14, 2018, https://www.nytimes.com/2018/03/14/science/stephen-hawking-life.html.

27. Niall Firth, "Stephen Hawking: I Didn't Learn to Read Until I Was Eight and I Was a Lazy Student," *Daily Mail*, October 23, 2010, http://www.dailymail.co.uk/sciencetech/article-1322807/Stephen-Hawking-I-didnt-learn-read-8-lazy-student.html.

28. Kitty Ferguson, email communication with the author, April 18, 2018.

29. "The Hawking Paradox," at 9:00.

30. *Hawking*, directed by Stephen Finnigan, 2013, YouTube, https://www.youtube.com/watch?v=hi8jMRMsEJo, at 49:00.

31. Kitty Ferguson, quoted in Kristine Larsen, *Stephen Hawking: A Biography* (New York: Greenwood, 2005), 87.

32. *Hawking*, at 49:30.

33. Much of the material in this and the next paragraph was drawn from Mason Currey, *Daily Rituals: How Artists Work* (New York: Random House, 2013); and Currey, *Daily Rituals: Women at Work* (New York: Random House, 2019). For specific individuals, consult the indices of each.

34. Currey, *Daily Rituals: How Artists Work*, 64.

35. Ibid., 110.

36. Twyla Tharp, *The Creative Habit: Learn It and Use It for Life* (New York: Simon & Schuster, 2003), 14, 237.

37. Isaacson, *Einstein*, 424.
38. Agatha Christie, *An Autobiography* (New York: Dodd, Mead, 1977), quoted in Currey, *Daily Rituals: How Artists Work*, 104.
39. John Updike, interview with the Academy of Achievement, June 12, 2004, quoted in Currey, *Daily Rituals: How Artists Work*, 196.

PHOTO CREDITS

INDEX

NOTE: *Italic* page references indicate figures.

"10,000-hour rule," 18–19

academic grades, 23–25
Accidental Billionaires, The
    (Mezrich), 202
ACT tests, 23–24, 26–27
Adams, John, 58
adult book clubs, 97
adversity, 148–51
Aesop's Fables, 163
"aha" moments, 230, 251, 252
Alcott, Louisa May, 47, 105–6, 150,
    232
Alice in Wonderland (Carroll), 74,
    114
Allegri, Gregorio, 50–51
Allen, Woody, 217
Alsop, Marin, 57
Alvarez, Luis, 26
Amazon, 5, 75, 143, 148, 159, 185,
    244
analogies, 161, 183
Apollinaire, Guillaume, 206
Apple, 75, 108, 135–36, 160, 170,
    211–13
Apple Genius Bar, 2

Archimedes, 158, 225
Aristotle, 114, 160–61, 205, 232
Ascham, Roger, 77
Asimov, Isaac, 95, 247
asking questions, 96
Asperger, Hans, 128
Asperger's syndrome, 128, 130, 131
attention deficit disorder (ADD),
    129–30, 131
Atwood, Margaret, 35, 222–23
Austen, Jane, 16, 32, 35
autism, 128, 130–31
autistic savants, 127
Avery, Oswald, 194

Baby Einstein, 2, 60–61
Baby Mozart, 60–61
Bach, Johann Sebastian, 15, 27, 115,
    175–76, 192, 216, 252
Bacon, Francis, 78
Bakker, Nienke, 117
Balanchine, George, 27, 148, 236
Baldwin, Neil, 214
Banaji, Mahzarin, 46
Bandello, Matteo, 238
Banksy, 145–46, 150

Barrie, J. M., 71
Baudelaire, Charles, 76
Beagle, HMS, 109–10, 166, 167
Beatles, the, 72, 228
Beautiful Mind, A (movie), 115–16
Becquerel, Henri, 102
Beethoven, Ludwig van, 4, 7, 27,
    123–25, 176, 251; bipolar
    disorder, 124; deafness,
    113, 115, 123–25, 131, 147;
    dreams and relaxation, 235;
    heredity, 12–13; passion, 108;
    productivity, 216
Bell, Quentin, 118
Belleville, Bob, 212
Bellow, Saul, 248
Benedict XIII, Pope, 42
Berlatier, Gabrielle, 113
Berners-Lee, Tim, 141, 159
Bernstein, Aaron, 93–94
Bezos, Jeff, 5, 7, 99, 204;
    academic record, 25; childlike
    imagination, 75; concentration,
    244; cross-border thinking, 159,
    167; curiosity, 79, 93; luck, 192;
    oppositional thinking, 173, 185,
    190; risk taking, 143, 148
bifocals, 156
Biles, Simone, 13–14, 21
Binet, Alfred, 22
biological inheritance, 11, 13–22
bipolar disorder, 114–20, 124
birth order, 16
black holes, 136–37
"blind-spot bias," 46
Blue Origin, 93
"blueprint theory" of genius, 16
Blum, Irving, 143
Blum, Joel, 129
Bold Ruler (horse), 15
Boleyn, Anne, 77
Boltzmann, Ludwig, 94
Bonheur, Rosa, 39
Boscovich, Rogerio, 91
Brahms, Johannes, 8, 115, 205, 246,
    249
brain size, 37

Brancusi, Constantin, 205
Branson, Richard, 7, 95
Breasted, James Henry, 41–42
Brennan, Chrisann, 212
Brennan-Jobs, Lisa, 212
Brin, Sergey, 26, 204, 205
Broca, Paul de, 37
Broken Column, The (Kahlo), 146,
    147
Brontë, Charlotte, 35, 45, 58, 192
Brontë, Emily, 35, 58, 192
Brooks, David, 18
Bruce, Lenny, 73–74
Bruno, Giordano, 138
Buck, Pearl S., 35, 215–16
Buddhism, 188
Buffett, Warren, 1, 7
Bunyan, John, 87
Burton, Tim, 44
Byron, George Gordon, Lord, 36,
    44, 63, 65, 129

Camden, William, 78
Capra, Fritjof, 244
Caravaggio, 218
Carey, Mariah, 13
Carlin, George, 73–74
Carlsen, Magnus, 115
Carmontelle, Louis Carrogis de, 53,
    54
Carrie (King), 149
Carroll, Lewis (Charles Dodgson),
    74, 114
Carver, George Washington, 205
Catch-22 (Heller), 150
Cavallino, Bernardo, 42
Cervantes, Miguel de, 94
Cézanne, Paul, 19–21, 52, 164, 165
Chagall, Marc, 205–6
Chain, Ernst, 200
Chaplin, Charlie, 231
Chappelle, Dave, 73–74
Charlotte of Mecklenburg-Strelitz,
    55–56
Chaucer, Geoffrey, 3
Cheever, John, 247–48
Chen, Nathan, 21–22

Chernow, Ron, 158
Chiang Kai-shek, 143
Child Genius (TV show), 51–52
childlike imagination, 64–76
Chopin, Frédéric, 19
Christianity, 38
Christie, Agatha, 248–49
Churchill, Winston, 26, 123, 136, 187, 199, 251
cities and genius, 204–7
Cleese, John, 74
Clinton, Bill, 126, 127
Close, Chuck, 123, 125–27, 217; *Bill Clinton,* 126, 127; daily work ethic, 247; spinal artery collapse, 125–27, 130, 147
Coleman, Debi, 212
Columbus, Christopher, 141, 173
Communist Manifesto, The (Marx), 141
compulsion, 106
compulsive productivity, 216
concentration, 237–49
Conduitt, John, 108
Confucius (Confucianism), 38, 100, 247
contrarian action, 173–90
Copernicus, Nicolaus, 138
Copland, Aaron, 205
copyright law, 165
Couric, Katie, 99
Coursera, 97
COVID-19 pandemic, 97, 139
Creating Minds (Gardner), 60
"creative destruction," 211
creative epicenters, 204–7
creative maladjustment, 113–33
creativity, 6–7, 27, 143, 160; and childlike mind, 68, 71; and exercise, 232–33; and mental illness, 114, 116
"creativity zones," 75
Crick, Francis, 64, 174, 194–97, 204
CRISPR, 197
Crosby, Bing, 13
cross-border thinking, 153–71
Crystal, Billy, 128

Csikszentmihalyi, Mihaly, 105
Cuban, Mark, 158
Cunningham, Barry, 67–68, 149
Curie, Marie, 22, 32, 64, 101–5, 192, 210; curiosity, 7; education and academic record, 25, 39; IQ, 22–23; passion and perseverance, 47, 101–5, 106; risk taking, 143
Curie, Pierre, 101, 102, 104
curiosity, 77–97

daemon, 3
daily ritual, 9, 247–49
Dale, Henry Hallett, 229
Dalí, Salvador, 227
Dante Alighieri, 3
Darwin, Charles, 52–53, 109–10, 141, 165–67, 192, 210, 251; concentration, 249; cross-border thinking, 165–67; dogs, 36; heredity and academic record, 12, 26; jokes, 187; passion, 109–10
Darwin, Erasmus, 65, 166
Da Vinci, Leonardo, 3, 8, 12, 13, 80–86, 84, 210; concentration, 237, 238–39, 244; curiosity, 80–86, 95, 154; genius gene, 2; *The Last Supper,* 238–39; longevity, 132; luck, 193–94; *Mona Lisa,* 82–83, 83, 180, 193–94; music and math, 161; obsession, 216; oppositional thinking, 177, 180; *St. John the Baptist,* 81, 82; *Virgin and Child,* 177, 178, 179, 180
Day-Lewis, Daniel, 1
daylight saving time, 156
deafness, 124–25
De Beauvoir, Simone, 12
Debussy, Claude, 205
Defoe, Daniel, 87
DeGeneres, Ellen, 99
depression, 129
determination, 106
Deutscher, Alma, 49–50, 56–57

Diagnostic and Statistical Manual of Mental Disorders (DSM), 114, 130
Dickens, Charles, 47, 115, 205, 232, 248
disabilities, 124–31, 147
discontent, 141–42
Disney, Walt, 26, 72–73, 75, 234, 251
DNA, 174, 194–97
Doudna, Jennifer, 197
Douglass, Frederick, 17
dreams, 65, 69–70, 225–30, 234–35
Dreyfus, Richard, 135–36
Dryden, John, 114
Duchesne, Ernest, 200
Dvořák, Antonín, 52
Dylan, Bob, 95

Eastman School of Music, 8, 17–18
Edison, Mary Stilwell, 213–14
Edison, Thomas, 4, 110–11, 141, 167–69, *168*, 251; academic record, 26; cross-border thinking, 167–69; among dropouts, 95–96; education, 94–97, 161–63; failures, 111, 148; luck, 192; obsession, 213–14, 215, 216; passion, 110–11; standardized tests, 23–24, 25–27; work ethic, 47, 110–11
EdX, 97
Eiffel, Gustave, 141
Einstein, Albert, 4, 6, 27, 30, 64, 69–71, 159, 205, 252; brain study, 6; childlike imagination, 69–71, 76; concentration, 239–40, 248, 249; cross-border thinking, 154, 159, 161, 170; curiosity, 79, 93–95; education, 26, 59, 60, 94–95; gender bias, 37–38; genius gene, 2; heredity, 16; jokes, 187; nonconformity, 136–37, 141; obsession, 209, 215, 216; oppositional thinking, 181–83; relaxation, 230–31, 205; specialization, 170–71

Einstein, Hans Albert, 231
Eliot, George, 1–2, 35
Eliot, T. S., 60
Elizabeth I of England, 8, 16, 77–79, 95, 97, 197–98
Ellington, Duke, 12
Ellis, Havelock, 16
Ellison, Larry, 204
"emergenesis," 16
Enders, John, 139
Engel, Susan, 92
Enriques, Adriana, 71
epigenetics, 16–17
Equal Opportunity Credit Act, 40
Ericsson, Anders, 18–19
Eve, 38
evolution, 93, 110, 141, 165–67
exercise, 232–33

face blindness, 126–27
Facebook, 201–4, 210, 222–24
failure, 148–51
Faraday, Michael, 52, 95, 192, 205
Faulkner, William, 216, 251
Faust (Goethe), 12, 91, 233, 234
fearlessness, 96, 155, 170
Federal Reserve, 144, 211
Federer, Roger, 1, 7
Ferguson, Kitty, 245, 246
Feynman, Richard, 28
Fischer, Bobby, 115, 242
Fitzgerald, Ella, 13
Fitzgerald, F. Scott, 150, 180–81, 206
Fleming, Alexander, 198–200, 210
Florey, Howard, 200
"flow," 105, 107
Flow (Csikszentmihalyi), 105
Fonda, Jane, 71
Ford, Henry, 184
"fourth wall," 240–41
"Fox and the Hedgehog, The" (fable), 153–54, 160, 167, 169
Frank, Anne, 87
Frankenstein (movie), 64
Frankenstein (Shelley), 4, 35, 63–67
Franklin, Aretha, 45

Franklin, Benjamin, 65, 87–89, 154, 155–57, 174, 186, 192
Franklin, Rosalind, 32, 44, 194–97
Franklin Gothic type, 156
Franklin phonetic alphabet, 157
Franklin stove, 156
Freud, Sigmund, 27, 60, 216; academic record, 25; curiosity, 79–80, 81–82; dreams, 225–26; jokes, 186; luck, 205; passion, 100; sublimation, 81–82
Fry, Art, 159
Fuller, Buckminster, 61

Galileo Galilei, 136, 137–39
Galton, Francis, 14–15, 16
Galvani, Luigi, 65
Gandhi, Mahatma, 27, 60, 136, 189–90
gaokao, 26, 27, 28
Gardner, Howard, 27, 60
Gates, Bill, 17, 51, 88, 95, 203, 204, 232
Gauguin, Paul, 100, 113, 217
Gauss, Johann Carl Friedrich, 174–75
gayness and sublimation, 81–82
Geisel, Theodor Seuss, 149
Gellhorn, Martha, 209
gender bias, 31–48
gender pay gap, 45
General Electric (GE), 168
general relativity, 70, 71, 94, 136–37, 154, 231, 252
genetics, 2, 13, 16–17
genius: definitions of, 2–3, 4–7
"Genius Anti-inertia Law," 205
Genius Aptitude Test (GAT), 28
"genius gene," 2
Genius Junior (TV show), 52
"genius test," 26
Gentileschi, Artemisia, 42–44, 43
Gentner, Dedre, 161
Gilot, Françoise, 218–22, 238
Girl with a Balloon (Banksy), 145–46
Gladwell, Malcolm, 18

glass harmonica, 156
Goethe, Johann Wolfgang von, 12, 91, 233, 234
Goncourt, Edmond de, 210, 253
Google, 25, 26, 48, 75, 132
Gorky, Maxim, 17
Gottlieb, Gilbert, 17
Gould, Stephen Jay, 23, 76
Graduate Record Exam (GRE), 28–29
Graham, Martha, 27, 60, 123
Grandma Moses, 100
Grant, Adam, 25
Great Gatsby, The (Fitzgerald), 150
Greatness (Simonton), 48
Greenberg, Jay, 49–50, 56–57
Greenspan, Alan, 211
Greenwald, Anthony, 46
grit, 47, 106, 168
Grit (Duckworth), 47
Gulf Stream, 157
Gurría, José Ángel, 40
Gutenberg, Johannes, 158

Hahn, Otto, 44
Hale, Bruce, 181
Hamilton (musical), 144, 158, 205, 234
Hamilton, Alexander, 144, 158, 205
Handmaid's Tale, The (Atwood), 222–23
Hanken, Jerry, 241–42
Harrison, George, 228
Harvard University, 8, 29, 39
Harvey, Thomas, 2
Hatshepsut, 41, 41–42
Hawking, Stephen, 1, 27, 174, 215, 244–46, 251; amyotrophic lateral sclerosis (ALS), 130, 147, 245–46; concentration, 244–46; gender bias, 37; on IQ, 22
Haydn, Franz Joseph, 176, 205
Heisenberg, Werner, 161
Heller, Joseph, 150
Hemingway, Ernest, 47, 115, 118, 150, 206, 209, 247
Henry VIII of England, 77

Hereditary Genius (Galton), 14–15, 16
heredity, 11, 13–22
Hertzfeld, Andy, 213
Hess, Robert, 241–43, 243–44
Hidden Figures (Shetterly), 45
Hildegard of Bingen, 42, 115
Hinduism, 38
homosexual passion, 81–82
Huffington, Arianna, 222
Hugo, Victor, 4, 248
Hulbert, Ann, 61
Hume, David, 94
Hungry Mind, The (Engel), 92
Huxley, Aldous, 72, 215
Huygens, Christiaan, 181–82

Imitation Game, The (movie), 128
"implicit bias," 46
In Search of Greatness (documentary), 100
"intelligence," 5
intelligence tests, 22–27
Intelligence Trap, The (Robson), 169
Interpretation of Dreams, The (Freud), 225–26
IQ (intelligence quotient), 22–30, 92
Isaacson, Walter, 211, 212
Islam, 38

Jackson, Andrew, 144
Jackson, Michael, 13, 71–72, 217
James, E. L., 35
James, P. D., 35, 181
Jamison, Kay Redfield, 114–15
Jenner, Edward, 136–37, 173
Jesus Christ, 136
Joan of Arc, 3, 136, 191
Jobs, Lisa, 108
Jobs, Steve, 5, 211–13; cross-border thinking, 160, 170; education and academic record, 26, 95, 251–52; failure, 148; obsession, 211–13; passion, 108; rebelliousness, 135–36, 141, 143, 148, 152

Joel, Billy, 228
Johnson, Boris, 78
Johnson, Edward, 214
Johnson, Lonnie, 159
Johnson, Samuel, 36, 57, 153
Joke and Its Relationship to the Unconscious, The (Freud), 186
jokes, 186–88
Joliot-Curie, Irène, 15, 105
Jonson, Ben, 95
Joyce, James, 27, 206, 243
Judaism, 38, 188
Julius Caesar (Shakespeare), 11–12, 224
Junto Club, 87, 94

Kahlo, Frida, 16, 74, 104, 132, 146–48; *The Broken Column*, 146, 147
Kahneman, Daniel, 18, 169–70
Kandel, Eric, 126–27
Kandinsky, Wassily, 12
Kant, Immanuel, 6
Kardashian, Kim, 1
Karloff, Boris, 64
Kauffman, Angelica, 38–39
Kaufman, Scott, 230
Keane, Margaret, 44
Keller, Helen, 87
Keynes, John Maynard, 106–7, 241
Khokhlova, Olga, 218, 219, 221–22
Kim Jong Un, 1
King, Martin Luther, Jr., 1, 27, 60, 131, 136, 137, 187, 188–90, 192
King, Stephen, 17, 149, 227, 247
Koestler, Arthur, 224
Kusama, Yayoi, 115, 120–22, *121*, 123, 131, 205, 247
Kuti, Fela, 4

Lady Gaga, 7, 12, 26, 58, 95, 154–55
Lamarck, Jean-Baptiste, 166
Lamb, Caroline, 63
Laporte, Geneviève, 219
Last Supper, The (da Vinci), 238–39
Lee, Harper, 35

left-handedness, 177
Leibniz, Gottfried, 214–15
Lennon, John, 228, 251
Les Demoiselles d'Avignon (Picasso), 123, *164*, 165
Levant, Oscar, 188
Lewy body dementia (LBD), 129
light bulb, 4, 167, 213
lightning rod, 156
Lincoln, Abraham, 1, 60, 95, 192
Lipton, James, 128–29
listening, 96; to music, 60, 225
Little, Christopher, 35
Little Women (Alcott), 105–6, 150, 232
Loewi, Otto, 229–30, 252
Lombroso, Cesare, 114
long arm (grabber), 156
Lorentz, Hendrik, 94
Lovelace, Ada, 32, 44
Lowell, Robert, 123
Lucas, George, 180
luck, 22, 44, 101, 191–207
lust for learning, 77–97
Luther, Martin, 136, 140–41

Ma, Jack, 7, 26, 95, 157–58, 251
Ma, Yo-Yo, 1, 7, 52
Maar, Dora, 218, 219, 220, *220*, 222
MacKinnon, Donald, 163, 169
"mad geniuses," 113–20
Magic Flute, The (Mozart), 74–75
Mahler, Alma, 40
Mahler, Gustav, 40, 205
Malthus, Thomas, 166
Mandela, Nelson, 136
manic depression, 114–20
Man of Genius, The (Lombroso), 114
Man Who Knew Infinity, The (movie), 128
Many Traits Quotient (MQ's), 27–28, 30
Mao Zedong, 143
Martin, George, 228
Marx, Groucho, 252

Marx, Karl, 141
math and music, components of, 161–63
Matisse, Marguerite, 16
Maxwell, James Clerk, 58, 94, 115, 182, 249
McBride, Michael, 199
McCartney, Paul, 71–72, 115, 228
McCormick, Cyrus, 158
McNamee, Roger, 223
medical catheter, 156
Meitner, Lise, 44
Melville, Herman, 118, 150
Mendel, Gregor, 16, 205
Mendeleev, Dmitri, 17, 227
Mendelssohn, Fanny, 33, 40
MENSA, 22, 51
mental disorders, 114–22, 241
mentors, 33, 46, 59–60, 252
Meredith, Rudy, 29
Merkel, Angela, 60
Mestral, George de, 159
Mezrich, Ben, 202
Michaelis, David, 237
Michelangelo, 3, 12, 17, 27, 85, 132, 243
Mickey Mouse, 72–73, 76, 234
Mill, John Stuart, 51, 105, 206
Miller, Zell, 61
Milton, John, 34, 147
Minotaur Leaning over a Sleeping Girl (Picasso), 220, 221
Miranda, Lin-Manuel, 144, 158, 205, 234
Miró, Joan, 205
misfits, 135–52
misogyny, 36–37
Missing Piece, The (Silverstein), 101
Moby-Dick (Melville), 118, 150
Mona Lisa (da Vinci), 82–83, *83*, 180, 193–94
Monet, Claude, 205
Monroe, Marilyn, 106, 142
Moore, Henry, 112
morality, 209
Morgan, J. P., 111, 168

Morrison, Toni, 27, 35, 47, 52, 87, 192, 235
Morse, Samuel F. B., 158
Moser, Mary, 38–39
Motherwell, Robert, 205
Mozart, Anna Maria, 50–51, 58–59
Mozart, Constanze, 240
Mozart, Franz Xaver, 16, 17
Mozart, Leopold, 50–51, 53, 54, 55–56, 58–59
Mozart, Nannerl, 50, 51, 53, 54, 55–56, 73, 161–62, 217
Mozart, Wolfgang Amadeus, 4, 8, 49–51, 124, 161–68; childlike imagination, 73, 74–75; concentration, 240, 244; cross-border thinking, 161–68, 163; education, 95; genius gene, 2; heredity, 13; obsession, 216, 217; oppositional thinking, 176, 176–77; prodigy, 49–51, 53, 54, 55–56, 58–59
Mozart Effect, 60–61
Mozart's Sister (movie), 55
Mrs. Dalloway (Woolf), 118–19
"multiple intelligences," 27
music and geniuses, 161–63
Musk, Elon, 17, 204, 205; concentration, 243, 244; cross-border thinking, 154; lust for learning, 91–92, 95; obsession, 210; oppositional thinking, 175, 184–85, 187; passion, 110, 111; rebelliousness, 141, 148; work ethic, 97
Musk, Kimbal, 91–92
Mussolini, Benito, 36

Nabokov, Vladimir, 12, 159, 247, 248
Nadal, Rafael, 1
Napoleon Bonaparte, 36, 191
Nash, John, 115–16
"natural selection," 166
"nature versus nurture," 14–22
neoteny, 75–76
neurotransmitters, 228–30

Neverland Ranch, 71–72
Newton, Isaac, 106–8, 128, 130, 242; concentration, 241; curiosity, 85; destructive tendencies, 214–15; luck, 192, 205; oppositional thinking, 173, 181–83; passion and obsession, 106–8; relaxation, 225
Nichols, Catherine, 31, 46
Nobel, Alfred, 209–10
Nocera, Joe, 211

Oates, Joyce Carol, 35
Obama, Barack, 144, 170
obscenity, 73–74
obsession, 106, 209–24
obsessive–compulsive disorder (OCD), 120, 122, 131
Off the Charts (Hulbert), 61
O'Keeffe, Georgia, 205
Olivier, Fernande, 218
Olmstead, Marla, 56
Ono, Yoko, 57
On Women (Schopenhauer), 37
Operation Varsity Blues, 29, 151
Oppenheimer, J. Robert, 71
"opportunity," 191–92
oppositional thinking, 173–90
optimism, 132–33
originality, 6, 55, 56–57, 65, 127, 224
oxymoron, 184, 186, 189, 190

Page, Larry, 205
pain, 115
palindromes, 175–77
paradox, 181, 182, 186
paradoxon, 181
Paravicini, Derek, 127–28
parental control, 151–52
Parr, Katherine, 78
passion, 9, 28, 63, 79, 82–83, 90, 93–94, 99–112, 213
Pasteur, Louis, 141, 198, 204
Pauling, Linus, 194, 196–97
Pavlova, Anna, 17
Peak (Ericsson), 18–19

Peek, Kim, 127
Pelley, Scott, 49
penicillin, 198–200
Peripatetics, 232
Peruggia, Vincenzo, 193
Phelps, Michael, 1, 7, 13–14
Phi Beta Kappa, 24–25, 26
"philosopher's stone," 107
photographic memory, 243–44
Picasso, José Ruiz, 59–60, 68–69
Picasso, Pablo, 19–21, 193, 218–22, 251; childlike imagination, 68–69; concentration, 238, 239, 243; cross-border thinking, 163–65; education, 95; gender bias, 36; heredity, 15–16; Les Demoiselles d'Avignon, 123, 164, 165; longevity, 132; Minotaur Leaning over a Sleeping Girl, 220, 221; mood disorder, 115, 123; obsession, 216, 218–22; prodigy, 51, 59–60; The Weeping Woman, 220, 220; women, 218–22
Piscopia, Elena, 38
Planck, Max, 161
Plath, Sylvia, 45, 58, 115
Plato, 11–12, 99, 114, 204–5
"play," 70
Player, Gary, 192
Plutarch, 87
Poe, Edgar Allan, 114
Polidori, John, 63
Pollock, Jackson, 52, 205
Polsky, Gabe, 100
polymaths, 155, 158–59
Post-it Note, 159
Pound, Ezra, 205–6
"Power" (song), 68
practice, 17–22
precox (precociousness), 52
preparation and luck, 191–207
Princeton University, 24, 29, 32, 39, 99, 205
prodigies, 49–62; definitions of, 51–52
"prodigy bubble," 59, 61–62

productivity, 216
"protester," 139
Proust, Marcel, 248
Pryor, Richard, 73–74
public library, 157

Raff, Joachim, 243
Rain Man (movie), 127
Ramanujan, Srinivasa, 128
"Renaissance man," 42, 154
Raphael, 3, 191
reading, 86–87, 89–94, 97
rebelliousness, 135–52
Redmayne, Eddie, 1
relaxation, 9, 225–36
REM sleep, 226–27, 229
"reverse chronology," 180
"reverse perspective," 180
Reynolds, Jock, 218
Rhodes, Cecil, 210
Rhodes Scholarship, 210
Richards, Keith, 228
Richmann, Georg Wilhelm, 89
Ripley, Amanda, 137
risk taking, 27, 29, 83, 143–46, 152, 201–4
Rivera, Diego, 205
Robson, David, 169
Rock, Chris, 73–74, 186
Rodin, Auguste, 27
Roebling, Emily, 45
Rogers, Will, 187
Romeo and Juliet (Shakespeare), 99, 183–84
Röntgen, Wilhelm, 198
Room of One's Own, A (Woolf), 34, 35–36
Roosevelt, Eleanor, 87, 92
Roque, Jacqueline, 219
Ross, Lillian, 217
Rothko, Mark, 205
Rousseau, Jean-Jacques, 35
Rowling, J. K., 28, 35, 67–68, 115, 234; academic record and test scores, 26, 28; childlike imagination, 67–68, 69; failure, 149; jokes, 188

Rushdie, Salman, 143
Ruth, George Herman "Babe," 108–9

Sabartés, Jaime, 239
Sacks, Oliver, 128
Sahl, Mort, 73–74
St. John the Baptist (Da Vinci), 81, 82
Salk, Jonas, 210, 222
Sand, George, 35
Sandberg, Sheryl, 32
sarcasm, 185–88
SAT (Scholastic Aptitude Test), 23–30
Satanic Verses, The (Rushdie), 143
Saunders, Michael, 39–40
savants, 127–28
Schiele, Egon, 218
Schoenberg, Arnold, 176, 205
school dropouts, 95–96
Schopenhauer, Arthur, 5, 36–37, 105
Schubert, Franz, 176, 205
Schulte, Brigid, 47
Schulz, Charles, 237, 244
Schumann, Clara, 33, 40
Schumer, Amy, 73–74
Schumpeter, Joseph, 211
"scientist," 88
Scott, Walter, 66
Secretariat (horse), 14–15
Sedlacek, William, 28–29
Semmelweis, Ignaz, 79
Sexton, Anne, 123
Shakespeare, William, 3, 11–12, 52, 205, 224; education, 95; heredity, 192; imagination, 188; IQ, 23; luck, 192–93; oppositional thinking, 173, 183–84, 186; passion, 99; productivity, 216
Shelley, Mary Godwin, 4, 35, 63–67, 69
Shelley, Percy Bysshe, 63, 65, 66
Shockley, William, 26, 28

Shostakovich, Dmitri, 13
Silicon Valley, 204, 206–7
Silverman, Sarah, 73–74
Silverstein, Shel, 100–101, 112, 247
Simonton, Dean Keith, 33–34, 48
Sinatra, Frank, 13
sleep, 9, 65–66, 226–30, 235
Small Fry (Brennan-Jobs), 212
Smartest Kids in the World, The (Ripley), 137
Socrates, 136, 204–5
Solomon, Maynard, 125
SpaceX, 91, 92, 93, 141, 175
special relativity, 70, 71, 93, 182
Spencer, Archibald, 88–89
Spencer, Percy, 198
Spengler, Joseph, 162
Spinoza, Baruch, 94
Sprague, Frank, 111
standardized tests, 23–24, 25–27
Stanford–Binet Intelligence Scales, 26
Stanford Online, 97
Stanford University, 95, 99, 205
Staw, Barry, 143
Stein, Gertrude, 69, 206
STEM (science, technology, engineering, and mathematics), 33, 170
Stern, Daniel, 35
Stickgold, Robert, 226
Stone, Douglas, 60
Straus, Joseph, 130–31
Stravinsky, Igor, 115, 176, 205, 227–28, 248
Strobel, Scott, 197
sublimation, 81–82
Summers, Lawrence, 37
Sun Also Rises, The (Hemingway), 150
"sunk cost syndrome," 168–69
Super Soaker, 159
Swift, Jonathan, 137
swimming flippers, 156

"talent," 5
Taoism, 188

Tassi, Agostino, 43
Taymor, Julie, 227
Teller, Edward, 161
Terman, Lewis, 22, 26
Tesla Motors, 184–85
Tesla, Nikola, 5, 12, 89–91,
    90, 111, 141, 169, 214,
    233–34, 252; adversity, 148;
    curiosity, 85, 89–91; mood
    disorder, 115; relaxation,
    233–34
Tesla coil, *90,* 91, 233–34
Tetlock, Philip, 169–70
Tharp, Twyla, 247, 248
Thiel, Peter, 205
"Think Different," 135–36
Thinking, Fast and Slow
    (Kahneman), 18, 169–70
"thinking opposite," 173–90
Thomas, Dylan, 58
Thoreau, Henry David, 232
Thorne, Kip, 130, 246
Titanic, 193
Tolstaya, Sophia, 40–41
Tolstoy, Leo, 40–41, 247
Topsy (elephant), 214
"Tortoise and the Hare, The" (fable),
    80–86
Toscanini, Arturo, 243
transmutation, 166
Trilling, Lionel, 218
troublemakers, 135–52
Trump, Donald, 1, 78, 139, 144
Tubman, Harriet, 7, 144–45
Turing, Alan, 1, 128
Twain, Mark, 94–95, 183, 187, 191,
    232

"unconscious bias," 46
Updike, John, 247, 249
Urban VIII, Pope, 137–38

Van Gogh, Vincent, 12, 17, 52,
    116–18, 205; cross-border
    thinking, 158; dreams, 227;
    mental instability, 113,
    116–18, 123; mortality,

131–32; passion, 99–100;
    rebelliousness, 136, 150–51
Vasari, Giorgio, 12, 83, 85, 244
Velcro, 159
Verdi, Giuseppe, 52
Verlat, Karel, 150–51
Virgil, 180, 201
Virgin and Child (da Vinci), 177, *178,*
    179, 180
Vogel, Jack, 187
Von Stade, Francis Skiddy, 39

Wagner, Richard, 180, 217, 227
Walker, Matthew, 226–27
Waller, John, 136, 199
Walt Disney Company, 60–61
Walter, Marie-Thérèse, 218, 219–20,
    221–22
Warhol, Andy, 106, 130, 141–43,
    145, 146, 165, 205, 247
war of the currents, 141, 214,
    233–34
Watson, James, 28, 64, 174, 194–97,
    204
Weeping Woman, The (Picasso), 220,
    220
Weiwei, Ai, 211
West, Kanye, 1, 7, 68, 75, 96, 115
Westinghouse, George, 111
"What Straight-A Students Get
    Wrong" (Grant), 25
"Why Individuals Reject Creativity"
    (Staw), 143
Why We Sleep (Walker), 226–27
Wilde, Oscar, 187–88
Wilkins, Maurice, 174, 194–97
William III of England, 107–8
Williams, Robin, 73–74, *74,* 114,
    128–30, 131, 217
Wiltshire, Stephen, 127–28
Winehouse, Amy, 123
Winfrey, Oprah, 86–87, *95,* 97, 99,
    148, 204, 210
Winklevoss, Tyler and Cameron,
    202–3
Winters, Jonathan, 129
Wolfe, Thomas, 247

Wonder, Stevie, 13
Wood, Grant, 225
Woolf, Leonard, 118
Woolf, Virginia, 16, 27, 32, 34–36, 205; education, 95; gender bias, 34–36, 44–45; manic depression, 115, 118–20, 123; *A Room of One's Own*, 34, 35–36
work ethic, 14–22
Wozniak, Steve, 160
writer's block, 232
Wyeth, N. C., 187, 248

Yale University, 8, 24–25, 29, 32, 39; Exploring the Nature of Genius course, 8, 11, 32, 130, 242, 253; Introduction to Classical Music course, 97; Listening to Music course, 231–32
"Yesterday" (song), 228

Zucked (McNamee), 223
Zuckerberg, Mark, 26, 95, 133, 201–4, 210, 222–24
Zyman, Samuel, 49

ABOUT THE AUTHOR

CRAIG WRIGHT is the Henry L. and Lucy G. Moses Professor Emeritus of Music at Yale University, where he continues to teach the popular undergraduate course Exploring the Nature of Genius. A Guggenheim Fellow, Wright has received an honorary Doctorate of Humane Letters from the University of Chicago, is a member of the American Academy of Arts and Sciences, and was awarded the Sewall Prize for Excellence in Undergraduate Teaching at Yale (2016) as well as the DeVane Medal for Excellence in Teaching and Scholarship (2018). He holds a Bachelor of Music degree from the Eastman School of Music and a Ph.D. from Harvard.